Other-Centred Therapy

Buddhist Psychology in Action

First published by O Books, 2009
O Books is an imprint of John Hunt Publishing Ltd., The Bothy, Deershot Lodge, Park Lane, Ropley,
Hants, SO24 0BE, UK
office1@o-books.net
www.o-books.net

Distribution in:

UK and Europe
Orca Book Services
orders@orcabookservices.co.uk
Tel: 01202 665432 Fax: 01202 666219
Int. code (44)

USA and Canada
NBN
custserv@nbnbooks.com
Tel: 1 800 462 6420 Fax: 1 800 338 4550

Australia and New Zealand
Brumby Books
sales@brumbybooks.com.au
Tel: 61 3 9761 5535 Fax: 61 3 9761 7095

Far East (offices in Singapore, Thailand,
Hong Kong, Taiwan)
Pansing Distribution Pte Ltd
kemal@pansing.com
Tel: 65 6319 9939 Fax: 65 6462 5761

South Africa
Alternative Books
altbook@peterhyde.co.za
Tel: 021 555 4027 Fax: 021 447 1430

Text copyright Caroline Brazier 2008

Design: Stuart Davies

ISBN: 978 1 84694 237 2

A CIP catalogue record for this book is available
from the British Library.

Printed by Digital Book Print

Other-Centred Therapy

Buddhist Psychology in Action

Caroline Brazier

BOOKS

Winchester, UK
Washington, USA

CONTENTS

Other books by Caroline Brazier

Buddhist Psychology (2003) Constable Robinson

The Other Buddhism (2007) O-Books

Guilt: an exploration (2009) O-Books

Listening to the Other (2009) O-Books

To David
my fellow traveller

NOTES ON EXERCISES

Welcome to Other-Centred Therapy. This book provides an introduction to a method of working which is founded on an understanding of human process that is both practical, and honouring
of our place in an experiential world. Grounded in the theory of
Buddhist psychology and in Western methodologies, it incorporates a positive and outwardly orientated view of the therapeutic
process.

The book is practical. It offers you ways to engage with
learning, not just through reading about models and examples,
but also through exercises and discussion points. These will help
you to integrate the methods and concepts which it presents. If
you have already read *Listening to the Other* you will be familiar
with the style of presentation offered here, and you will find that
this book will help you to carry on and develop your skills. If you
are new to the series, these notes will give you guidance on how
to use the materials effectively.

Learning to counsel is a process which inevitably involves
engagement with others. A book cannot replace an attendance
based training programme, and in this case it is not intended to.
Learning therapeutic method in a group is an important part of
the process of skills development. It offers opportunities for
practice, where staff and peers can give feedback and offer
comments, and for dialogue which integrates learning through
active discussion of implications. The materials are intended as a
supplement to regular training courses, offering a perspective
which is different from that taught on most Western therapeutic
training programmes. As such is it both complementary and
challenging.

This book can be used as the basis for individual learning or
for learning in groups. It might be used on a training course by
students or by counselling team members who wish to develop

1

their skills. Although simply reading it will help you to reflect on your practice and integrate other perspectives, you will gain more from it if you use the material as it is set out, treating it as a study programme, and trying out the exercises and other activities which are offered to help you explore and refine your skills.

Group and Solitary Learning

Counselling and therapy skills are best taught in groups. Getting feedback on the quality of your work and seeing different people working is an invaluable aid to learning. It is a reminder that there are many possible approaches and no one method is "right". As counsellors grow in competence, they start to see alternatives and to build up a repertoire of responses to any given situation. They start to build a sense of what may result from different styles of intervention and what approach may suit a particular person or circumstance best. Learning in a group can assist this process as you see how other people work.

This book is designed so it can be used by groups who wish to develop their skills together, on the other hand, you may be trying to develop your skills without having a group of people to work with. For this reason, most of the exercises in the book are presented in forms which you can use if you are working on your own. This way you can develop your skills as well as reflecting on issues relating to the therapy process.

Working on your own offers the advantage that you can proceed at your own pace. If you are already a therapist, you can integrate your learning as you go in your regular work. The theory builds sequentially, so it is sensible to work through it in the order presented, but you will be able to review your learning and look back at previous sessions as new situations arise in your practice.

If you are working through this material in isolation, one way of integrating the material and getting feedback is an on-line peer group. If you want to link up with other people who are studying with this book to share experiences of the exercises you can contact us at courses@amidatrust.com. We will put you in touch with others who are in the same position and offer a point of reference for any queries which you have, or introduce you to our on-line learning community.

A few of the exercises included in the book are offered specifically for groups. Where this is the case, it is indicated on the exercise and an alternative is given. Mostly though, the exercises are presented in a form which you can do on your own. If you are working in a group, most of the exercises in the book can form a basis for counselling skills exercises, even though this is not necessarily indicated in the instructions. (To do so every time would be repetitious.) You can start off by doing the activity individually and then work in pairs to share what you have learned, taking turns so that one person is 'counsellor' and the other 'client' and then vice versa. Alternatively you could use other formats:

- working in groups of three with the third person acting as observer and giving feedback to the counsellor on their facilitation skills (see the instructions in session three) or
- each person undertaking the exercise individually and then sharing responses using a stone passing circle (see session one for a description of this method.)

Practicalities

Many of the exercises given include drawing or writing. You will need big sheets of paper, so you might like to invest in a child's drawing book, a flip chart or a roll of lining paper. It is useful to keep a folder of the work that you do as you go through the sessions so that you can look back through them. Alternatively you can keep a record of your work using digital photographs.

When you are using this book, make time to do the exercises.

Each session contains between two and three hours of practical activities as well as your reading time. If you are using the book as a home learning programme, you may like to set aside a regular time to work, ideally in a quiet space where you can be sure of not being interrupted.

Support

Personal therapy is a requirement on most counsellor and therapist training programmes. This is with good reason. If we are going to do therapeutic work, we need to learn to face emotional reactions in ourselves and others. Clients generally come into therapy because, for one reason or another, they feel out of their depth or isolated in their situation. They feel overwhelmed and want to escape from the feelings that are coming up.

Hearing other people's experiences, counsellors are likely to be reminded of their own personal stories. Sometimes this can be distressing. Unless we learn ways of sharing these feeling responses, we may find ourselves thrown by the emotional impact of the work we are doing. We cannot really give support to others unless we are able to face difficulties without mentally running away. Also, at a simple level, we need a familiarity with emotional material and a language for talking about it not just at a theoretical level, but also through having faced it ourselves.

Facing our own experiences is important in helping us to develop our capacity to understand others and not impose our views on them, but it can be difficult. If, as you read this book and undertake the exercises in it, you find yourself reacting with strong emotions, you may feel the need of someone to talk to. If you find things being stirred up for you which you feel you do not want to handle on your own, do not be afraid to seek out support. If you are already working as a counsellor or therapist, you will have a supervisor. It may be that you can talk to this person about your feelings. If you need more than is appropriate in a supervision relationship, however, find a counsellor in your locality. Your supervisor may be able to advise you, or you can find listings in local directories.

Through listening to the stories of people's lives and the multitude of feeling reactions which they experience, we are ourselves touched and changed. The courage and spirit which people demonstrate in terrible circumstances can be uplifting and humbling. The despair and hopelessness which others feel can be equally affecting. We are the recipients of many treasures, but in order to receive cleanly, we need to explore our own experience with honesty.

Keeping a Learning Journal

Thinking about your learning process as you go along will improve your capacity to get more from the exercises. Whilst you are using this book, you may wish to keep a learning journal. This in itself can be a useful way of focusing your study.

There are many ways of keeping a learning journal, but in particular you may like to:

- Record the exercises you have done (perhaps with photos of drawings)
- Write about your process in doing the exercises. Record what you have learned
- Write about how you apply learning in your work
- Write about incidents which happen in your work or leisure contexts, where you observe instances of things discussed in the book
- Write about other reading you do, or about material from TV, radio, lectures or workshops which you come across which has relevance
- Read back over earlier entries and annotate them in the light of your later learning.

Since a learning journal can be interactive, keeping it in a computer file can be a creative way of working, as it allows you to go back and expand previous entries. You can also include photographs and other media. If you do this, whilst you may want to add comments to earlier entries, do not censor your first reflections by deleting bits. It is useful to look back and see how your thinking has progressed.

Such journals can be shared with others on line, but be careful in anything you write to observe good standards of confidentiality and to protect the identities of anyone you refer to.

Orientation and Language

This book presents a model of therapy which is based upon the understanding of the mind and its conditioned nature which is offered in the Buddhist teachings. You will find the theoretical material which supports this model in my previous book, *Buddhist Psychology*[1]. By contrast, *Other-Centred Therapy* is intended to be complementary to this volume and to provide a more methodological focus.

In keeping with this more practical outlook, I have tried to simplify the theoretical content by putting the concepts into more everyday language. I have mostly avoided use of Sanskrit (Skt) terminology, putting the original terms into the notes at the end of this book. The only exceptions to this are where a Sanskrit term is simpler than the English alternative. (For example I use the Sanskrit word *rupa* to describe the "perceived object which is invested with particular psychological energy" because it is simpler than repeatedly using this rather clumsy phrase). The end notes also offer more detailed discussion of some of the Buddhist theory which underlies this therapeutic method. If you are interested to understand the links between methodology and Buddhism, you will find that reading these will help to elaborate the theoretical context.

There are some problems in using English terms to present

Buddhist theory in the Western context, since some terms which I use have other meanings in Western psychological literature. Attachment, conditioning and object-related theory are all important components of a Buddhist approach and have specific, technical meanings. The same words are, however, also used in Western psychology with different meanings. As reader, it is important that you appreciate this distinction and recognise that when I use these terms I am doing so intending the meanings associated with a Buddhist approach rather than the Western one. This will be explained as the terms arise, but bear this in mind if you dip into the book at different points.

In particular, an other-centred approach makes considerable reference to our relationship with the object world. Mental states are described as being object-related. Objected-related theory has its roots in a particular understanding of conditioning presented in the Abhidharma, the key Buddhist psychological text[2]. This term in particular can cause confusion, as it is similar to the term object-relations theory used by Fairburn, Winnicott and Guntrip in Western psychodynamic psychology. The two meanings can be distinguished by the observation that Buddhist object-relation theory is framed in the singular. It is Buddhist object-related theory which will be explored in this book.

The Structure of the Book
This book contains fourteen sections, or 'sessions'. These sessions include exercises and suggested reading, and will take you through a programme of skills development in a sequence which builds from initial concepts to more sophisticated ideas and methods. They could thus be used as the basis for a teaching programme.

If this is the case, each session will take at least two to three hours and students will need to pre-read the material in their own time before meetings. Having copies of the book will enable them to revisit themes and re-read theoretical materials. If time allows, however, there is sufficient material included in each session for you to devote far longer to it.

Working on your own, of course, you have more flexibility. Nevertheless, the book is intended to work as a whole, so it may be most fruitful to aim to complete each session within, say, one or two weeks.

Notes on Professional Terminology

The terms counselling and psychotherapy have both been used in different ways in the past and there has been a lack of clear distinction between the them. As a broad generalisation, counselling tends to be seen as specific, issue-centred, and shorter term, whereas psychotherapy has been seen as concerned with deeper personality change on a more generalised level and consequently usually involves longer term working. In practice, however, the two disciplines are not so neatly divided and practitioners may often work at both levels on different occasions depending upon the needs of the particular therapeutic relationship. In this book I have used the terms 'counsellor' and 'therapist' fairly inter-changeably. It is up to the reader to decide which term he or she feels most comfortable with

Also, as will become clear, because its methodology tends to be outwardly orientated, an other-centred approach to psychotherapy may dwell on practicalities as much as on 'inner' thoughts and feelings, but does, nevertheless work at the level of whole personality transformation. The situation regarding terminology is further complicated by the statutory regulation of professional titles, which seems likely to be introduced in the UK shortly. This new regulation will no doubt have implications for the professions and will define boundaries between them more sharply. It may also create a new group of practitioners who listen to others in a caring and helpful way who do not have a professional term available to them. This may result in new fields emerging.

Whatever the future brings, the skills involved in listening and responding to others in ways which are therapeutic will no doubt continue to be used. Reflecting on these skills and on the implications of their underpinning theoretical framework, with its assumptions about values and about the nature of society is vital to the integrity of our work and our professions. This book offers a means of doing this.

Another issue for a book of this kind is that of gendered pronouns. For ease and clarity, I have adopted here the same convention which I used in *Buddhist Psychology* which is to use the feminine pronoun, *she*, to refer to the therapist and the masculine pronoun, *he*, to refer to the client, except where there are good reasons to do otherwise. This is not intended to carry any implication other than the need for succinctness and readability.

Further Study
This book includes suggested reading at the end of each session. For other information on training and resources, you are welcome to make contact with the Amida training programme through our website www.buddhistpsychology.info or by contacting us at:

Amida Trust
The Buddhist House
12 Coventry Rd
Narborough
LE19 2GR

SESSION ONE

Roots, Ethics and Society

This session will explore
- Counselling in a social context
- The therapeutic value base
- Therapy and spirituality
- Ethics and responsibility
- Counselling as spiritual practice
- Ethics and values as a foundation for therapeutic change

Ever since our earliest ancestors began to communicate with one another they have probably tried to make sense of their lives. They have tried to understand the world and their position in it, the processes of life and death, and the meanings of relationships. They have tried to understand the impact of their environment upon them: the seasons, the forces of nature, the growth cycles of plants and animals, and the transient beauty of these things. In the past they have pursued their curiosity and fears in artistic expression, or in fields such as religion, philosophy or literature, or indeed through intimacies with family and mentors, have sought advice and guidance in such matters. They have approached seers and oracles for insight into the unseen forces. They have struggled in contemplative isolation, or gathered in academies to discuss and tease out the fundamental underpinnings of human existence.

Against this background, psychology is a young discipline. It has grown strong only in the last century or two. Its roots, however, go back into the earlier human struggle to understand our nature. Psychology's early theorists, for example William James, Sigmund Freud and Carl Jung, all brought to their studies a perspective which reflected both the old and the new. Of their time, these thinkers were influenced by the wider social discourse of a changing intellectual scene, and its need to reconcile the old religious order with the rise of the scientific paradigm. In respect of this, they located the human psyche in a territory demarcated by the uneasy but creative tension which grew up in the space between these old and new perspectives. They grounded their understanding in the daily, material world and expressed their observations in the language of the spiritual.

The Social Impact of Psychology

Psychology has had a massive influence on modern society. Its impact is such that our present culture and ways of thinking incorporate the psychological perspective without even recognising it. Ideas of subconscious motivation, repression, and the assumption that people carry into adulthood damage resulting from childhood trauma, have all come into our everyday ways of thinking and interactions.

Many people believe that their lives are driven by unseen influences of attraction and repulsion, and they frequently feel powerless to overcome these. Such thinking is perhaps not so different from that of our forefathers. Perhaps our gods just come in different guises.

Conversely, psychology has become a mechanism for our advancement. Its concepts are integrated into the tool kit of everyday life, embedded in our commercial and creative processes. People employ psychological theory to improve the efficacy of advertising products or to coerce the public into particular behavioural patterns.

The predominating culture of ideas which are in the public domain conditions a society. For that society's members, it creates common ways of viewing the world, people and situations. So the growing interest in psychology has conditioned our culture. It pervades popular fiction and drama and it influences public policy. For example, we have seen its influence in shaping twentieth century attitudes in fields as diverse as education and child rearing, public policy and the conduct of warfare.

These influences have, of course, not been consistent. Theories have been proposed and contradicted and styles of provision have changed radically as new interpretations and research arose. Old methods have lost popularity, only to return years later when new theory was brought in to support them. Surveying such changes one cannot necessarily determine what ideal psychology espouses, if, indeed, as a field it is united in its view, but one can conclude that it shapes our ways of thinking and probably also that it creates wariness. People are afraid of damaging others and of themselves being damaged psychologically.

The Rise of a Therapy Culture

The past twenty or thirty years have seen an increasing popular interest in counselling and therapy. The human potential movement and third wave of therapeutic theorists, led by people like Carl Rogers, Abraham Maslow and Fritz Perls, popularised psychology and psychotherapy in the 1950s and 1960s, taking it out of the hands of medical experts, and creating a more egalitarian philosophy. Set between the analysts and the behaviourists, it positioned itself as a new and different movement. Users of psychological services were no longer patients, but clients. This change of terminology was introduced by Carl Rogers as something of a protest against what he saw as the authoritarian attitudes of the profession. It is interesting to us that the change involves a shift of implication, relocating the recipient of therapy from a medical or healing context to a consumerist one.

The human potential movement bore fruit in the decades which followed, but it was really not until the 1970s and 1980s that it gained popular momentum in the UK. Ideas of personal transformation and fulfilment were growing with the flowering of new ideas in the late 1960s, and this gradually influenced a growth in voluntary sector and service user led organisations in the decades which followed. Most of the established counselling training courses in the UK, for example, have developed since the 1980s and 1990s. Our own Amida training course was founded in 1981, and, although it changed its name and orientation in 1995, has operated continuously ever since.

EXERCISE ONE: LOOKING AT HISTORY

Take a sheet of paper and draw a line from left to right across it. Mark dates along the line from 1960 to the present. (If you were born after 1960 you may like to start with a more recent date, but you can still do the exercise using your impressions of earlier times).

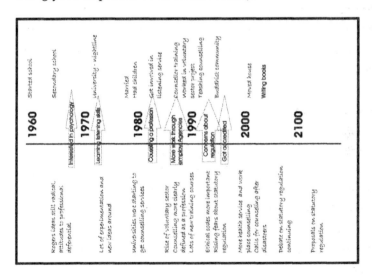

Above the line, note down the major life events and life stages which you have gone through, putting them against the dates when they happened. Below the line, note down

---

what sort of psychological awareness you think there was in society and any developments which you are aware of which affected the therapy professions.

Mark arrows crossing the lines where changes or events in the psychological consciousness of society impacted upon you.

The popularisation of psychology and its wayward offspring, the personal growth movement, has led to a plethora of self-help books and an industry of personal development workshops, manuals and resources. Not only this, but it has infiltrated our thinking and shaped our culture. In his 2004 book, *Therapy Culture*, Frank Furedi shows how modern culture has absorbed therapeutic thinking, demonstrating that terms, such as self-esteem, stress, trauma, syndrome and counselling, have all found there way into popular publications in a steadily increasing wave over the last twenty years. This shift of culture, Furedi argues, has changed the nature of our society and influenced the activity of the mass of people.

The triumph of therapeutic culture is most striking in Britain, a society that was formerly associated with reserve, understatement and reticence. During the 1960s and 1970s, stoic Britain was frequently contrasted with the let-it-all-hang-out ethos of the US. But after the unprecedented display of public emotionalism over the death of Princess Diana in 1997, it is difficult to sustain the myth that Britain is the land of the stiff upper lip[3].

Furedi also argues that, with the increased emotionalism of modern society, there has arisen a predominating view that people are vulnerable to damage from life events and not able to handle their consequences without professional intervention. Offering counselling has become a standard response to large scale disasters. People are not expected to be able to weather such experiences without professional intervention. In this, ironically, we could see that the early attempts at democratisation of the psychological therapies by Rogers, Maslow and Perls and other leaders of the humanistic therapy movement seem to have come full circle, reintroducing a professional mystique to what might otherwise be ordinary human situations.

Therapy has always had its critics. Whether or not one agrees with the particulars of these observations, if one is involved in the profession, it is important to reflect on the social role which, as counsellors or therapists, we play. The profession holds the intention of changing people's mentality. We can look at specifics and argue about issues such as influence and freedom, but if nothing else, we have to accept that our raison d'etre as a profession is to help people to change the way they think, the way they see things and the way they act. Furedi would argue that we have done this very effectively and that the whole of society has shifted its psychic energy in consequence

But how do we determine what direction this change should take and what the ideal, towards which we assist people, is? Who defines mental health? In the past, women have been locked up in mental asylums for having illegitimate babies; homosexuals have been given aversion therapy so that they could fit into heterosexual society. Do we as a profession still espouse such values? What will therapists of the future make of our current values?

The psychological orientation of society runs deep. History will be shaped by decisions made in a psychologically orientated milieu, not least because our decision makers are selected on the basis of their appeal to a therapeutically minded audience. We no longer, apparently, look for tough warriors, but appreciate those who can be tender and expressive, or slick and professional. If responsibility for such changes can be laid at the feet of a more therapeutically orientated culture, then as therapists, collectively, we carry a heavy responsibility. So at the outset of this book, let us consider the role which, as practitioners, we occupy, and the message which we convey through our work.

The relationship between our profession and such social trends is complicated, though. Do we create the mind-set of our age, or is our work shaped by society? We can look at the influence that we have, both on the micro-scale in each therapeutic relationship that we take on, and on the macro-scale of social trends, but it is often hard to determine whether we are authors or servants of the process. What we can conclude is that we play an important part in the propagation of ideas and values in society.

EXERCISE TWO: THERAPEUTIC CULTURE
AND SOCIETY

From birth, to marriage and parenting, through to bereavement, people's experience is interpreted through the medium of therapeutic ethos. Numerous studies of this subject have noted that conventional moral meanings attached to concepts such as guilt and responsibility lose their salience in circumstances where the therapeutic ethos gains influence.[4]

Reflecting on the quote above and other examples given in the text, how much influence do you think therapeutic attitudes have on society? Do you think the influence is good or bad?

Now take two newspapers, one tabloid and one broadsheet. In each of them, go through and highlight any references to counselling, or to psychological factors.

What sort of things are being said about the psychology or society or individuals and the role of the counselling profession?

Do your observations equate with those quoted by Furedi?

If you are able to find old newspapers, compare the references in those to the examples which you found in modern ones. What changes do you observe?

Therapy, Methods and Values in Society

If therapy is influential on our modern culture, it is probably important to inquire into how it is influential. What messages does it convey? How does this vary over time? For example, as we have already reflected, the influence of psychological understanding on educational theory has been strong throughout the twentieth century, but it has not been consistent. Educationalists have drawn on their knowledge of mental process but have come to different conclusions at different points in time.

In a similar way, psychological theorists have not always agreed on the nature of human process or on how it is best facilitated. If, for example, we look at how psychotherapists approach anger, we find little agreement on its management or even its value. Some will see it as something to be understood in terms of underlying unconscious motivation, which needs to be interpreted. Others see it as something to be "got out" through expressive methods. Others still see it as something to be contained through behaviour modification programmes. Within these broad differences are many subtle variations, not just of understanding, but also of advice on how to act towards it.

Behind such differences, lie differences of understanding and of values. Is anger something problematic, or is it a resource? Is it something undesirable or even "bad", or is it something wholesome? Does it lie in some place in the psyche, waiting for an opportunity to be expressed, or does it arise as a new phenomenon in each instance as a result of a stimulus, and then disappear without trace? We can apply similar questioning to other emotions.

Psychological methods depend upon a theoretical understanding of the way that people think and act. In order to help someone to change, we need to have a theory about why they are doing or feeling as they do. This does not necessarily mean we have a complete explanation of the situation. Psychologies rarely make such simplistic claims. It does mean we have some theory of the person, at least implicitly.

Theory rests upon a world view. It is grounded in a value system and a way of thinking: a paradigm. A culture which values courage is likely to have a theory of the person which emphasises the building of strength and the efficacy of "grin and bear it" methods. One which values justice may encourage people to think of their rights and getting retribution. One which values expressiveness may be more appreciative of softer qualities in the person.

The paradigm which is operating in any culture is, by definition, at least partly unrecognised. It is so deeply associated with the basic assumptions of those who are immersed in that culture that it is assumed to *be* reality. The paradigm is the shared frame of reference by which those living in the culture act. It is only glimpsed by inference and when it is contrasted against a different paradigm.

So therapeutic methods represent the deliberate manifestation of the therapist's understanding of human psychology, their theory base, and this in turn is grounded in a world view, a set of values and ways of thinking, which make up the cultural paradigm in which the therapy takes place, and which is probably unconscious.

In the light of this, as a book on therapeutic method, this work cannot ignore the importance of the paradigm from which such methods arise and within which they are embedded. So, let us reflect on what values our therapeutic practice embodies.

EXERCISE THREE: VALUES

Take some small pieces of card. On each of the cards write one of the following:

COURAGE	UNDERSTANDING
EXPRESSIVENESS	FORGIVENESS
HONESTY	VIRGINITY
SEXUALITY	PEACEFULNESS
SENSTIVITY	RESTRAINT
REMORSE	GREED
HAPPINESS	GUILT
RIGHTEOUSNESS	COMPASSION
INTIMACY	AFFECTION
EQUANIMITY	VENGEANCE
INTEGRITY	PIETY
ANGER	CALMNESS
FAITHFULNESS	RESPECTABILITY
GRIEF	PITY

You can add other elements to the list.

Now arrange the cards in a line from "most desirable" to "least desirable", according to what qualities or emotions you think the therapy which you practice embodies. What do you think you support in people whom you counsel? What do you think are ideal?

Now rearrange the cards, grouping them according to different paradigms. What might a psychotherapist from the 1930s have valued? What might a Muslim therapist value? What might a humanistic therapist value?

How accurate do you think your impressions are? Are they realistic or based on prejudices?

Finally, think back to your attitudes before you started to be interested in therapy or personal growth. How would you have arranged the cards then? Have your attitudes changed?

Therapy and Spirituality

The value base of the counsellor is particularly significant if we reflect that, as many people have hypothesised, therapy can be seen as occupying the same slot in society which religion has done in the past. The therapist is seen as the confessor, offering private space, behind closed doors, in which the therapeutic relationship unfolds, the intimacy of the session protected by the temporary vows of celibacy which professional codes of ethics confer.

This intimacy, coupled with the mystery of the counsellor's real identity, for personal details are generally not revealed, creates a powerful ambiance in which the therapist can be imagined to be fount of all knowledge and a source of unconditional love. Despite careful attempts to equalise the relationship, the counsellor can often be perceived as a guru type figure.

Those counsellors whose model of psychology includes the psychodynamic concept of transference (i.e. that the client will bring patterns of relating from early significant relationships into the therapeutic encounter) will appreciate the power of such relationships, but nevertheless may overlook the real social factors which contribute to the therapist's attributed power. The tendency of clients to perceive their therapists as knowing, powerful, psychologically healthy, and infinitely compassionate is not just grounded in their own pathology. It is also embedded in the view of society, and the roots of such perceptions are bound up in the inheritance of the religious lineage, which counsellors are recipients of. In this secular age, the hunger for spiritual leadership often falls at their feet and the natural human instincts for devotional practice and religious ecstasy are satisfied through the rituals of the therapeutic relationship.

EXERCISE FOUR: THERAPEUTIC RELATIONSHIP

Recall instances where you have gone to someone professional for advice or support. It might be that you went to a counsellor, or it may be that you sought help from someone else like a teacher, spiritual leader, or a superior at work. Try to identify five instances.

What sort of framework did the encounter have? Was it time limited? Was it in a private space? Was it in a special place?

How did you feel before the encounter, during it, and after it?

What sort of expectations did you have of the person? What did you imagine they thought of you?

How did you see their life? What did you imagine it was like? How realistic was this?

Reflecting back, does the idea that there is some parallel between the counsellor and the priest make sense to you?

How does this affect your sense of your own role as a counsellor or therapist?

EXERCISE FIVE: PRIESTS AND COUNSELLORS

Divide your page into two columns. In the first column make a list of attributes or functions which you think the priest traditionally held or was ascribed.

In the second column, try to think of a parallel attribute or function which the counsellor or therapist has today.

Compare your two lists. How far do you think the two roles equate? How do they differ?

Given the power of the therapeutic relationship, and the quasi-spiritual frame in which it unfolds, as counsellors, we have a responsibility to look at the value base from which we operate.

Ethics and Responsibility

The responsibility which we have as counsellors has two levels. First of all, it is vital that we work with integrity. Working within an ethical frame which puts the client's interests at its centre, and which, at a gross level, protects them from mal-practice and exploitation, provides a first level of safeguard. The power of the relationship is contained by well tested rules of engagement. In general such a framework is provided with good reason, and creates the boundary for good practice. Occasionally such boundaries may be appropriately varied, but any such variance needs to happen with a valid reason. As a supervisor once said to me, "If you break a boundary, do it with your eyes wide open!"

The second level of responsibility is both more profound, and more difficult to define. As we have already discussed, the therapist conveys a value base. Their practice is grounded in a set of beliefs and mores which informs their responses. Clients will sense these values in the flicker of facial responses of which the counsellor has no awareness. Probably the client has no awareness either, but will be deeply influenced. There is research which suggests that clients become more like their counsellors in their values and attitudes during the course of therapy, and that this happens most strongly with clients of person-centred counsellors, who attempt most strongly not to influence.

Whilst codes of ethics create a boundary which can be monitored, the values by which a person lives are often invisible. Even where someone strongly espouses a position, the likelihood is that they will actually act upon other beliefs and currents of which they have little awareness. It is in the nature of the paradigm that it is unrecognised. Our assumptions about what is so are just presumed to be inalienable truth. We do not question them, or even articulate them to ourselves. The frame of reference is not questioned; the cultural conserve is maintained. It's just "how it is".

In exercise three, you investigated some of the elements

23

which might or might not be in your world view, but such experiments are blunt tools, giving only a superficial indication of the issue. To be more aware of our assumptions requires a willingness to be vigilant in our interactions with others, to notice the sticking points and discrepancies, and to allow their otherness to teach us. Counselling is a wonderful opportunity in this respect. It forces us to look more closely at the relationship and at the person to whom we are relating and to see beyond our habitual viewpoints. If we can enter the relationship in this honest way, and not all counsellors do, it releases us from our grosser prejudices.

In this way, counselling might be seen as a spiritual practice. By listening to others, we deepen our appreciation of our own limits and assumptions and we have the opportunity to move beyond them into relationship with another. We embrace the mystery of the unknowable in our attempt to deeply understand.

At the same time, both we and our clients are embedded within shared cultures and even our agreement on the nature of good mental health may simply be a collusion within that viewpoint.

EXERCISE SIX: WALKING IN OTHERS' SHOES

Think about someone with whom you are working currently. If you are not undertaking counselling work, think of someone whom you work with in another context, or are offering support to.

Imagine the person sitting in the room with you.

Reflect on the person whom you are holding in your mind's eye. Who is this? What really underpins their life? What is

---

important to them?

Try to imagine yourself in the other person's shoes. What is it like to be them? What inspires them? How do they see you?

Be aware of how much you know, but also of what remains mysterious.

Spend time sitting in quiet reflection, holding the person in your thoughts.

Counselling as a Spiritual Practice

Counselling can be seen as an opportunity and even as a spiritual practice. We can feel deeply appreciative of the other person and our encounter with them. We can feel privileged to be in their presence. In this we may feel touched at a level of spirit as well as emotion and intellect.

The process of counselling can thus be inspiring, and this is no bad thing, since inspiration can create a condition for ethical practice. The person who is inspired is not jaded or falling into cynicism, but gives the energy of their inspiration to the work. On the other hand, inspiration, without the devotion and discipline which follows it, can be flaccid and self-indulgent. The role of the counsellor is not just concerned with wanting to do good and help others. It also requires rigour and commitment. This, itself can be seen as a spiritual practice.

As counsellors, our responsibility to our clients is to be available and to ground our being in wholesome attitudes and values. Creating availability involves making therapeutic space in our minds. It means letting go of preoccupations and, as far as we are able, being willing to go beyond our habits of thought and view.

This space is what is known in phenomenology as the *epoche*[5], created by "bracketing" our prior knowledge and viewpoints so that we can observe and respond afresh. The *epoche* is never perfect, but this does not prevent us attempting to create it.

Here, then, there are effectively two sorts of activity which allow the space to be created:

- Letting go of preoccupations, we are basically looking for a calm, clear mind which is not busy with other matters from our lives and will not interrupt the attention we give to our clients.
- In attempting to create the *epoche*, we also become more aware of the way that our expectations and assumptions, our frame of reference, distorts our view of others. We notice the interruptions and the thoughts which intrude.

We can think of both of these activities as having parallels in spiritual practice. Meditation, for example, has two basic forms[6]. The first, stopping or *sammattha* meditation, involves clearing mental space. The second, insight or *vipassana* meditation, involves investigating elements of experience.

Clearing mental space and becoming aware of our blocks to being really available to the other is a basic practice for the counsellor. It provides the ground on which the session can rest.

MEDITATION EXERCISE

If you read *Listening to the Other* you will already have a quiet space in your home which you have been using for reflective exercises and as a base to go back to in order to

---

relax and reflect on your work. If you have come straight to this book, you may now like to take time to create such a quiet corner in your home. This place should be somewhere where you will not be disturbed. You need to be able to sit comfortably, either on a chair or cushion on the floor. You might like to have a blanket to wrap around you as you sit. Your area may have a focal point to help you to build associations of calm and peace, which might be flowers, pictures or photographs, candles or natural items such as pebbles or shells. Start your meditation there.

A common definition of meditation is that it involves holding the attention upon a wholesome object. Different objects are used in this way, including real or imagined ones. One meditation method involves paying attention to the breath. This was presented in *Listening to the Other*. Other meditation methods might involve visualisation. If you already have a preferred meditation practice, you may like to do this. Otherwise, if you are new to meditation, a nice practice to start with is to use a candle as your focus of attention.

Before you start, find a position in which to sit which is comfortable but in which your body is alert. Traditional meditation positions mostly use a low cushion on the floor and involve sitting with pelvis tilted forwards and an upright spine, so that your abdominal area is extended, and you can breathe deeply into the region of the naval. This is the best way to sit, but it does not work for everyone. You can achieve an approximation to it if you sit well forwards on an upright chair, with your feet flat on the ground. Experiment with different ways of sitting, and ideally find a position where you can breathe deeply, where your spine is straight and your shoulders aligned, and in which you can remain still for a period of time in a comfortable relaxed way.

Once you have decided on your position, and you have sufficient undisturbed time available, take a candle and light it and place it in front of you so that it is in your line of sight as you sit (if you are using a chair, you might put the candle on a low table.)

Sit down and close your eyes. Take a few minutes to settle into your meditation posture. Feel the way that your body makes contact with the ground or chair. Breathe out slowly and deliberately, and notice how your body sinks a little as you do so. If you feel tense, you can repeat this a few times.

When you feel ready, open your eyes slightly so that you can see the candle. Focus your attention on the flame. Notice how the candle flame moves and changes. Notice its luminescence and its transparency. Spend a few minutes watching, keeping your mind on the flame. When you find yourself wandering off into thoughts, gently bring your attention back.

After a little while, as you look, allow your eyes to close again slightly, gradually letting the lids drop, but holding your attention on the candle flame. See if you can hold the image of the flame in your mind even when your eyes are closed. Keep opening your eyes slightly to "top up" the image.

Start by sitting for five or ten minutes each day. Do not push yourself to go beyond what is comfortable. Gradually build up your time until you can hold your attention on the candle for around twenty minutes.

This sort of exercise will help you to develop a calm, steady presence. It will help you to be more focused and open when you are working with clients.

EXERCISE SEVEN: EXPLORING EPOCHE

After you have spent a period of time in meditation, spend five minutes noting down any thoughts or distractions which came into your mind. What sort of things intruded on your meditation? How effective was your concentration on the candle?

How well did you see the candle? Can you describe the different shades of light which you saw in the flame? What did the wax do? Did the flame smoke at any point, if so, why?

If you found it difficult to answer these questions (and this is not a sign you did the meditation wrongly) what was your mind doing whilst you were watching the flame?

You can repeat this reflective exercise several times, but do not feel you have to do it every time you meditate, as it may affect the attention you give to the meditation process if you are trying to make sense of it or remember it as you go.

Ethics and Values as a Foundation

Whilst the practice of counselling can be equated to a spiritual practice, to the deep, mysterious connection between two human beings, our presence as counsellors is primarily intended to be the catalyst to a process of change for the other.

The process of developing our capacity to set aside personal agendas and to hear the depth of the other's story is an important part of the counselling relationship. This in itself is not easy, and our ability to give such quality attention is something which develops over time. The counselling itself can be seen as a training in meditation.

Likewise, our ability to look at our own process is something which we can develop. We can notice our preoccupations and distractions, and see how our understanding of the other is limited and imperfect. This takes more vigilance, for as we become experienced, it is easy to fall into complacency. Good supervision can help us to tease out some of our blind-spots, but we are always in danger of assuming that what we hear and see is the correct interpretation of the situation. Both these aspects of our practice are, if you like, professional skills. They relate to how we act within the counselling space, our ability to create good conditions, and to perform certain mental tasks in a time-limited session. Our basic life assumptions will manifest in our assumptions about what the client is saying, so personal growth work can never be eliminated from our training and development as counsellors, but the work we do in looking at our own process needs to draw our attention to our biases rather than supporting our prejudices. The *epoche* is never perfect, however. Our values and preferences will always manifest in our responses, even if at a subtle level.

Being a counsellor is not really something we do, it is something we are. It is work which requires us to be present as human beings, not as robots. In therapeutic work we may have techniques to draw on, but basically, when we sit in the client's presence, we are most effective when we are simply present as ourselves. We are, in this respect, our own tool box.

The training which we do is a process of honing, and it is important. It sharpens our perception and brings to focus our areas of capacity or of limitation. Training puts us under the microscope and leads us to look more closely at our responses. It helps us to clean up our vision and see others more directly.

At the end of the day, however, our skills and awareness rest upon a foundation of who we are. This foundation is not something which we can muster up for the duration of the therapy hour and then discard. By its nature, it is woven into our being. Nor is it even ours alone. It is part of the culture in which we operate, the values which we assimilate, the social conserve. It is "common sense"; what everyone thinks. It is the received wisdom of our group.

This book starts with an exploration of values, because values are foundational to our work. As we have seen, psychology and Western culture are closely inter-linked. Concepts and assumptions about the nature of the human experience are passed back and forth, sometimes resulting in surprising interpretations. Waves of thought and fashions in ideologies flow through these processes and it is hard to determine what originates from where. Looking back after a passage of time, we may see the effects of our profession and be dismayed, or we may appreciate its contribution to the process of civilisation.

So, it is valuable to develop awareness and the ability to critique these assumptions. Our clients are also immersed in a culture which has been infiltrated by ideas which may or may not be psychologically healthy. They may have learned to think of themselves as vulnerable and needing help, as damaged and needing healing, as dependent and needing to find independence, because such ideas are prevalent in our society. We may well be swimming in the same soup.

It is important, as counsellors, to ground our lives in wholesome values. Our own beliefs and preoccupations will influence our work. This does not mean that our clients will take on our belief systems in a simplistic way. It is more a matter of offering them a greater space to explore and not intruding upon it with unhelpful concerns and preconceptions.

If our views are grounded in a different perspective, if they implicitly call into question social dogmas, if they are solid in their confidence in the good and the worthwhile, then we will offer a space that is wider, and more open to new possibilities. We will not confine our clients to the doctrines of our times, but will challenge them to question and embrace other perspectives.

In the next session we will explore the nature of this foundational layer. We will look at how, as counsellors, our way of being offers conditions to our clients, and at how those conditions may be conditions for good, or for harm.

References and Background Reading for this Session

Bates, Y & House, R, 2003 *Ethically Challenged Professions* PCCS Books, Ross on Wye

Bond, T *Standards and Ethics for Counselling in Action*, Sage, London

Furedi, F, 2004 *Therapy Culture* Routledge, London

Harvey, P 2000 *An Introduction to Buddhist Ethics* Cambridge University Press, UK

Keon, D 1992 *The Nature of Buddhist Ethics*, Palgrave, US

Masson, J 1988 *Against Therapy* HarperCollins London

SESSION TWO

Grounding the Counsellor

This session will explore:
- Faith as an underpinning factor in therapy
- The ideas of Gisho Saiko and Carl Rogers
- Connection and separateness
- Attention and focus
- Grounding
- Refuge and sanctuary

In session one, we explored the way that psychology and counselling has been influential in shaping Western culture in the latter part of the twentieth century and how, at an individual level, the counsellor is influential on the client. We saw how this is, in part, grounded in the nature of the counsellor's role, and how this role bears the inheritance of many qualities which were, in the past, the province of the priest.

Whatever belief systems underpin a society, these beliefs will influence the lives of its members. Likewise your attitudes and values will communicate themselves in subtle ways to your clients and will influence the counselling process. If you are concerned with achievement, your clients may become more goal orientated, seeing success in material or intellectual attainment. If you believe that life is a struggle and it is important to face its grim reality, your clients are likely to spend their time talking about the bad experiences which they have had. Some counsellors use up boxes of tissues, others laugh more.

Beyond all these beliefs, however, some people exhibit a quality of presence which is not really founded in any particular beliefs. This quality above all makes someone a good therapist. It is often hard even to frame in words, though we might call it faith. It is a sort of confidence in life; a relaxation of the spirit, which trusts, in the words of Julian of Norwich[7] that 'all's well and all shall be well, all manner of things shall be well'.

Such trust is not a Pollyanna-ish disregard of reality. It is a deep acceptance of what is, and a trust that beyond the vicissitudes of daily life there is a stability in the universe which is benign and holding.

Faith as an Underpinning Factor

In *Listening to the Other* we explored the ideas of a Japanese teacher and Priest, Gisho Saiko. Saiko, who was a devotee of Carl Rogers, and developed his own theory of the counselling relationship. He saw the counsellor and client as meeting within a context of faith.

Saiko represented his theory as a diagram of two overlapping triangles. These two triangles represent counsellor and client. They face each other. The diagram is traversed by a line which separates the conscious engagement of the session (above) from the unconscious communication (below). This results in the upper, conscious parts of the relationship being contiguous but separated and the lower, unconscious parts overlapping one another. The overlapping area is below this line, and represents the shared psychic space of the therapy session.

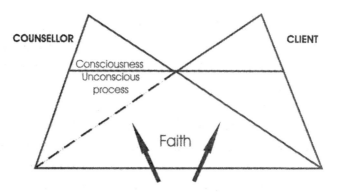

When you look at the diagram, one thing which you will notice is that the two upper triangles representing counsellor and client are equal in size. This represents a person to person meeting. Whilst some models of counselling might see the counsellor's triangle as bigger or more powerful, Saiko emphasises the equality of the two participants in the counselling relationship. This is a person to person encounter.

In his paper *A Dharma-based Person-centred Approach in Japan*, Saiko[8] compares this type of therapist-client relationship with the I-Thou relationship described by Martin Buber[9]. It is a relationship characterised by respect and open communication.

The lower part of the diagram represents the unseen underpinnings of the therapeutic relationship. In this part of the model, the mundane world of human interactions is grounded in unseen connections. It is rooted in the infinite, the transcendent and the eternal. The human world rests within a spiritual context, which percolates up through the depths of the interaction. Unseen, and often unacknowledged, our day to day being is inevitably connected with the bigger forces which shape our lives.

At the start of the counselling relationship, the counsellor is in touch with these forces. Grounded in a confidence in the process of change and in an awareness of the spiritual benevolence which underpins life, she or he is the holder of the faith. This is faith is represented by the fact that below the horizontal line, the counsellor's triangle is drawn with a solid line. The counsellor is aware of the spiritual source. Initially, the client's triangle is drawn with a broken line below the line, for the client is, in all likelihood, not.

For Saiko, the counsellor's grounding in faith was rooted in a faith in Amida Buddha, the focus of his religious tradition, but he was able to present his theory in more universalist terms in non-Buddhist or secular contexts. For counsellors of other backgrounds, then, we can understand this source to be framed in whatever spiritual language feels comfortable. Amida means without measure, so you might like to think in terms of the infinite. Grounding our practice in a confidence in the measureless qualities of life, in the bigger picture, we bring a calm and availability to our work and so support our clients to discover a similar groundedness.

Saiko's model assumes a universally available spiritual resource. His faith is in an omni-present influence, which is there for everyone, but is not always recognised. As the counsellor and client participate in the therapeutic relationship, they are in the field of the same spiritual support, but the client is not aware of it. Gradually, as the relationship continues, the client comes to trust the source and in some sense catches the counsellor's faith. As the relationship progresses, the client begins to trust the resources on which the counsellor is drawing.

Gisho Saiko's model is simple, and as such is eloquent. Whether or not we share the specifics of Saiko's spirituality, the recognition that the vital element which the counsellor brings into the counselling relationship is the element of faith is important.

We have already seen how influential the values which a society holds can be on the psychological health of that society and also how values inevitably underpin our counselling work. It is therefore good for us to explore our own values and to test out what faith we are conveying to our clients.

EXERCISE ONE: FINDING OUR GROUND

Take a large sheet of paper and some chalks or paints.

Sit in your quiet space and spend a few minutes settling yourself. Close your eyes and breathe deeply. Ask yourself:

What is it that I ground my work as a counsellor in?

Try not to find intellectual answers, but, rather, to arrive at some sort of felt sense of your work. You can help this process by imagining yourself sitting with clients and asking yourself "how does this feel, what am I relying on?"

When you start to get an intuition, look for a colour which represents that sense. Start to draw on your paper. You might just want to create swathes of colour, or might have distinct shapes or images in mind.

Allow your drawing to grow spontaneously. Add more shades and shapes. From time to time sit quietly with your eyes closed and check the felt sense.

Your drawing will grow out of your experience, but inevitably it will be a mix of representation of what you are feeling, and things which have arisen out of the drawing process itself.

When you have finished, sit with your image in front of you. Allow yourself to look at the image and then to close your eyes and check the feeling that arises as you look at it. Alternate short periods of looking at the image with periods of reflection. Finally, sit quietly and allow your sense of grounding to develop.

Unseen Connections

One of the interesting aspects of Saiko's diagram is the way that the two triangles inter-penetrate. Counsellor and client are, on the surface separate, but, in the unseen levels of the interaction, their worlds meet and inter-mingle. Each has some areas of separation and privacy, unknown, mysterious territory of the mind, but much of their experience is superimposed.

This diagram reflects the experience of therapeutic relationship well. Although, in one way, psychological separation is maintained, in quite uncanny ways we can often sense one another at a very embodied, intimate way.

When I sit with a client who is talking brightly about her how she is solving her various troubles, I may feel a tightness in my chest which speaks to me of sorrow and tells me that she is maybe not as happy and confident as she is presenting herself to be. On another occasion, when I share an image of a bird flying the nest which comes to me spontaneously during our session, the client has tears in his eyes as he tells me that he has just left the person he loved. I can notice the feeling welling up and feel the bitter-sweet tenderness it expresses.

Such experiences are uncanny. It can feel as if we are privy to the other's world in a way that is both privileged and unsettling. We may explain the phenomenon by talking of deeper levels of empathy, but often the experience of such times is of touching the other's being, and even entering their psychic world, in a profound and real way. The felt sense of another's unspoken grief speaks to us through the chatter of their conversation in a way that leaves us with a feeling of having known them profoundly.

In the opening chapter of *A Way of Being*[10], Carl Rogers describes an encounter with a woman who attended one of his groups. The woman was in some distress in her life. She was angry, prickly and beneath it all, very lonely. She felt no one could understand. After one of the sessions of the group she made a mildly disparaging remark about Rogers. His response was to put his arm around her shoulder. Later she wrote to him to tell him how she had been deeply affected by this moment and in it had sensed his deep concern for her. She had felt his humanity, his genuineness; his love.

You seemed so genuinely concerned the day I fell apart, I was overwhelmed... I received the gesture as one of the first feelings of acceptance... that I had ever experienced.[11]

The woman continued to describe her feelings, talking of the importance of the connection she had felt with Rogers on that occasion. Rogers, himself, then reflects:

This woman, of course, was speaking to me, and yet in some deep sense she was also speaking for me. I too have had similar feelings.[12]

At moments of deep understanding and emotional impact, we may feel very closely connected with our clients. We may feel that we share emotional process with them. This feeling of touching the other's world is, for many, at the very heart of the therapeutic experience, (although other therapists would be wary of such emotional entanglement.) In such human encounters, we may have a profound sense of some important connection having occurred, which transcends the ordinary levels of communication. We may feel that we have stepped into the other's world and breathed their breath with them. We have shared at a level of greatest intimacy.

As Rogers describes, the time when we feel such a connection, is often a point when layers of pretence seem to drop away and we relax in the other's presence. The client feels heard and seen, and as therapist too, we feel a level of connection which is not simply intellectual and professional, but engulfs our whole being. We feel completely present to the other.

But such feelings are, of course, slippery. It is our way, as humans, to distort and add and interpret. We filter and shape what we hear according to the templates in our own minds. We enjoy emotional arousal, but do not question whether the experience is really shared or whether it is simply that we both have simultaneous, different responses to a single trigger. Have we indeed shared the experience, or have we simply each had a profoundly affecting experience at the same time?

Rogers is careful to say 'similar' feelings. His quality of empathy is an 'as if' experience, in which the counsellor experiences what the client is saying 'as if seeing the world through his eyes'. If that 'as if' steps over into a semblance of psychological merger, we have almost certainly stepped from experiencing the client's world into identification. We have lost an appreciation of their otherness and confused their identity with our own.

Psychological theory struggles with the question of human connection. Do we ever really see others as they are? Is there a meeting? Or is the distance between us and the inevitable mystery of the other an unbridgeable gulf? In this book we will return to these questions.

EXERCISE TWO: EXPLORING CONNECTION I

Think of an experience in which you felt the sort of profound connection or shared understanding with a client, or with another person.

What did you experience? How accurately do you think it reflected what the other person was feeling? Write about the experience for five minutes, describing what you thought and felt.

Now imagine showing your writing to the other person. Try to imagine being them and reading your account. Imagine yourself as them responding to the piece of writing. As them, write for a further five minutes to give

---

your response and share your experience.

Read both pieces of writing and ask yourself, soberly, what the nature of the connection really was.

If you do this exercise relating to an experience you had with a friend or peer, you might consider discussing the experience with them and seeing how accurate your sense of their response really was. Do bear in mind, that even when people believe there is close correlation between their perceptions, objective research does not necessarily back this up.

EXERCISE THREE: EXPLORING CONNECTION II

If you have the opportunity, work with partner on the following exercise.

Sit opposite one another in silence for five minutes. You may look at one another, or not, but you may not speak. Ask yourself: Who is this in front of me?

Try to get a sense of the other person, and feel what it is like to be them.

After five minutes you may talk for a further five minutes and compare notes. Continue to explore the question: Can we know one another?

Now spend five more minutes, again sitting in each other's

> presence in silence with the original question.
>
> Spend the last five minutes debriefing. What does it mean to know another person? How do we feel most deeply connected? Is the connection real or delusory?

The nature of our relationship with the client is a subject for further discussion elsewhere, but what we can identify from these examples and from our own practice as therapists is that often there is a feeling of profound connection with the client. In such times, as we have seen, there can be experiences in which we feel some emotion or intuition arising in us which seems to have no source in anything which we have consciously observed or heard in the other's story.

There can be occasions when we not only see their distress or struggle, but also feel something which mirrors their experience. We sense their distress or joy in our bones. Such moments seem to touch a way of being which is different and which takes us into a field of interaction which seems to be on a different plane to that which has gone before.

This sort of experience is often referred to as *contagion*. The term is a good one, for it carries with it an implication of a transfer of experience which happens on a level which is not seen, but which comes about through a kind of person to person contamination. We catch the other person's feeling as we might catch a cold. In such moments, the sense may be of not simply hearing the person before us, but of tapping into a universal truth. Rogers sees this in terms of the particular instance putting us into contact with a common human state:

So there is both the satisfaction in hearing this person and also the satisfaction of feeling one's self in touch with what is universally true[13]

Saiko, on the other hand, sees the therapeutic connection as something which takes place within the spiritual dimension. In his model, there are not just two parties involved in the meeting. He senses a third omni-present force for good, which supports the encounter, and which is discovered through it.

Both theorists are describing a process whereby at the heart of the counselling, in the deeply personal experience of connection between two people, a universal dimension appears. This universal dimension is uplifting and inspirational, and indeed may well be the motivating factor for both counsellor and client, a holy grail of the profession. However it is described, the sense of touching a shared experience which is beyond ordinary description lies at the base of many therapists' motivations.

Attention and the Felt Sense

Our mental states are dependent upon what we are giving attention to at any one time. Whatever thoughts, images, conversations or experiences are at the forefront of our minds, these will condition our mental process in the moment. If we look at a pleasant pastoral scene we probably feel calm and happy. If we look at broken glass and graffiti by the bus stop we may feel irritated or depressed. If we look at an envelope from the tax authorities we may feel anxious. If we look at a baby we may feel tender. The object of attention is highly significant in the creation of mental states[14].Changing the object of attention changes the mental state. Intensifying our attention is likely to intensify the emotional reaction.

During the counselling session, if we are working effectively, we will naturally be working with strongly focused attention. The subject of that attention will, however, vary. Depending on what we give attention to, our felt experience will also vary. To some extent we can make deliberate choices about where we place our attention, and it is part of the skill of the therapist to direct attention to different foci and to move between them, checking the different possible fields of perception.

As therapist, our focus of attention might be:

- The client (what is said, gestures and facial expression, body language, voice tone etc)
- Our own experience as counsellor (reactions, resonances, impulses to speak or act, body responses etc)
- The scenario being described (location, characters in story, events etc)
- A stable external source (values, beliefs, the physical space of the room, silence etc)

The client can likewise shift attention to different elements in the counselling process. These might include:

- The therapist
- Their own experience in telling the story
- The story itself and elements in it
- A stable, external source

It will be apparent that the two lists are equivalent. The client's experience and choices mirror those of the therapist. The different possible focuses mirror the different possible objects of the therapist's attention.

What may be less apparent, however, when one considers these choices, is that, when they interact, in some instances the client and therapist will be looking in the same direction, by giving attention to the same object, but in other situations the two may be looking in different, or even opposite directions.

If the therapist's attention and the client's attention are both on the story which the client is telling, then both will have the same (or at least similar) objects of attention. They may therefore experience parallel feelings, helping the therapist to empathise with the client. Of course, as we will see, this is not a straight-forward process, because the therapist's perception will not be the same as that of the client, but trying to align in their vision of the story may be one way to improve the empathic under-standing between them.

If the therapist's attention is on the client and the client's attention is on the story, then the therapist's experience will be conditioned by the view of the client, and their visible reactions of happiness, sadness or anger, whilst the client's experience is conditioned by the various scenes which are unfolding in their account of an event.

If the client's attention is on the therapist and the therapist's attention is on the client, each will find themselves reacting to the other. Here, on the one hand, there is the possibility of oppositional responses, where the two fall into counter-part roles. The therapist sees the client's vulnerability and the client sees the therapist's caring response, so that a kind of symbiosis develops. On the other hand, the two may align into a shared position. The therapist sees the client's anger and feels outrage on their behalf, which the client sees and consequently feels even more angry.

There are many possible permutations. We will return to look at ways in which different objects of attention condition different mind-states in future sessions, for it is central to this approach.

Grounding

In the last session, we looked at the way that meditation can be used to help us create a calm, quiet space in ourselves so that we can be open to the other person's story. In order to listen well, we clear the mind of intruding thoughts as far as possible. This clarity is the ground in which the counselling takes place.

Because mental states depend upon the object of attention, although we talk about a meditative exercise as a process of clearing the mind, really it is a matter of turning the mind to something inspiring or calming so that it will not be pulled away onto more mundane matters. When we are faced with something compelling, we naturally give the single pointed attention which meditation is intended to foster. Deliberately calming the mind means learning to give this kind of attention to the ordinary and the wholesome.

A skill which depends upon this kind of single pointed attention is the skill of grounding oneself. This skill is very helpful to the counsellor. The term grounding is commonly used to describe a method whereby the attention is focused on an object external to oneself, usually in the physical environment, in order to evoke a calm, quiet mind and body state. Often the focus of such an exercise is literally the ground on which one walks or sits, but it need not be.

Grounding involves paying attention to physical sensation but it also involves allowing a sense of the symbolic aspects of that experience to develop. It is particularly about establishing contact with a physical reality outside the body, but also about sensing the universal dimension within the immediate.

Thus grounding has some similarities with meditation. Its focus is on a benign object and it involves both mind and body, but it differs in placing a stronger emphasis on the bodily aspect of the process and on the supportive nature of the external presence.

EXERCISE FOUR: GROUNDING YOURSELF

You may wish to make a recording of this script so that you can play it to yourself as you practice the exercise. If you do so, speak slowly and allow spaces between the sentences and paragraphs so that you will be able to take plenty of time in following the instructions.

Start by sitting in your quiet space. Sit on an upright chair in a position where your body is comfortable, but straight. You back should be aligned and your weight evenly distributed on the seat. Your feet should be flat on the floor, so if your chair is too high you may need to put a book or a firm cushion under them. Check that your head is straight and evenly balanced on your neck.

Experiment with moving your head slightly backwards and forwards to find the right point where it feels comfortable and your neck feels free from strain. You can imagine a piece of string tied from the top of your head going up to the ceiling, pulling you up straight. Relax and let the imaginary string hold you upright. Close your eyes or let them go out of focus, looking at the ground in front of you.

Check that your shoulders are not tense. Pull them up towards your ears, then let them drop to release tension. You can repeat this several times. Let your hands sit comfortably in your lap.

As you settle into your position, breathe slowly and evenly. Give particular attention to the out-breath, lingering a little over it.

Now bring your attention to the parts of you which are in contact with the chair. Feel the way that you thighs and buttocks are supported by it. Maybe you can feel it with your back too. Notice your feet as they are in contact with the ground.

Focus your attention on all these places of contact. Try to

do this in a feeling way, not just holding it as an idea. Feel the outline which your body makes on the chair, and where the points of greatest pressure are. Imagine that someone has created a map of the points of pressure with the points of heaviest pressure marked in the deepest shades. Where would those deep shades be? What tone would they be in? Allow the lower part of your body to sink a little so that the outline which you are making on the chair increases its size and the shades on your pressure map increase in depth.

See if you can feel the texture of the chair beneath you, or of the carpet or flooring beneath your feet. Where is your body most sensitive to the different textures? Feel the solidity of the seat and of the floor. Notice the way your body is supported by the physicality of them. Try to let yourself be supported further.

Now imagine your breath flowing down through your body. Feel it flowing into the chair and through it into the floor. Feel yourself connecting deeply with the earth beneath, the energy flowing down into the core of the planet.

Now imagine that you are part of a huge oak tree. Your deep, gnarled roots stretch down into the soil.

Feel your contact with the earth through your body, and going down into those imagined roots, and imagine your trunk stretching tall and straight, with branches stretching up and outward, high into a summer sky in the bright summer sunshine.

Feel any tension flowing out of your body, down into the roots, deep in the ground. Breathe deeply and enjoy the feeling of being supported by the earth.

When you are ready you can stretch and start to move your body slowly, open your eyes and bring your attention back to the room around you. As you move, walk tall, continuing to plant your feet firmly.

Grounding is a basic skill for the counsellor. To be able to feel calm and release bodily tension before we see our clients, helps us to offer the sort of attention which is likely to be helpful. It brings us present. Like meditation, it creates a more focused mental state, and brings that calm into the body as well as the mind.

It can also be noticed that the grounding exercise, like Saiko's diagram, locates the main source of support in the space beneath us. In doing the exercise, we symbolically evoke the experience of a benevolent presence which underpins life.

We feel beneath us the holding quality of the universal dimension. We learn to trust the forces on which we depend, to trust life, and in doing so, we become able to transmit that trust to others.

Refuge and Sanctuary

What underpins our existence? In what do we take refuge? What is the thing in which we place our confidence? What is the object of our faith? Saiko was a Buddhist and his view of counselling was grounded in his Buddhist faith. Refuge is a central aspect of the Buddhist life and for Saiko, his sense of the presence which underpinned his work was of something which he would have seen as a source of refuge.

To take refuge means to place our trust in something. The term is used in the religious context to describe an act whereby a person places their faith in the core tenets of that religion, but the word can also be used in the secular context to describe the act of seeking support and succour at a time of peril. We might think in mundane ways of taking refuge in a hut or cave during a storm, or of falling back on a set of ideas with which one has long been familiar.

A similar concept is that of sanctuary. If you visit Durham Cathedral in the north of England, you will see on its great oak door an old brass knocker, shaped like a lion's head with a ring in its mouth. This knocker is the sanctuary knocker. It became famous because anyone who grasped it could not be taken by the law. Criminals would come to seek help by clinging to it, thereby gaining a thirty seven day stay of execution in the Cathedral, before they could be deported.

The sanctuary knocker is a particular example of refuge. It reflects the wider use of churches as places of sanctuary. In a holy place, one may be protected, safe from attack. Those who intend harm would not venture into God's house to do it, at least in theory. In practice, history has revealed many who did not share such scruples.

In the last session we saw how the counsellor might be compared with a priest in occupying the same social place as confessor and source of wisdom as the priest did in the past. Similarly, we might think of the counselling room as a place of sanctuary or refuge for the client. The private space with its firm boundaries and protective wall of silence allows secrets to be shared and burdens unpacked away from the threat of retribution or judgement. The counsellor, as confessor, provides the listening ear of the priest, presiding over this safe space in which the world's troubles are held at bay.

Different therapists will offer sanctuary in different ways. Some will create it through their quality of presence, their belief in the client's capacity to grow, and their consistent warmth. Others will create it through their groundedness and common sense practicality. They will hold an optimistic no-nonsense view of life's difficulties. Others still will bring their beliefs and values to bear on the situation, relieving the client of personal guilt through their insight into social, political, or spiritual contexts.

Each of these offers a form of faith. The faith may be the confidence which the therapist has in the client and his ability to work through whatever arises. It may be in the processes of ordinary life and the human capacity for survival. It may be in a spiritual truth which underlies all our experience. Thus each counsellor offers their own style of refuge, and the efficacy of their work depends upon the faith in which it is grounded.

EXERCISE FIVE: REFUGE

Reflect upon the image of the Durham door knocker.

Are there times in your life when you have felt the need for sanctuary?

Where have you gone? What was the sequence of events?

How did it feel before you reached your place of sanctuary?
How did it feel when you got there? What was the outcome?

Take five minutes of silent contemplation to explore the process. Reflect on the experience of longing for sanctuary and of attaining it.

Express your process in a piece of creative writing, either in poetry or prose.

References and Background Reading for the Session

Buber, M 1970 *I and Thou* Charler Scribners Sons, US

Rogers C.R. 1961 *On Becoming a Person*. Constable, London

Rogers C.R. 1980 *A Way of Being* Houghton Mifflin Boston

Unno T 1998 *River of Water, River of Fire: An introduction to the Pure Land tradition of Shin Buddhism*, Doubleday, New York

SESSION THREE

Object Related Identity

This session will explore:
- The creation of identity
- Objects and identity formation
- Sub-personalities
- Empathy
- Empathy and perception of the object world
- The client's need to empathise

The mind is conditioned by the object of attention. Thus we can say that our mentality is object-related[15]. The world which we perceive creates our mentality and our mentality creates what we see. This is the basic working of the human condition and the trap which it creates. A self-reinforcing cycle of expectation and reaction means that we build around us a psychological wall to keep out the things we fear and resist. We protect ourselves from anticipated troubles with comforting familiarity.

In this session we will look at the basic model of mental process which will form the context for the methods offered in this book. The model is one which I have set out in greater detail in my earlier book, *Buddhist Psychology*[16] so I will not go into the history or derivation of the understanding in depth in this book. For the sake of readability, I will also avoid using technical language as far as possible and stick with English equivalents.

Protecting Ourselves

The reality is that life is unpredictable. Many of our troubles come unannounced and most of the time we live in uncertainty. One day we may be healthy and the next we may discover that we are suffering from a terminal illness. We may be driving along a quiet road when a drunken driver comes round the

corner in the opposite direction. We may be holidaying in the sun
when our resort is hit by a tsunami17. All of us have friends
whose lives have been torn apart by unforeseen disasters, even if
we have not experienced them ourselves. On a day to day level,
we know the unpredictability of ordinary things: the car breaks
down; a letter gets lost in the post; we get sick.

Some troubles are more predictable. We get older and our
health changes. Things wear out. Our children become teenagers
and then leave home. Our parents age and grow frail and
eventually die. We try to take things in our stride, but at a
psychological level, we create defences to help us to cope. This is
completely understandable.

According to the model which Buddhist psychology offers, the
process whereby people create their psychological defences
basically has three stages:

Firstly we distract ourselves with sensory experiences.

This first level of response is common-place. We have a rough
day at work, and we just want a comfortable evening in front of
the television; an argument with a close friend, and we pop into
the supermarket for a packet of chocolate biscuits. This is what
most people think of as a normal way of carrying on. We do
things to blot out thoughts about what has gone wrong. Mostly
this distraction is physical. It includes all the usual indulgences,
like drinking or smoking or overeating.

Sensual distraction happens through all the physical senses.
We watch, taste, touch, listen, and savour distractions. The imagination, according to this model, is included as one of the sense
organs[18]. It perceives thoughts and dreams and visualisations.
We also distract ourselves with day dreams or compulsive
worries.

Secondly we create a sense of identity.
With time, our patterns of distracting ourselves become habits. We have our preferred way of escaping from daily troubles. In this way we tend to go round the same behavioural patterns repeatedly until we begin to identify with our habits. We start to build up a sense of identity based on the things which we associate with.

The identity is supported by a series of action patterns, each with other associated objects. For example, a person might distract himself by playing football. Gradually he builds up an identity based on his love of playing the game. This identity might be associated with being a member of his football club, wearing its strip, going to the pub where his team congregates, and so on.

Most of us have a number of different ways of distracting ourselves, each of which has an associated world of objects and experiences. Many of these, in themselves, provide other sensory distractions. The football player may enjoy going to the pub after the football game or telling ribald jokes in the changing room. Together these many faceted distractions create a complex web of associations and preferences which is particular to each individual, and which becomes the identity.

Whilst sensory distractions are transient, and serve to draw our attention away from the immediate source of trouble in our lives, identity has the advantage, and disadvantage, of persisting. Because we tend to repeat our patterns of distraction and seek out familiar situations to help us to reinforce them, the identity which arises as a result has the illusion of being permanent. In a world of unpredictable disasters, creating a sense of identity which feels secure and fixed has its attractions, even if it is basically illusory.

EXERCISE ONE: IDENTITY AND DISTRACTION:

Think about a client with whom you have worked. Try to identify ways in which this person deals with the stress or pain in their life.

Can you identify first level sensory distractions which they have used? Can you see ways in which these move into being supports for identity?

The cross over is not easy to distinguish. Indeed, it is probably not important to know, because if a distraction has become established enough for you to have heard about it, it is probably supporting their sense of identity in some way.

Reflect on your client's ways of creating and maintaining identity.

Thirdly we seek oblivion.

Whilst the sense of identity protects us from most of the difficulties which we encounter in life, there sometimes comes a point when a person feels so overwhelmed by their situation that they can no longer face continuing. Perhaps at this time, the things which have been important aspects of the person's identity have fallen away. Perhaps a loved one has died or the person has been uprooted from their home environment.

Whatever the circumstances, if the need to escape becomes strong enough, at some point a person may tip over from their struggle to maintain an illusion of permanence into just longing for escape and oblivion. This last stage may be the end of the line, the descent into becoming seriously suicidal, or to depressive addictions in which the person just longs to bury everything under a haze of drugs. It may on the other hand be a transitory despair which we sink into periodically, in which we reject the world and long to just give up.

These three levels of defence are part of the normal process of human function. For the most part, as you can see, we use the first two stages. Only occasionally do we fall into the third.[19]

EXERCISE TWO: SEEKING OBLIVION

Think about clients whom you have worked with who might have passed into the final phase of escape.

What sort of thing do you think contributed to tipping them over the edge in this way?

What did you find helped in this circumstance?

Could you identify times when you have felt similarly low, which might help you to empathise with the person?

Objects and Identity

According to the model which we are exploring, the creation and maintenance of identity is closely related to things which we do, and with the world which we inhabit. In particular it is linked initially to the objects which we use to distract ourselves. These become important to us not just because they bring immediate relief, but also because they come to support our sense of self. Our sense of identity is associated with many sorts of objects. Some were originally sources of distraction, but many are just part of the world which has grown up for us associated with the original activity. The football game might have been the original distraction, but the clothing and the football magazine and the photographs of players all become part of the new identity to be embraced alongside the game itself.

In using the word "object", we are here talking not just about physical objects like ice cream or beer or a new dress, but also about more abstract objects, like the name of our football team or a designer label. We are talking about perceptual objects. The term is technical. It refers to things which are perceived through any of our senses. An object might be a place or a sound, an image or a person, a brand-name or even an idea (for we must remember that the mind is also considered to be a sense organ in this model).

The objects which support our sense of self are part of our story about our self. Objects which are very important to us in defining our identity are ones to which we are likely to feel a strong pull. Because our identity is important to us as a means of warding off difficulties, we tend to cling tenaciously to things which support it. This means that we form strong attachments to certain things and resist giving them up. We also tend to seek out those things which help to maintain our self world. We feel compulsively drawn towards them.

One can think of many simple examples of such activity. We have our regular newspaper and rarely buy a different one. We walk to work along the usual road rather than trying a new route. We feel a quiet pride when someone praises the type of car which we drive. Habits persist. We feel an irrational sense of ownership when we see something which is 'like one that I have at home'.

It is interesting how frequently people who live overseas hanker for particular products from the home country. The British crave Marmite and Branston Pickle, the Americans crave Oreos, the French crave baguettes and French cheese. Such objects have a particular attraction because they are also associated with other more abstract, yet powerful, object, like 'my nationality' or 'my childhood'.

So objects cluster together, forming worlds which support particular aspects of our identities. Most of us are complex and have many facets to our identity, what in some systems of psychological theory might be called sub-personalities[20], but which we can also think of as different identities, or even different selves.[21]

EXERCISE THREE: DISCOVERING PERSONAL WORLDS

Take a large sheet of paper. Think about different 'identities' which you have. These might be connected with different roles you play, or different interests. They might just seem to be different moods you go through.

For each of these identities, draw a small circle on your piece of paper. Scatter them around to cover the whole page.

Now take each identity in turn and think about the objects which you associate with it. Remember that the term object includes people and places. You can use the following questions to help you:

- Where do you feel this identity most strongly?
- What people do you spend time with when you are occupying it?
- What clothes do you wear when you feel like this?
- What do you like to eat / drink / do when you are like this?
- What images do you associate with this?

- Is there music or literature associated with it?
- Does this identity have associations with a political or social view?
- When did you first experience this identity?

When you have finished exploring one identity, move onto another. After you have marked as many objects as you can around each identity, look at the overall picture. Does one identity predominate? Are there some objects which support more than one identity? Are some identities newer than others?

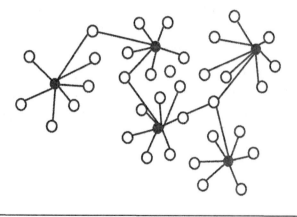

For each identity there are many objects. These objects help to keep in place the psychological defences which convince us that there is safety and permanence we can rely upon at times when the world seems threatening and unfriendly. They make us feel as if we are a special case.

EXERCISE FOUR: CLIENTS' PERSONAL WORLDS

Choose one of your clients with whom you have been working for a while. Repeat exercise three, identifying and exploring your client's different identities and the objects which are important in supporting them.

Notice the gaps in your knowledge and ask yourself why they are there, if they are important, and how you might remedy them if necessary.

Implications for Counselling

Our identities are supported by the things which we collect around us. Whether these things are material objects, people, ideas or cultural norms, they create a world in which we can feel secure and "at home". We create pockets of the familiar to protect ourselves from seeing the unknown and the frightening. This is a normal human pattern.

In this book we will look at ways that counselling and psychotherapy method can draw on this recognition of the importance of the object world. The following points will provide a summary of some of the areas which we will explore and give you an idea of the scope of this theory. We will return to the specifics later.

- People tend to seek out and re-create the object worlds which support their sense of identity, either by associating with real objects, or by conjuring them imaginatively
- When someone's object world is changed or a central object is lost, the person may feel disturbed and even become mentally unstable

- When clients talk about their experience they talk about the objects which support their current identity
- If a person shifts the focus of their attention and places it on different objects, their mental state, and sometimes their sense of identity, will change as a consequence
- People may have several distinct identities each with its own object world
- Through focusing on the objects which a person presents, we can work at the level of personality change without the person feeling intruded upon
- Many objects take on symbolic significance, not just as pointers towards the person's own identity[22], but also as reminders of, or connections to, other significant objects (especially people or religious figures), who in turn are significant in supporting the person's identity.
- In focusing on the objects which a person presents, as therapists, we enter into the client's world and see it as if through their eyes. We place ourselves alongside them and develop our capacity to empathise.

As we listen to our clients, they describe to us their object world. As they tell us about their lives, one after another the significant objects which maintain their sense of stability and of who they are will be paraded before us.

Empathy

Tuning into the world of the client is a core skill for any therapist. This means having *empathy* for the client. The development of empathy involves a concentration of our natural curiosity about other people. It also requires an ability to step out of our own viewpoint and see the world from another's perspective; that of the client.

In *Client Centered Therapy* Rogers describes empathy as follows:

It is the counsellor's function to assume, in so far as he is able, the internal frame of reference of the client, to perceive the world as the client sees it, to perceive the client himself as he is seen by himself, to lay aside all perceptions from the external frame of reference while he is doing so, and to communicate something of this empathic understanding by doing so.[23]

When we read this description, the first thing which is apparent is that Rogers is talking about achieving a perception which is parallel to that of the client. The counsellor enters into the perceptual frame of the client, setting her own expectations and views aside in the process. The perceptual frame which is adopted includes both the client's world view, and his view of himself. As the counsellor steps out of her own frame, in other words creates an *epoche*[24], she imaginatively stands alongside the client, viewing things as if through the client's senses.

EXERCISE FIVE: EMPATHIC UNDERSTANDING

Rogers writes: *can I enter (the client's world) so sensitively that I can move about in it freely, without trampling on meanings which are precious to him? Can I sense it so accurately that I can catch not only the meanings of his experience which are obvious to him, but those meanings which are only implicit, which he only sees dimly or as confusion?*[25]

Reflect on your own work as a counsellor, or your interactions with friends. Think of one session or encounter in which you have been involved recently and ask yourself Rogers's questions. Were there specific moments which you can identify when you felt this level of understanding for your client? Were there points where

---

> you shared something with your client which seemed to
> crystallise what they were struggling to understand?

EMPATHY LAB EXERCISES

Developing skill in empathic understanding is the foundation of
therapeutic practice. If you have the opportunity to work with
others, whether in a peer group or on a course, using this opportunity to actually practice skills and give feedback is immensely
valuable.

The empathy lab exercise has become a common means of
developing therapeutic skills. If you have undertaken a
counselling or therapy training you will probably be familiar
with this form of work. It involves working in *triads*. One person
is counsellor, one client and the third person is observer.

The client needs to be willing to share something from his or
her own life. This does not need to be painful, but it should be
something which is meaningful (it might, for example, be
something you are proud of or moved by, but it could also be
something you are struggling with.)

The counsellor counsels, attempting to understand as deeply
as possible what is being said. Use a reflective style. Check out,
have I understood this? Was this what you were saying? Does
that imply...? Do not be afraid to interrupt or even to voice your
hunches, so long as you do this tentatively.

The important thing is to communicate what you have understood. In that way you can check out your level of empathy and
keep as close as possible to the client as he talks. It is rather like
a footballer practicing shadowing a team-mate. You need to
follow the client through every twist and turn of their story, and
the only way to do this is through very small steps and very close
attention.

After an agreed time (five or ten minutes is usual) stop the session. Now is the time to give feedback. The client should feedback first, sharing at which points he or she felt best understood and at which points the counsellor seemed to misunderstand. The counsellor then also gives feedback, sharing his or her sense of which points were most significant.

The observer can facilitate this early part of the feedback by asking questions and prompting investigation. They may then give their own observations on the process.

Empathy lab exercises are about skills development, so you may take the opportunity to be more active than you would be during an actual counselling session with a client. Nevertheless, even with a client, being actively empathic is a good way to deepen your connection and demonstrate your level of empathy (or discover its limitations). So long as you remain tentative and willing to change direction if proved wrong, the client will appreciate your attempts to understand, even if they do not result in perfect comprehension.

EMPATHY LAB: VARIATION ONE

Empathy lab exercises can be varied in order to develop skills in particular ways. Once you are familiar with the form, you can experiment. One variant on the method is to do a five minute counselling session as described above. Afterwards, the three people involved each write for five minutes about what they noticed, before giving feedback.

Record:
- your memories of the process
- key points in the client's story
- key interventions made by the counsellor
- points of understanding or of misunderstanding

After five minutes, compare your answers before discussing the session in the usual way. Sometimes the discrepancies between them can be very revealing.

EMPATHY LAB: VARIATION TWO

One of the difficulties with empathy development is that often the counsellor only shares part of what he or she has understood. This variation on the empathy lab exercise helps you to 'get at' some of the hidden material. It is particularly good if, as counsellor, you have difficulty voicing non-verbal cues which you observed. It forces the counsellor to voice observations which are more tentative; things he or she heard and intuited.

Start by doing a counselling exercise in the usual way, with counsellor (A) and client (B) and observer (C).

After five minutes, swap chairs so that the counsellor sits in the chair which the client was sitting in, the client moves to the observer's chair and the observer to the counsellor's chair. (This physical re-location is important in order to help you make the switch of roles)

The counsellor (A) now role-plays the client (B), starting from the beginning of the story, but allowing him or herself to go spontaneously with whatever direction emerges. This may mean using imagination. The observer (C) is now counsellor and responds in an empathic style to what (A) is saying. Of course, (C)'s view will be affected by having watched the session, but predominantly he or she should focus on what (A) is actually saying. The original client, (B), becomes observer. Watching the session, (B) may feel that (A) has a very good understanding of his or her situation and may gain insight. Alternatively, it may become apparent that (A) was missing the point of (B)'s story and had a different view of what was going on. Often, in role as client, (A) will express feelings, details or hunches which he or she was not expressing in the role of counsellor.

After this second session, sometimes it can be helpful to go back into the original configuration for a further five minutes. When you do this, you will probably see a deepening of empathy. Whether or not you use this last stage, there will be a need for de-briefing and feedback. It is useful to reflect on whether (A) was expressing more understanding when role playing (B) than when in the counsellor role. If this is the case, discuss how the material which emerged might have been expressed in the original counselling scenario.

The "As If" Quality of Empathy

In *On Becoming a Person* Carl Rogers offers another description of empathy:

To sense the client's world as if it were your own, but without ever losing the "as if" quality...To sense the client's anger, fear, or confusion as if it were your own without your own anger, fear or confusion getting bound up in it is the condition we are endeavouring to describe.[26]

This extract offers similar definition to the one quoted earlier, but it clarifies that Rogers viewed empathy as an 'as if' quality. In other words, he was careful to avoid an implication of psychological merger. The counsellor always maintains an ability to regard the client's process and the shared dynamic of the therapeutic relationship, whilst at the same time immersing herself completely in it. She attempts to be both in and out of the stream of the client's experience. If this ability to remain in an 'as if' position is lost, the therapist simply falls into identification. In this case, although she may feel very close to the client, she in probably confusing the client's world with her own.

We can think of this mode of engagement as involving keeping the observer mind active. A part of the counsellor watches what unfolds. This part exists alongside the part which actively engages with the client, commentating inwardly on the process. Alternatively we can describe the activity by using the metaphor of having one foot in the river and the other on the bank.

Such descriptions imply a splitting of attention, but really, it is probably truer to say that we are constantly switching between a viewpoint where we are immersed in the client's world, and a somewhat more objective one. We probably cannot actually hold both positions simultaneously. The important thing is that we do not lose our ability to observe and bring objectivity into our perception. To be empathic and not simply get lost in the client's material, demands mental agility and concentration.

There are, of course, issues about how well we can really perceive the world of the other person. We may hear their story and understand the scenario, metaphorically standing alongside them and regarding their object world, but do we really respond in the same way to it as they do? As one develops skill in empathy, one gradually develops the ability to tune in better, but our ability to really step into the other's shoes is always only partial.

Acknowledging this partiality is important. If we start to believe that we are in perfect empathy with the other, this is probably a warning that we are slipping into identification. It probably means that we are not really understanding the other person, but, rather, are imposing our own interpretation upon their circumstances and feelings. When we are really in empathy, there always remains a degree of mystery and an edge of curiosity. We yearn to know them and their world a bit better.

It is probably this hunger to know more which the client senses in us. The client notices if we have genuine interest and concern. The therapist strives to understand and make psychological contact but is humble about her ability to do so, always struggling to look more deeply and questioningly into her perception. When the client senses this, he probably feels reassured at the humanity of the counsellor. He too reaches out across the gulf which separates all humans from one another, and tries to explain; to communicate more precisely.

In the first chapter of *A Way of Being*[27] Rogers describes the impact of those moments when client and counsellor seem to touch across the void of this isolation.

I have often noticed that the more deeply I hear the meanings of this person, the more there is that happens. Almost always, when a person realised he has been deeply heard, his eyes moisten. I think in some real sense he is weeping for joy. It is as though he were saying "Thank God, someone heard me. Someone knows what it is like to be me." In such moments I have had the fantasy of a prisoner in a dungeon, tapping out day after day a Morse code message, "Does anybody hear me? Is anybody there?" And finally one day he hears some faint tappings which spell out "Yes."[28]

This moving image seems to encapsulate the feeling which can come upon us in those moments of recognition that we experience from time to time in our work with clients. The connection feels like a meeting. Something feels complete. In that moment we both relax, resting in the experience of communication. Such moments are infrequent. They stand out in their specialness, just because they are uncommon. They become the memorable landmarks of long therapeutic relationships.

But even here, the understanding is never really complete. We do not occupy the other's mental space. Rogers talks of us hearing '*more* deeply'. The term is relative, not absolute. Even in these moments of deep encounter, the mystery of the other is present, and indeed, the emotion we both feel is probably as much in recognition of the majesty of this mystery, as it is of its bridging. We come into the presence, but we do not occupy it.

EXERCISE SIX: EMPATHY AND IDENTIFICATION

Take a sheet of paper and divide it into three columns. (Make these columns wide enough for you to be able to write in them.) Choose a client with whom you have been working for a while.

In the first column, think about your relationship and how good you feel your empathy is. Write down some thoughts about this.

In the second column write "ways in which this client is like me."

In the third column write, "ways in which this client is different from me"

Use these two columns to explore how similar or different

---

to them you sense that you are. Then reflect on what you wrote in the first column.

Repeat this exercise with a number of other clients.

Reflect on the overlap between feelings of being able to empathise and feelings of being similar. Of course this exercise does not necessarily indicate that there are problems if you find a high correlation between similarity and empathy. When we empathise we tend to find aspects of our own experience which are similar to that of the client, but this is a secondary process, triggered by our recognition of their experience. On the other hand, a high level of correlation may be an indication that you are too closely identified with your client and not appreciating differences.

Ask yourself what is going on in your own case.

Empathy for the Client's World

The nature of empathy is something which bears some reflection. What is it to sense another person's world? Do we need to be able to see its contents, or simply to see the person's reaction to them? If we are to empathise with a person's anger, fear or confusion, do we achieve this by seeing the person get angry or frightened or confused? Or do we experience it through standing alongside them and looking at the thing which evokes anger or fear or confusion?

To achieve the sort of understanding of the client's experience which Rogers is describing we have to be able to get into resonance with our clients. We need to get alongside them and look at the world as if through their eyes. This is not a matter of dissecting the minutiae of their reactions by observing their sadness or frustration, but rather, it is a matter of seeing how things look through their eyes, and in doing so, feeling an echo of their experience.

Rogers was interested in the experience of perception. Sometimes he is misunderstood and seen as someone who reflected feelings, but in fact he denied this strenuously. At the Second International Forum of the Person-Centred Approach, which was held at the University of East Anglia, in Norwich in 1984, when it was suggested that this was the case, Rogers said emphatically that he did not reflect feelings, but rather, that he was concerned to understand the client's way of perceiving[29].

In order to understand another person's reactions, our best approach is to try to get into a viewpoint which is parallel to theirs. If we can look at the world as if through their eyes and, in seeing it, direct our attention towards those objects which draw their attention, then we may start to get a felt understanding of how it is for them. Just as the mentality depends on the object of attention, so too, feelings are conditioned by the world which we inhabit.

If I want to frighten you, I do not tell you to have fear, I tell you about the forthcoming hurricane or the raging epidemic or your probable tax bill. For the most part, we are not frightened of fear or other emotions, though of course there are exceptions, such as when someone fears getting into a panic attack which they have experienced in the past. Mostly if we actually look at a feeling, it starts to dissipate.

Our fear or anger depends upon perceptual objects. These may be real, or, in the case of most of what is talked about in therapy, may be perceived by the mind's eye. Even when we fear depression or anxiety or grief, that emotion itself becomes a perceptual object which conditions our response. We look at "depression" and feel dread at the thought of its return. We look at "anxiety" and feel nervous that it may overwhelm us.

In the definitions quoted in this session, it is apparent too that Rogers' view of empathy had much in common with the object-related model. He was interested in what people give their attention to. This is the study of perception.

The study of perception brings with it an implication that in order to have perception, there must be a perceptual object. So in order to empathise with the client we need to be able to enter into that person's object world and place ourselves in relation to it, so that we can experience that world 'as if' looking through his eyes. Empathy is a process of entering another person's world of objects, feeling the pull of those which have become the supports for identity, and the rejection of those which threaten to destroy it. It means inhabiting another person's story and getting a feel for its' unfolding, as if from the inside. When we can do this, we can stand shoulder to shoulder with our clients and share breath with them.

Clients Need to Empathise

In his paper, *The Necessary Condition is Love*[30] my husband, David Brazier, wrote about the importance of the development of empathy, not just as the means by which a therapist comes to understand a client, but also as a process which is positive in itself. This process, he argued was something which benefited the counsellor and which should therefore also be of benefit to the client.

The creation of identity is primarily a function of our fear of life. People become caught in patterns of distraction and self-building because they experience distress as they try to engage. Small disappointments[31] and larger ones lead people to retreat into themselves. Yet the drive to connect is also present and as part of our fundamental nature[32] it goads us to try again to build relationship. However imperfectly, we relate to others.

In therapy, whilst the counsellor's task is often presented in terms of her ability to empathise with the client, in actuality, its healthy orientation is towards helping the client to empathise with others. In exploring together the world the client presents, therapist and client deepen their appreciation and respect for that world and the people in it. In other-centred work, this task becomes explicit. The client's exploration of their world becomes central and their attempt to reach a closer, more empathic connection with those others who are important to them becomes a focal task.

This process can take different directions. It may focus more upon the barriers of misconception which the client has created over time, or may be a more direct attempt to understand the reality of those others' lives. In either case, our purpose is still to help the client to establish a relationship with the world that is solidly grounded, empathic and respectful.

David has written of the need to esteem[33]. If we esteem, we respect the otherness of the object of our esteem. Esteem is something which we can only do across a divide. We look, we appreciate, we honour, and in doing so, we allow the other to be as they are, not part of our functional world, but separate and whole. This is the quality of empathy, and it is this which we would offer to those with whom we spend our working hours. When people are able to empathise, the isolation of self-interest is transcended. The person grows, walking in the shoes of many, and yet, in keeping esteem for them, does not simply warp their image into another facet of self, but rather, allows them to flourish in tact. Empathising, we open our hearts and love.

References and Background Reading for This Session

Brazier C, 2003, *Buddhist Psychology*, Constable Robinson. London
Beech, C and Brazier, D 1996 *Empathy for a Real World* in Hutterer, R, Pawlowsky, G, Schmid, P & Stipsits, R (eds)1996 *Client Centred and Experiential Psychotherapy: a paradigm in motion* Peter Lang, Frankfurt am Main, Germany

Brazier, D 2009 *Love and its Disappointment* O-Books UK

Rogers, C. R. 1951 *Client-Centred Therapy*, Constable London

Spinelli, E, 1989 *The Interpreted World: An Introduction to Phenomenological Psychology*. Sage Publications. London

SESSION FOUR

Conditioned View

In this session we will explore:
- Self worlds and self-world phenomena
- The creation of the self-world
- Self-fulfilling prophesies and expectations
- Facilitating exploration of the self-world
- Rupa: the phenomenal object

People shape the context of their lives to a much greater degree than they often recognise. This is true at a practical level as well as psychologically. When a client tells a counsellor their story, it can sometimes seem as if they have been victim of circumstances. The life situation in which they are embroiled seems intractable and choices seem to have disappeared or become completely invidious. Such restriction may not, however, be objectively there.

On the one hand, a person may feel that there is no alternative to their current position, but on the other hand it is unlikely that, if another person were placed in the same situation, they would act in exactly the same ways. No two people act the same. That other person would have their own set of perceptions and responses which would lead them to tackle a difficult scenario differently. Such different patterns of response put people on different paths as each response has consequences and is followed by further responses. So each person creates a life track which grows not only out of external circumstances but also out of the person's conditioned responses to them. Even if they experience similar events, the outcomes may be very different. They would not necessarily fare any better, but they would fare differently.

Mental conditioning

We inhabit worlds which reflect our mental structures. Our mentality is conditioned by the worlds we are exposed to, but equally we create worlds which mirror our emotional constitution and our sense of identity. The relationship is cyclical.[34]

The world we create, which is being described here, is not the physical world of objective reality. It is the personal world which we perceive. It is the world of perceptual objects which support our identity; the things we think of as "mine"[35] or those things we feel association with.[36] We can call this the self-world.

We create our self-worlds in two ways:

- We seek out things which support our sense of self. We choose friends, environments, possessions and so on which reflect our sense of who we are, or who we would like to be. We visit places with which we identify and choose a profession which suits what we think of as our nature.

- We perceive the things which we encounter in ways which support our sense of how the world is and who we are. In other words, even when we can't choose our location, we still choose to notice those aspects of the world in which we find ourselves which reflect our sense of self. This might mean our attention is caught by the décor of a room, or the books on the shelf, the garden out of the window, or the conversation of our host. Each person in the same situation will notice different things and what they notice will reflect their sense of self.

As you can see, one level of this creation process takes place at the practical level, and one at the mental level. At a practical level we actively choose some of our life circumstances, but at a mental level we also choose how to see what happens to us unbidden. The two levels are both driven by the desire for identity, and ultimately by existential fears of instability, loss and impermanence.

EXERCISE ONE: DIFFERENT WORLDS

If you are working in a group or pairing: each person should write for five minutes about a room you are all familiar which is not the one that you are currently working in (eg. somewhere you go for coffee or the entrance hall).

Compare your descriptions: What similarities and differences are there? Are there differences in what is noticed; in the priority given to certain things; or in the descriptions of things? Are there any mistaken perceptions? What do these differences say about your different current preoccupations, and identities? What might have conditioned these differences?

If you are working on your own: Write for five minutes about a room other than the one which you are currently in (say, your bedroom). Now imagine that you are your mother coming into the same room. Write a description of the room as seen through her eyes. Use the questions above to explore the differences of perspective between the two views.

Choice in Environmental Conditions

People's mental worlds are configured in particular ways. Our habits tend to run along well worn tracks. People often re-create again and again similar conditions in their lives. This can be why some social improvement schemes do not work. Even given the same initial start, different people will make different use of the same resources, and what they do will be conditioned by their past experience. When Mary's husband leaves her with two small children and a pile of debt, she may see no way out and sink into depression, or she may feel overwhelmed with anger and resentment and vow to turn her life around by making some radical career choices.

Some differences can be put down to active choice. People gravitate to places which suit their preferred lifestyle. They decorate their houses and choose clothes according to personal taste. They choose friends who have similar interests and move in circles where they are likely to continue to meet other like-minded people. Their career choices and relationship choices determine many things about their world.

Many things in our lives are not consciously chosen, however. They may be determined by habit-patterns, or by virtue of the fact that they have similarities with things which have gone before. People are often attracted to others who remind them of people whom they have known in the past. They play out old patterns of relationship.

A lot of therapeutic interest goes into such occurrences. Some of these things may even be genetically programmed. For example, our attraction to others may be based on familial likeness or species determined preferences for the ideal mate. Whilst we like to imagine that we have autonomy, it is probable that far more of our day to day activity is determined by such influences than we imagine.

So, the world which we inhabit is fashioned. Some aspects of it, of course, are not of our own making at all. We do not choose for our loved ones to die or that the company we work for changes its management, direction or collapses, but many other things are, in one sense or another, chosen by us.

The things which influence these choices, though, even when we think we are actively choosing, are often hidden; buried in layers of unconscious motivation. Ultimately, they are connected in some way with preserving our identity. In one sense we choose, but in another that choice is conditioned, and hardly under our control. In one sense we create our own worlds, and in another we are at the mercy of our histories and life circumstances. We believe we are rational yet our actions are determined by forces which we are unaware of; forces which, for the sake of preserving our sense of security, we prefer to ignore.

EXERCISE TWO: ROOTS OF THE PRESENT

Take a large sheet of paper.

At the top of your paper, write down a sentence which summarises your life at present. Do not write too big as you need to leave plenty of space for the rest of this exercise.

At the bottom of your paper, write down a sentence about your life ten years ago.

In the space in between the two descriptions, map out the choices and changes which have occurred between the two points in your life (single words will do.)
Most of these changes will not be isolated, but will have involved a sequence of events, so link these together with lines to show the stages in the change process.

Think about how much the changes in this middle section were

---

a) conscious choices
b) choices conditioned by your expectations and habits
c) unavoidable events. Of course many things will be complex; circumstantial but also conditioned by your response.

Choose a few significant events to explore in more depth and write about them, trying to identify your own part in them, as well as what was objectively unavoidable. If you feel unsure, imagine someone you know well in the same circumstance and think about what they might have done.

Mental Conditions

Whilst some aspects of our self-world are in the physical world and can be seen by others, other aspects of the self-world are to do with the ways in which we see the world. Our perception of the world is coloured by our mentality. This colouration has a number of aspects.

Selective view

Our attention tends to be drawn to things which fit with our interests and our world view. This is sometimes quite obvious and happens on both gross and subtle levels. A young man at a party will probably notice all the attractive women in the room, whereas a young woman may well view the women in a different way to the way, comparing their clothes with hers, for example. A mother, entering her teenage son's bedroom may notice dirty socks and mugs on the floor, whereas his teenage friend notices his computer. A gardener, walking along the road, notices the plants in gardens, whilst someone who has an interest in architecture notices the facades of the buildings.

Such differences of interest can mean that two people in the same place may have quite different experiences. Even the same person may have different experiences on different days. On a bad day, we see all the cobwebs and chipped paint around the house, whilst on a good one we appreciate the view from the window.

Differences of interpretation

Whilst our attention may be drawn to different phenomena in our environment, even viewing the same phenomenon, different people may see it differently. Two people faced with the same scene may put quite different interpretation onto it.

When my twins were small, on one occasion both lost a tooth on the same day. They put the two teeth side by side under the pillow of the bed which they shared at the time. In the night, the tooth fairy came and exchanged the two teeth for two shiny coins. The next morning, the two children came running downstairs. One was very cross and the other very excited.

"The tooth fairy didn't come!" the first grumbled.

"Look, the tooth fairy left me two lots of money!" exclaimed the second.

It took quite a long time to convince each of them that their view of what had happened was wrong. Each had expectations about the fairness of the universe which led them to interpret the situation in a particular light.

Appropriation

When we bring something into our self-world, in some sense we are always appropriating it. We impose our view onto it and either identify with it or create our identity in distinction to it. We use it as an indicator[37] of our identity. Sometimes such appropriation is subtle. Other times it is more obvious.

In my paper, *Empathy for a Real World*[38] I described how women joining a research group all described the group room, in which we were working, in a self-referenced way. When asked to write about their experience, their responses included a lot of comment on décor and furnishings, mostly in terms of what "I like" or what "I don't like". The style of these comments seemed to indicate that their perception of the neutral space of the meeting room was being filtered through a process of selection and rejection according to criteria of personal comfort or familiarity. They were mentally making the room their own.

This sort of appropriation of neutral objects is, of course, the basis of the creation of the self-world which happens all the time, but in some situations it becomes particularly overt. In this particular research group, the issue of 'sense of self' was something which concerned the women. They frequently stated that they felt that they lacked identity. In fact what became apparent through the process of the research was that the women's sense of self was almost entirely projected. They perceived almost everything which they commented on with a high level of identification, even though this identification was not recognised or acknowledged.[39]

Mistaken view

The tendency to look for confirmation of our identity in the world around us can sometimes lead us to actually distort our perception in order to make it fit with our expectations. We see what we anticipate. In small ways this happens all the time as we add our personal interpretation to perceptions. In this way we are sometimes said to inhabit an unreal world.[40]

Occasionally we realise that we have completely misinterpreted a situation because we had expected it to be otherwise. I recall in my teens giving my phone number to an attractive young lad who I met at a school dance. Two days later the phone rang and I was delighted to hear a young male voice on the other end. We arranged a date for the following weekend. I was so excited that I told all my friends that I was now going out with the boy I had met.

We had three further phone calls, but it was only when the boy turned up on my door step, that I realised that it was not the lad I had danced with. It was my friend's boyfriend who was trying to double time her and date me behind her back. Red faced I backed out of our arrangement with muttered excuses. Such is the influence of expectation on our hearing!

EXERCISE THREE: MISTAKEN VIEW

Recall an incident when you made a mistake in your interpretation of something you experienced through your senses – you misheard something or misinterpreted what you saw.

What do you think lay behind the misinterpretation? Did it reflect some interpretation which you commonly make? Mistakes of this kind can be amusing, often because they tell us something about our presumptions about the world.

Write about your experience.

Self-Fulfilling Prophesies

The world with which we identify is powerful in conditioning our mentality. We create a perceptual world either by choosing to put ourselves in a particular environment or by our reactions to our situation and our habitual mental processes. This perceived world supports our expectations, and reinforces our sense of who we are. The world which we encounter mostly fits our expectations because we tend to see what we expect to see. We adjust our view of the real world according to the blue-print we have in our minds already. Our identity becomes a self-fulfilling prophesy.

In this way, the self can be seen to have two aspects, the

identity, or aspect which we think of as 'me' and the self-world, which is our perceived environment. The self-world includes things which we think of as 'mine', but also includes our perception of things which we do not necessarily identify with. It is our assumption of reality.

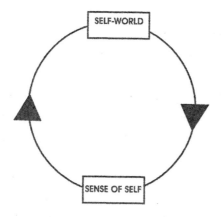

The idea that we create our own world extends not just to our perception of a neutral environment. As we have seen we may choose to associate with particular things in order to support our sense of 'how things are'. We structure our lives in order to support our sense of self.

Not only do we manipulate our perception and our physical environment to create these conditions. We tend to invite other people to play roles in our worlds. We seek out people who fit with our patterns of relationship, and we re-play old scripts. Also, we behave in such way that we invite the other people, who happen to wander into our worlds, to respond to us according to the pattern of our expectations. Not only do we choose to associate with people who have roles in our life script, but also we teach people, whom we may not necessarily have chosen to associate with, how to fit into our personal stories.

Working Within the Object world

When people talk about their experience, they naturally talk about their self-world. People, who have not yet been educated into talking the language of therapy, often talk almost entirely about their self-world rather than about themselves. Whilst their sense of self may be undefined and abstract, their sense of important people and events in their life is strong. Emotions and ideas are mediated through the events and nuances of ordinary experience.

To some degree the rising influence of a culture which is psychologically aware has turned people's attention more directly towards their feelings and thought processes, but you will still find many clients who begin their sessions with long stories about the people in their lives. Such a person may seek therapy, or indeed be directed to it by a well meaning friend or partner, in order to 'get in touch with their feelings'.

As we saw in *Listening to the Other*[41] hearing the client's story is an important starting point. When people feel heard, they naturally move on in their lives. This does not necessarily require a lot of focus on feelings or identity. An object-related approach is particularly concerned with hearing the person's story; the description of their world, its significant objects, whether people, places or other things, and events that happen there. From this, emotions, confidence, insight and life decisions will naturally flow.

Because this approach builds upon people's natural enjoyment of story telling, it is particularly helpful in circum-venting the resistance which many people experience when their attention is turned onto their own process directly. It allows the frame of reference to be gently explored and tested. They do not feel personally exposed.

Mentality and Identity

So far we have talked about the mentality and the identity

without differentiation. Both mentality and identity are conditioned by the self-world. Both serve to create it.

The nature of self is something which has been the subject of much contention in Western psychology. Some theories have used the term 'self' to describe that part of us which we recognise and identify with. Others have included in the definition psychological material which is unconscious and hence not available for identification. Since this book is primarily concerned with the practicalities of therapy method, let us not repeat these largely linguistic discussions on the nature of self here, other than to note that the subject is contentious.

As we have already seen, the models which we are using here take a very broad definition of the self, including in it not only the material which are associated with the person, but also the self-world that is perceived. Likewise, it includes not only the part of the self which is identified with, but also the broader set of mental phenomena which condition the mode of that perception.

Self-material includes both the perceived self-world and the accumulation of habit, thought, emotion and attitude which make up the person. Within this latter material I find it useful to distinguish the *identity*, or sense of self, which is the aspects of self-material with which we identify, or which we recognise as 'me', from the other aspects of self associated with the person. These latter, unclaimed aspects can be referred to by the broader term *mentality*.

The word mentality describes a person's orientation to the world; the part of their self-material which is not the self-world, but which perceives and acts in relation to it. The mentality is not necessarily reflexive; it is not necessarily perceived as 'me' or 'mine' and much of it is probably assumed to be just 'seeing the world how it is'.

Self-Consciousness and Flow

Because our society has tended to become more psychologically aware, people have tended to literally become more self-conscious. They think more about their personal process and emotional state. In fact there is little evidence that this makes them happier or more psychologically healthy.

In common parlance, when we talk of someone being self-conscious, we are usually implying that the person has a problem. Their awareness of their own part in things is preventing them from functioning well and they are getting tripped up by the awkwardness of that awareness.

The common advice to someone who is self-conscious, say, when he is asked to make a public speech, is to suggest he places his attention on the audience, or the subject matter and distracts himself from his self. This shift of focus away from the self, towards the other, is very characteristic of the other-centred approach.

EXERCISE FOUR: SELF-CONSCIOUSNESS

Think of an occasion when you were self-conscious. What led up to the occasion? Why do you think you were self-conscious on that particular occasion? What did you do to overcome the inhibition?

Write about your experience.

When we read Rogers's description of the therapeutic process in his paper *A Process Conception of Psychotherapy*, he describes the self as:

...becoming increasingly simply the subjective and reflexive awareness

of experiencing. The self is much less frequently a perceived object, and much more frequently something confidently felt in process[42]

This description echoes a view that the person is most healthy when they are fully engaged with what they are doing or with the person to whom they are relating, rather than when they are self-consciously observing their experiences.

In the description which follows the passage above, Rogers describes how a former client is surprised to realise how his life has changed. Having noticed that these changes have occurred, he does make a link between the changes and his therapy, but this is only at the prompting of the researcher. He has been too busy living life to think about his mental state. Mental health means getting on with life, not endlessly ruminating on our mental process.

This being the case, we can see that if a person grows more psychologically healthy, their concern with identity will diminish and their involvement with the world will increase. We may therefore talk more generally about their mentality, as the identity comes to have less importance. The mentality will still be conditioned, though probably in a less rigid way than before, and likewise their view of the world will be more open to innovation and change.

At the same time, however, we should be cautious in acclaiming the person who feels themselves to be without identity. Such a state is not necessarily what it seems. The person who feels that they lack identity, or who talks of having a poor sense of self, is still very pre-occupied with the matter of self. This person is not in the flow of their experience, but caught in a backwater. Their feeling of lacking identity is usually either:

- A state in which they have a negative view of self to which they are strongly attached (i.e. I am an identity-less person; I am worthless; I am damaged.)

or

- A state in which the person is completely focused on their self-world to a degree where their sense of self is not defined.

Sense of Self Built on Negative Worlds

The objects which support our sense of self are not necessarily comfortable. Much of our self-structure is built up in reaction to events in our lives which are significant, and which make us who we are. Even when our lives have been shaped by difficult or traumatic events, the objects associated with those events are conditions for our sense of self, just as much as objects which we enjoy identifying with. This situation often creates ambivalence. A person knows, on the one hand, that a memory or a way of behaving is unpleasant and yet, on the other hand, cannot let it go and move on.

We frequently find ourselves working with clients who cling tenaciously to stories or ways of behaving which are destructive and negative. They may seem desperate to change, or find new interests, yet keep repeating the same accounts of their earlier experiences, and resist any suggestions of a different view or new activity. When we understand, however, that such phenomena may be supports to their identity, and that even a negative identity is protective against life's unknown forces, we can start to appreciate why they are so difficult to relinquish.

In addition, the fact that an identity is supported by a frightening or unpleasant self-story can make it very difficult for the person to unpick the associations and responses which form the foundations of that identity. The abuser or the traumatic accident acquires a haunting quality; a presence which is neither directly perceived, nor relinquished, but which continues to condition the self for years after the event. We will look at the way that such elements can have a strong hold on the self-structure, and at ways of working with these negative perceptual objects, in more detail in the session six.

Object-Related Approaches

Because the mentality depends upon the objects to which we give attention, and because our sense of identity is intimately connected with our perception of the world, when we explore the object world which someone presents to us, we indirectly explore that person's mental process.

The self-world mirrors the identity, so gaining understanding or making changes, real or perceptual, within the self-world will bring about changes in the mentality and in the sense of self. This way of working has the advantage of being direct and not inducing self-consciousness.

There are many ways in which a therapist can help a client to explore the objects in his world. This book will offer different methods for doing this. Broadly, object-related work falls into two categories, based on two directions which may be taken in the investigation:

Exploring the power of the object

The first direction which the therapist may take involves exploration of the perceived objects, as they are experienced. She may help the client to explore the hold which these objects exert on him. What effect does it have when his attention is drawn to the object? Why does the object have significance? What is its function in holding the sense of self?

The object that is given significance in the self-world is a pointer towards the identity[43]. Object-related work involves highlighting powerful objects, their context, and appearance. It involves empathically appreciating the object world, and, in so doing, making it more vivid. Theoretically, this mode of work can be framed as a therapeutic exploration of the impact which these significant objects have on the psyche. In practice the client experiences a shared exploration of his life experience.

The perceived object, which is in fact part of the self-world, is called a *rupa*[44]. Strictly speaking rupa is a quality or colouration which is added to the object itself. In this sense it has no existence. It is simply a phantom, a perceptual illusion. It is distinct from the object, as a real thing which has existence. For practical purposes, the term can be more loosely used to describe things which have strong significance for a person and which condition his mentality. In doing this we need to remember that it is the object's significance, and not its actuality, which make it rupa.

The significant object exerts a strong pull upon the person. The fact that a rupa is in one sense illusory does not negate its real power to shape and direct a person's life. In one of his early teachings called *The Fire Sermon*[45] the Buddha talks about the way that everything that has connection with the senses is on fire. The eye, the ear, the nose, the tongue, the body, the mind, are all drawn to the world of rupas[46]. They are hooked and inflamed by objects, and as a result are drawn into the processes of attraction or aversion[47] which are the foundation of identity formation. In other words we are strongly drawn to things which we identify with and reject forcibly those which we see ourselves as different from, defining our identity through a sort of 'like me, not like me' process. This process is driven by our urgent drive to escape from life's painful aspects.[48]

The process of self formation and object conditioning is not, then, a benign or passive one. In this understanding of mental process, the image is one of entrapment and burning passion. It offers a powerful diagnosis of the human predicament. Caught in a world where our fate is not in our own hands, we are pulled by our emotions towards anything which seems to offer security or distraction.

We seek the illusion of control, but inevitably sickness, ageing and death, and all life's other disappointments and troubles overtake us. It is this which feeds our fascination with our object world, and it is behind our object world that the pain of life's afflictions hides.

Exploring the reality of the object behind the rupa

The objects of the self-world point towards our identity. Their power to entrance us derives from the associations they carry and the fact that they are given energy by their rupa quality. These objects, for the most part, however, also exist as things or people in their own right. They are real people or real places or real things to which we attribute personal significance and from which we derive a sense of our enduring nature.

A second type of investigation in object-related work is to explore the reality that lies behind the self-world. This work involves challenging perceptions and investigating the truth of situations. Of course such a process is always partial, but the gradual recognition of a world of "others", who have independent existence and are not dependant on our being, is the path to maturity.

Working with Rupa

I use the term rupa in this book, both because it is a simpler and shorter term than "perceptual object", which would be a Western alternative, and also because the term rupa has particular implications. It suggests not just a neutral process of perception, but one which carries psychic energy. The rupa-ness of the object is in its power to fascinate us and to draw our attention. This power arises because of the object's role in creating identity. We are caught by things that are rupa for us because they maintain our sense of self.

Identifying significant objects

Clients describe worlds which are made up of rupas. When we listen to clients, they present us with a series of objects which are significant in their self-world. The first skill which a therapist needs to develop in order to work in an object-related way is to listen for the significant objects in the story; those with strong rupa power. This means giving careful attention, and hearing which things in the client's story carry emotional energy. It can take a while before the client reaches the object in the story which carries the most powerful significance, so listening and waiting may be important at the start of a session. It is also useful, however, to remember the first object which is mentioned. This frequently turns out to be something significant which was passed over with little thought in the opening moments of the session.

Significant objects are often people, but sometimes they may be things. Abstract concepts may also have rupa qualities, but in general, for this kind of work, concrete objects are most useful. In some ways, the identification of a particular significant object does not matter as the self-world is redolent with connections. There may be a number of possibilities and whichever point you start with, so long as the object has energy, the resulting inter-action is likely to bring you back to significant places.

This process is not as directive as it sounds. In fact, it is close to the ordinary process of empathic reflection. It is simply that, instead of adopting a bias towards investigating the implicit question "but how is it for you?", as many Western therapists do, the other-centred therapist leans towards enquiry into the object world which is being presented, and in particular to the most significant objects within it.

If your object-related work is embedded in an empathic understanding of the client's world, you will naturally hear the particular significance of some elements in that world and will draw the focus towards those elements in your responses. If you have good empathy skills and simply follow the client's process without the common bias towards reflecting feelings, you may well find yourself naturally following the client's line of attention and naturally draw that attention towards the most significant rupas.

EXERCISE FIVE: RECOGNISING RUPAS

If you are working in a group: do a piece of counselling practice, about five minutes long. At the end of the time, both counsellor and client (and observer if you are working with an observer) should record the session by writing down the sequence of rupas presented. Remember that rupas are any objects spoken of. For these purposes include people, places, physical objects or events. Do not include abstract concepts (though these are rupas).

If you are working on your own: Reflect on a recent piece of counselling which you have done and identify the series of rupas presented. As an alternative you can listen to a radio broadcast in which someone talks about their life and then record which significant rupas were mentioned. This latter method has the advantage that if you record the programme or use a "listen again" feature on the internet you can check back over your notes and observe the biases in your perception and your level of accuracy in recall.

Since many counsellors have trained themselves to listen out for feelings, spending time simply practising this shift of orientation is valuable.

Amplifying the rupa

When the client talks about significant objects in their world, it is common for the therapist to encourage them to talk about their feelings or thoughts. By contrast, working in an object-related way the tendency is for the therapist to be interested in the rupa quality of the object.

Hearing the significant objects in the client's story is often a matter of listening for the point where the person's voice becomes charged with emotional energy. Sometimes this is obvious. On other occasions, you may find yourself testing the water a bit with a few exploratory questions. At this point, the therapist will try to intensify the attention which the client is giving to the object. Let us look at an example of what might happen.

Let us imagine that Susan has been having difficulties with her supervisor at work. She finds the woman overbearing and critical. After a particularly difficult encounter, Susan arrives for therapy in a very emotional state.

"I've realised something," she says. "That woman reminds me of a teacher I had at school."

"That's interesting," responds her counsellor, "Can you tell me a bit about that teacher?"

"Her name was Miss Richards. She was a real tyrant."

"Uhuh, I'm getting a picture of a formidable woman. Can you describe her some more. What was Miss Richards like? I mean, how old was she? What did she teach? How did she talk? What sort of clothes would she be wearing?"

EXERCISE SIX: RESPONDING TO RUPA

As you read this short extract from Susan's therapy session, if you were therapist, consider what you would be thinking and saying at this point.

How would it be similar or different from the responses of the therapist described here?

As you read the account of this short interaction, you will notice that the client has already identified a parallel between the supervisor at work and the teacher. Clearly there is a lot of energy behind this association. Had she not made this connection herself, the therapist would probably have invited her to talk more about the supervisor, and the connection might have emerged from that interaction. As it is, the teacher was mentioned with some energy, so is evidently powerfully rupa. The therapist therefore asks her client to tell her more about Miss Richards.

When a person has a powerful reaction to a person in their current world, that reaction is often fired by an association between that person and a significant figure from the past, often, but not always, from childhood. Many therapists would pick up on such a connection, but the other-centred therapist pursues it in a particular way, keeping the focus in the object world. The choice to pursue the earlier figure comes from the strength of Susan's insight. Object-related work may focus on past or present figures.

So, let us look in detail at the responses so far. The counsellor's initial invitation is open. She simply invites Susan to tell her more. Although this counsellor's response is a question, a simple reflection might have led to the same material. An other-centred therapist working with an empathic reflective style might simply have responded "A teacher?" and so offered the same invitation to explore the rupa.

This initial invitation to say more evokes two pieces of information: the teacher's name and that she is a tyrant. These are two subsidiary rupas to be remembered and perhaps re-introduced: 'Miss Richards' and 'tyrant'. Since both are descriptive of the teacher, the therapist stays with the original line of enquiry, focusing on developing a feel for the teacher as a presence.

Here, the emphasis of the enquiry is on the visual aspects of the scene. The therapist is keen to 'see' what the teacher is like, and asks specific questions about the woman. She is amplifying the visual sense for both Susan and herself. She asks the teacher's age and clothing, inviting Susan to form a clearer picture. Notice that the therapist does not respond in a way that says "tell me how you felt"; the implication of her response is "tell me what you saw."

Creating a visual image is usually an important aspect of this kind of work. Sometimes other senses may be involved. The senses are the doors through which we perceive the world and sensory data is the precursor of feeling reactions and associations[49] which are the building blocks of the mentality. When the rupa is intensified, it moves from being a remote idea or fleeting impression into being a perceived reality, and it is then available for exploration in the therapeutic process.

There are, of course, situations where such intensification is not needed and could even potentially be harmful. We will discuss this in session six. Mostly, however, the process of therapy is one of investigation and it works best when we explore the images and objects which haunt us in a direct way. The counsellor is an accompanying presence, who supports the client's investigation of the mysterious territory of the mental world, and gives courage and support for what may be an emotionally taxing experience.

The impact of working with the rupa element can be powerful, and we will revisit Susan's experience in the coming sessions and see how the amplification of the image can lead to cathartic change and insight.

Subsidiary rupas

In this sort of work we do not necessarily need to stay with one rupa. Often a piece of work starts focused on one rupa, but then moves on to others. In Susan's case the first rupa presented was the supervisor. We can see how behind the image of the supervisor, lurked the powerful rupa of Miss Richards. It is possible that in subsequent interactions it will emerge that behind Miss Richards lies another figure. Because we repeat the same patterns of relationship through life, it is common for us to add layers of rupa one on top of the other.

This layering is interesting, and one function of this sort of work can be to reveal the history of a particular pattern. Such investigation may throw light on current patterns of relationship and behaviour, and may free the client from some of the more pernicious influences of past associations. It is not, however, always necessary, or even desirable, to retrace the history of a particular pattern back to its earliest origins. Other-centred work is not necessarily concerned with the psychological archaeology that preoccupies some other schools of psychotherapy.

Since rupas are basically dynamics which support the identity, a quality perceived in, but not pertaining to, the object to which they have become attached, it is possible to work with any layer of the process. Susan was clearly ready to explore the relationship she had had with Miss Richards, so this provided a good direction for her therapy. It would also have been possible, in this mode of therapy, to work with the image of the supervisor without looking into its historic antecedents. Indeed, the choice could have been left with Susan. Her therapist's response might simply have been to re-present the two women and to allow Susan to choose her own direction. She might have said, "So there's your supervisor, and your teacher..."

References and Background Reading for this Session

Brazier C 2001 *Buddhist Psychology* Constable Robinson, London UK

Brazier, D 1995, *Zen Therapy* Constable, London (these books give the background to conditional relations and object-related theory as presented in this book.)

Tsering, G T 2006 *Buddhist Psychology: The Foundation of Buddhist Thought* Wisdom UK (this book offers a useful overview of basic Buddhist concepts. The reader should however be aware that the orientation and some interpretations offered by Geshe Tsering are not the same as those used in this book.)

SESSION FIVE

A Sense of Place

In this session we will explore:
- Seeing the rupa in context
- Abstraction and trust
- Making things concrete
- Facilitating scene setting
- Exploring the scene
- Dismantling the scene
- Objects and the therapy room as containers for rupa

In the last session we looked at the way that the self-world is created and maintained through expectations, habitual ways of viewing things and of acting. We also looked at the way an other-centred therapist might identify and amplify significant objects in the self-world, referred to as rupas. In this session we will continue this exploration. In particular we will explore the way that we can ground the work we are doing by focusing not just on the rupa itself, but also on the context in which it arises. To see how this might work in practice, we will return to our imagined session with Susan to see how her therapist might continue to facilitate her exploration of the rupa.

Placing the Rupa in a Specific Context

When she arrived for her session, Susan was emotional about her work situation. The encounter with her supervisor had upset her, but Susan herself had already linked this in her own mind with her experience at school. Clearly the relationship with her teacher, Miss Richards, still represents an important source of rupa energy for Susan.

The rupa still seems associated with a powerful and frightening authority. It conditions particular reactions in Susan which have now affected her response to her supervisor. In order to explore this pattern of conditioning, and perhaps reduce its potency, Susan and her therapist may now want to look at the story more directly. What is it about Miss Richards that is now being reflected in the relationship with the supervisor? What is it about the memory of her school days which inflames Susan's feelings?

Whilst Susan can talk about her teacher and describe details of her behaviour and appearance, the real power of the rupa is in the pull that it exerts on the senses. The reaction is not simply a cognitive process. It is a process which is felt at a bodily level. Thus exploring the power of the rupa involves not just talking about it, but imaginatively re-experiencing it. In order to understand the rupa's power, Susan and her therapist need to revisit the memories of Miss Richards in an experiential way.

This process is not without its complications. Indeed, we are playing with fire[50], so the therapist must be sure not to let the client get burned a second time. In the next session we will look at how a therapist may need to help the client regulate the level of emotion with which he is working.

In this case, though, Susan's therapist has confidence that, at present, the material is not overwhelming Susan, and so she invites her to look more closely at it. Having begun to hear the story of Susan's relationship with Miss Richards, the therapist is now aware that if they are going to bring the scenario to life, a first step will be to slow the client's process down and make the scene more vivid. The therapist is interested in placing the image of the teacher in a context and exploring not just the relationship with the person in isolation, but also the scene in which she appears.

Finding a specific example of a scene in which the rupa appears is usually more helpful than exploring the figure in the abstract or the general case. Recalling a particular place, and then looking at specific details of an incident which took place there, brings the issue to life in a way that a more generalised description cannot. For example, let us imagine a person called Roger who reports having been the sort of child who was teased a lot. Perhaps he was never chosen when the class were asked to pick teams for sports. He probably has a vague memory of feeling miserable and left out.

Let us now imagine that Roger is asked to recall a particular occasion when an incident of this kind happened. He remembers an afternoon when Mary was team captain, and made a sarcastic remark when she was asked to take him onto her team. Recalling the scene, Roger suddenly feels much more aware of just how painful and humiliating the experience was. As he recalls the incident, he starts to picture of the playground, the crowd of on-looking children, the wire mesh fence, the overhanging trees, and Mary's red face as she spoke; tears well up in his eyes.

This sort of recall includes both the drama of the incident, and the apparently superfluous detail of the context in which it happened. Roger not only remembers that Mary spoke unkindly, but he *sees* the lines of the netball court on the tarmac of the yard, the fencing, the trees and the red faces of children on a cold day. These details are part of the scene in which the rupa is embedded. They have themselves taken on rupa energy by association. Recalling them brings Mary's comments vividly into Roger's present experience. It is also likely that in his everyday life, seeing a similar playground or having to choose partners in a group exercise, might bring up emotions in Roger even as an adult.

Memory is often sparked by details. We hear a favourite tune or smell a scent of wall flowers, see a family picture album or lie down on an old counterpane. Such small things evoke memories of incidents or relationships in ways that simply talking about those relationships cannot. It is often the sight of the loved one's coat on the hook, or the scent of tobacco which brings tears of grief long after a death.

So it is that exploration of a powerful rupa often begins with the establishment of a scene, and that scene with the establishment of the small details which it contains. The rupa is given a context and thus its power is invited to become apparent.

Abstraction as a Distancing Process

If detail brings a scene to life and puts a person in touch with its emotional impact, the absence of detail can offer a means of diminishing the emotional energy of a memory. When clients first start to talk about significant figures or life events, they often gloss over details and talk about people or places in generalised ways. This is a protective pattern. We are less likely to be emotionally affected by abstract ideas than we are by objects which appear real to us. When we talk theoretically about a situation, it tempers the emotional impact of the story.

In the early stages of a counselling relationship, and later too, clients will tend to express their story in ways that do not really engage the scene. This behaviour may have a number of psychological motives. Firstly, as we have seen, it may be protective of the client because it diffuses emotion. Also, though, the use of a rather distanced description may be a protective strategy because it is a way of testing out the counsellor's ability to understand and listen. By talking casually or indirectly about a painful event from the past, the client discovers how much on his wavelength the counsellor is. Does she pick up the fact that the incident has emotional significance or does she fail to notice the hints which are given?

This sort of testing out is not usually conscious. In the early stages of therapy, the client is often motivated by a need to discover how trustworthy the therapist is and how able he or she is to sense and contain painful material, but, unless the client is very self-aware, this need is only rather vaguely sensed.

Even when a client talks about issues of trust and enquires into the therapist's skills, he will probably not be aware of all the unconscious strategies which he is also using to assess these matters. Without consciously intending it, he will be looking for signs of what the therapist can handle and how perceptive she is. He will notice what she reacts to and how she handles sensitive information.

This is not surprising. People rarely feel comfortable to launch into the depth of their emotions immediately. In fact, to do so is abnormal, and, although to some extent the special circumstances of the therapy room over-ride normal reticence, a client who leaps straight into an explicit account of his life may be showing an inappropriate level of trust. Usually people want to know that the person whom they are confiding in will be able to understand what they are saying and that they will not be overwhelmed by it or treat it disrespectfully.

Talking about an aspect of the problem without committing emotional energy to the disclosure, can be a way of testing the waters. It allows the client to see whether the counsellor will appreciate the depth of distress which is only obliquely being hinted at. If the counsellor is in empathy with the client and hears the significance of what is said or senses that layers of meaning may be being obscured, then the client may feel ready to venture deeper into the material, but also, if the counsellor is really in empathy, she will also hear the client's fear around trusting her and will tread carefully.

This means that the counsellor may judge it best not to bring too much attention to the client's hidden distress. A gentle allusion and a respect for the person's process may well be more appropriate. The client will usually appreciate an acknowledgement of the seriousness of what is being said, but may not want to be pressured to reveal more at an early stage. Some space to grow comfortable in the relationship will probably be reassuring.

The use of abstraction as a way of distancing painful memories doesn't only happen as a means of testing trust.

Abstraction can also be a way in which people protect themselves from facing some things at an emotional level. This is because, whilst they are discussed in abstract terms, objects do not become vivid to the imagination, and so do not carry as much rupa energy. Indeed, the abstract concept wraps a sort of protective blanket around the rupa itself, insulating the person from repeating the raw experience with which it is connected. This means that a person can talk about a distressing subject and yet not be touched by its emotional impact.

People who are facing a big trauma or loss often become very adept at talking about the event without experiencing its power. They tell you about their cancer or their divorce in a great deal of detail. They discuss their symptoms and treatment or their custody battle and financial arguments, but such disclosure is without emotional energy because it is distanced and abstracted. It functions to protect and even to inoculate the person against their emotion. It creates a verbal barrier which is erected as soon as anyone tries to discuss the real impact of the situation.

Even when a person expresses a great deal of emotion, there may still be a distancing process going on. Since sensory distraction is the first layer of defence against painful aspects of reality, the sensation of expressing emotion can itself sometimes be a distraction from the pain of a distressing event.

Most counsellors from time to time encounter a client who cries endlessly and loudly about his problem, but never seems to reach catharsis or resolution. In such situations, the counsellor may feel quite distanced from the emotional display. Usually, eventually, the person finds the courage to face the reality and move beyond the defensive tears. At this point a shift of expression is evident and new, raw emotion surfaces. Now the counsellor may suddenly feel a wave of response as her heart is touched by the reality of the new tears.

Trust is a foundation for therapy work, and is particularly important for imaginative replay of past scenes. Establishing trust ultimately depends upon the therapist's trustworthiness, as well as the client's ability to trust. Only by demonstrating this trustworthiness through her genuinely caring attention, can the therapist offer the conditions for real therapy to take place.

EXERCISE ONE: DISTANCING AND TRUST

Explore your own experience of distancing strategies. Have you noticed yourself using abstraction or intellectualisation to cope with difficult feelings and circumstances? Have you noticed yourself testing trust in this way? Can you recall a time when you came to trust someone whom you had previously been wary of, so that you let go of the barriers and defences to share the emotion which lay behind them, and if so, how did this come about?

Explore these questions either in a counselling exercise or in your learning journal.

Reflect on clients whom you have worked with. Have they distanced material in similar ways?

Finding a Time and a Place

In order that the client to feel safe enough to explore experiences in a meaningful way he needs to develop trust in the therapist. The client needs to feel that the therapist will hear and understand, and that her response will be motivated by genuine caring and compassion. He needs to sense her humanity and her presence[51].

If these conditions are in place, the therapist can help the client to look at his experience more directly. She may invite an exploration of the powerful rupa figures which relate to his issue in ways that anchor them in specific examples and make them concrete. Usually this means identifying a time and place where an incident happened in which the rupa was powerfully present.

The first step which the therapist takes is often to slow the client's process down. Because the common human response to painful memories is to skim over the surface facts of a situation without really entering into the felt sense of the scenario, grounding the exploration in the specific example means bringing the details into focus so that there is time for feelings to emerge.

Even after such an invitation, sometimes a client will continue to respond in a rather generalised way. This may be an indication that the therapist has intruded too fast or that the client is still distant from the emotion and needs help to re-contact it. The therapist might need to back-track and discover where the real focus of the client's energy is directed. She might simply ask, "I'm wondering where your mind is now…"

In the case we are describing, however, let us imagine that the therapist's invitation is well timed and Susan responds immediately by alluding to a scene. The emotion which she expresses as she does so indicating that this way of working is probably going to be useful. So, let us return to Susan's experience.

Susan's therapist asks, "Do you remember a particular day which you associate with Miss Richards?"

"Oh, yes," Susan's face flushes, "there was that day she gave us all detention because Laurie was late…"

The counsellor here simply invites Susan to recall an instance where the rupa was powerful. This direct approach is often the most effective. It cuts through any distancing that may be going on, by asking her to find an actual example.

There are now a number of rupas for the therapist to choose from. Susan earlier called Miss Richards a 'tyrant' and has now mentioned 'the detention' and 'Laurie', but all elements of these are linked to the same scene. Her energy is still with 'Miss

Richards' and 'that day'. From her flushed face and agitated voice, it is clear that there is a lot of emotional charge to the story now, and the therapist is keen not to rush to talk about its conclusion.

Instead she continues to elicit and amplify the detail of the scenario. In particular she now feels a need to make the scene more concrete.

"So tell me about that day. Let's go back to before Laurie arrived late. What lesson was it? Where were you? What was the classroom like?"

Susan responds to the therapist's line of enquiry. Guided by further questions, she describes the classroom: the desks, the other girls, the light streaming through the windows, the poster boards on the walls. This is the room in which the incident happened. As the scene begins to emerge, it creates the context in which the event can be replayed.

EXERCISE TWO: FINDING A TIME AND PLACE

Think of an issue which is problematic for you in your life at present. In doing this exercise, you will not need to disclose this issue to anyone else.

Having thought of an issue, now cast your mind back to your childhood and try to identify an incident which has some relationship to this issue. It might be a time when something similar happened, or when you first experienced the emotion or behaviour in question. You may not even know why a particular incident popped into your head.

If you are in a group working in counselling triads, take it

---

in turns to use the space to explore the incident. In particular focus on making the scene in which the childhood incident took place as vivid as possible. Recall where you were, who else was present, what sort of things were around, what sort of light, colour, temperature, smells you associate with the scene. Try to feel yourself back in the space.

If you are working on your own, write a descriptive passage about the place where the incident happened, recalling as much detail as possible.

Notice what effect recalling a specific incident and place has. Does it throw any light on the issue that you thought of?

Scene setting has a number of purposes.

- Firstly it makes the story more real. Whilst details can be glossed over in dialogue, once a location is evoked, the characters and events tend to "come alive".
- Secondly, entering the scene evokes a mild trance state in which the client is imaginatively in touch with the sense qualities of the object world.

Scene setting is an empathic activity. Although the therapist is asking questions of Susan, and appears directive, in fact she is following her process very intently. The questions are exploratory, and are used to create the scene, which will be the therapeutic container for the subsequent investigation of the rupa, 'Miss Richards'. They do not direct Susan towards a particular conclusion, and if it seems there is any resistance from

Susan, her therapist will stop and explore what is behind that reticence. If anything, the therapist is slowing Susan's process so that the development of the scene can be more thorough, which will in turn make the incident more realistic.

The picture of the classroom becomes more vivid, and as it does so, her therapist watches Susan's movements and facial expression closely. She notices that Susan is now gesturing to parts of the imagined classroom as she speaks and that her eyes are following different directions to the places where her various friends would be sitting. Instead of talking about the experience as an event in the past, the scene has become real enough for Susan to be feeling herself participating in it.

Most of us recognise the feeling of being completely immersed in a world which only exists in our imagination. This sort of mental state is quite normal when we are caught up by a story or memory. Rather like a waking dream, we are transported into another place. This is a sort of mild trance state. This is not something unusual. To many people, the word trance has connotations which are far more dramatic than the term actually warrants. The reality is that we are all in some sort of mild trance most of the time.[52]

EXERCISE THREE: TRANCE STATES

Recall a recent occasion when you were so absorbed in reading a book or watching a film that you were completely in the world being portrayed by it. Probably you only realised that this was the case when something interrupted you and you realised that time had gone past and your cup of tea grown cold.

Reflect on the experience. How did it feel to be completely

> absorbed in another world? How did you become so
> absorbed? What was the strongest impression that you
> were left with?
>
> Write about the experience.

Scene Setting: A Refuge and a Springboard

Recalling and recreating a scene from the past is often an emotional experience. Before moving into exploring a significant event in this way, it can be helpful to establish a broader context first. This is not only because this context is evocative, but also because it will give the client a point of reference to return to. For this reason the time and place which is first explored is often one that has pleasant associations, and that existed before an unpleasant incident occurred. This creates a place of refuge for the client.

This process of creating a refuge becomes particularly important where one is working with someone who has memories of serious abuse. In such cases it may be unwise to revisit the scene itself, but establishing "safe" psychological places to which the client can go, which predate the traumatic event itself may be very helpful. We will look at this kind of work in the next session. Revisiting positive stories provides a resource for the client. Too often people's identity is supported by unhappy memories and accounts of times when things went wrong. Knowing it was not always so, a person is freed to explore and look honestly, balancing dark memories with lighter ones.

Susan's therapist encouraged her to look immediately at the scene in which the incident took place. Had the whole scene been too frightening for Susan, though, her therapist could have invited Susan to start by recalling a childhood time which was pleasant, and creating that scene in her imagination. Revisiting a happy scene can be a useful prelude to other therapeutic work, in that it offers a positive association or *anchor* which can be returned to if the other scene becomes too distressing. Also it creates a reminder that there were good times in the past as well as bad and re-dresses any tendency for the therapy to itself dwell on the negative, creating negative tracks in the mentality of the person.

Frequently the initial scene is a springboard from which the client can go on to re-experience an event. It is a jumping off point for the work which is to come. Recreating the place in which a significant event took place can be very powerful in evoking a resurgence of memories. Peripheral details captivate the feel of the occasion and can even be more evocative than the details of the actual event. This is because the event itself may have been remembered many times. Revisiting the memory over the years may have, to a degree, desensitised the person to its original impact. Layers of remembered memories may have misted over the facts, clouding genuine recall, and adding layers of interpretation and distortion. After we have gone over an event many times in our thoughts, it can be hard to distinguish genuine memory from more recent accretions. We remember the memory we recalled last time, not the original incident.

The small details of the background scene, however, are fresher. Not contaminated by the mind's distancing processes, they can sometimes be highly evocative. Different senses also play their part. Whilst the visual or verbal memory may have grown jaded and exhausted itself, smell or taste can take us back through decades in a moment. Music can touch our hearts and we can recall being young once again.

Sometimes setting the scene is enough. I have worked with clients where simply imaginatively re-creating a sitting room or a bedroom in the space of the therapy room has brought cathartic tears and a sense of resolution which has needed no investigation. At such times, it may be that the incident itself never needs replaying because the work has been done.

Later the client may want to recount the event and tell you the meaning of previously hidden aspects, but this is often simply an explanation, offered for your benefit, a kind of token of gratitude for the work. The client has been released from the spell which was binding him in silence for so long. Other times a person guards his privacy. No need to tell all, he gives his thanks and departs.

The scene provides a context for the event. Background detail may:

- Be less emotionally charged, providing resources for the client to draw on if the experience of the event itself is too threatening. or
- Spark and intensify emotions as they point to the incident itself which is being remembered.

In both these aspects, the scene helps the counsellor to tune in to the client's world and deepen her empathy for the client's situation. Returning to our example, the counsellor can not only hear about Susan's world, but also enter it alongside Susan. In this way the process of scene setting helps her to establish a good working alliance. Creating the scene has a number of functions:

- It enables Susan to get deeply in touch with the sense elements in the scenario in a way that is less threatening than talking immediately about the central event.
- It gives the therapist an opportunity to bring herself into line with Susan's world and allow her own responses to be conditioned by it.
- It helps to establish a robust working alliance.

EXERCISE FOUR: SCENE AS REFUGE

Think about the scene which you evoked in exercise two. What sort of feeling was associated with this scene? If it was reassuring, in what sense might recalling this scene provide a psychological place of refuge for you? If it was disturbing, can you imagine yourself in a situation which was pleasanter, before the emotive event occurred? Can you visualise this place? Could you imagine this place creating a place of psychological safety for you?

Experiment with the idea of creating refuge through recalling pleasant or neutral events and scenes from your early life. Notice the way that evoking such memories affects your general mind-state.

Amplification of the Trance

As we have seen, the engagement with the scene produces a mild trance state in the client. Facilitating the development of this trance is one of the important skills in object-related work. We call this skill *amplification*.

Sometimes a client will naturally enter this kind of trance state when they are talking about an event. When this happens there is clearly no need for amplification, and sometimes there may be a need to offer *distancing* or *containment* as we will see in the next session. Often, though, the other-centred counsellor will use methods to intensify the experience so that the object world becomes more vivid. Recalling the peripheral detail of the situation brings the scene to life. Just as in theatre, it is the action of minor characters, as well as of the lead parts, which makes the play believable, so too the incidental elements create the backdrop, enabling the client to enter into the scene.

In summery, then, we have already seen three basic methods which the therapist might employ after the rupa has emerged. These are:

- Slowing the client's process down.
- Identifying a specific time and place, probably before the significant incident occurred.
- Asking questions about peripheral details of the scene.

Language

Linguistic factors are also important in the process of amplification. Small changes of language help to intensify the development of the scene.

As Susan's session continues, her therapist asks, "Where are you sitting? Where is Miss Richards?"

You will notice that at this point the therapist begins to talk in the present tense instead of the past tense. This is probably spontaneous, for the therapist is in empathy with Susan, and is feeling the temporal shift that has occurred naturally. She may not even be aware that it has happened. It may just feel right to speak in this way. Sometimes, though, a therapist might make a deliberate choice to switch tense. If Susan were having difficulty getting in touch with the scene, a deliberate change into the present tense might help her to make the leap.

As Susan describes the room, the therapist also enters into the scene imaginatively. Guided by Susan's responses, she too is exposed to the objects in Susan's world. She starts to allow herself to be conditioned by them. As she does so, she starts to get a felt sense of being the girl in the classroom. She might indicate this shared sense of the scene by including herself in her reflections.

"So we are all sitting waiting…"

To verbally include oneself in the scene can be a risky strategy in some situations. It may cause complications, as the therapist may be attributed various qualities which really belong with the characters from the past. In this way, the therapist could lose her role as a source of neutral support.

In this scene, however, there are many girls in Susan's class. Other people are in the room who are not particularly significant to the event. It is therefore possible for her therapist to follow her intuition and to slip into the scene anonymously. She feels safe to be silently present with Susan.

These, then are further strategies which intensify the client's experience of the scene.

- Shifting the tense into the present.
- Bringing the therapist into the scene as invisible companion to the client.

Both these strategies involve the use of subtle shifts of language. Evocative language can also help the client to enter more fully into the scene. To achieve this, the therapist might speak in ways which border on the poetic, rather than using normal conversational styles of speech. Because the situation is becoming dramatic, this does not feel as artificial as it might sound. For example if you are working with a scene which occurred on a winter night, you might say, in a dramatic tone, "so we are standing in the doorway, the wind is lashing around us and we can feel the chill seeping into our bones…"

This kind of response is not like the sort of reflection that might be used in ordinary counselling, which might be something like, "You were standing on a doorstep wondering what to do." It draws the client into a scene, using the sort of language which is more commonly used in storytelling. It picks up allusions from the common heritage of literature and culture uses it to amplify the atmosphere.

EXERCISE FIVE: LINGUISTIC MICROSKILLS

If you are in a group, work in triads. The client should describe a scene from their life. The counsellor should experiment with using different tenses in their responses. Do not tell your client which form you are going to use. Notice what effect it has if you respond to your client speaking in the present tense rather than past tense, and using 'we are...' instead of 'you are..'.

Get feedback from your client on the effect which the different modes of counselling have.

If you are on your own, try to be more aware of your use of language in counselling sessions. Make notes on your observations. Experiment (judiciously) with expanding your range of responses.

Use of Space

The scene is not only amplified by what is done, but also by what is not done. The space which is left by the therapist is an invitation to the client to explore further and to experiment. What is not said can be more potent than what is spoken. Imagination needs space.

In theatre the dramatic pause intensifies the action on stage. In radio, a silence heightens tension or humour. In dramatic therapies, an empty chair can be more evocative than one in which a person who is acting an auxiliary role in the drama is asked to sit. The empty space allows a person to visualise the room or the person without hindrance.

This is why, if we move into action therapies, we usually keep props simple and to a minimum. The space allows the client to "see" their world without the complication of interpretation through unsuitable objects.

So two further strategies can be employed in evoking the scene:

- Creating atmosphere through use of descriptive or evocative language
- Leaving spaces for the imaginative process

Observation and Intensity

The level of intensity and observation which the counsellor is able to bring to the therapy is a crucial element in its efficacy. If you watch an experienced counsellor, one of the first things that you will notice is the level of concentration which is involved in her work. Counselling students are often amazed by how tired they are after even a ten minute counselling exercise if they have been concentrating well. To keep this level of focus for an hour, and then another hour, requires practice.

The focus which the counsellor holds is not directed single pointedly. It has to be flexible and move between different fields of attention. Whilst, in object-related work, the client's attention is single-pointedly focused upon the scene, the therapist is entering the world which is being created alongside him, holding in mind the different objects within it and allowing her imaginative energies to tentatively fill in gaps so that she can offer further questions or test out hunches about the scene. Everything is held lightly, on the one hand vivid enough to allow her to develop a feeling for the client's world, but on the other hand, constantly open to change as new information emerges.

Alongside this soft but focused attention, the therapist is also watching the client intensely. She notices facial expression, constantly asking herself "Are we on the right track? What else is going on?"

This process of observation is partly about looking for

evidence that the client is in the flow of the scene, and not just going through the motions of it, and partly about noticing the reactions which occur. These reactions guide the therapist in highlighting particular objects, and in spotting features in the physical layout of the scene that may not have been described so far.

As we have already seen, when someone is imaginatively immersed in a scene, he will behave as if he is really in the place. He will look about him as he speaks, gesture with his hands towards imagined people or objects, or assume particular postures. Noticing when this happens can help the therapist to spot new aspects of the story. When this happens, the therapist may use the observation in a variety of ways.

- She may use the observation as the basis for a further question, for example "What is over there?" (following the client's line of sight with her own)
- She may mirror the body language with her own. This may draw the client's attention subtly to his own gesture, or it may simply communicate resonance on a level which is barely conscious.
- She may, rarely, comment on her observation, for example, saying "you look frightened of him." This latter response would be rare, as it would tend to pull the client out of the scene into self-consciousness.

Usually her intention will be to facilitate the establishment of the scene as a trance and to allow the exploration to unfold in a fluid way, following the client's attention and energy.

EXERCISE SIX: SETTING THE SCENE

If you are working in a group: practice scene setting. Work in triads with counsellor, client and observer. The counsellor should invite the client to describe a place that was important in the past. The client need not reveal why the place was important or what happened there.

If you are working on your own: try to bring this form of working into your client work. You can start in a low key way, simply being more aware of the scene when your client is talking. You may also like to experiment with the method by imaginatively returning to a scene from your past and writing about it as if you were present in the location.

In both cases here are some guidelines to help you:

Invite the client to tell you what is in the space they have chosen (so what sort of place are we in?).

If it is not clear from the way that they frame their response, ask the client whereabouts each item is (Where is that? How close? Over here? And what's over there?). Ask them where they are (so where are you standing now?) and what is close to them (what can you see immediately in front of you? What is to your side?).

As the person talks, imaginatively enter the scene yourself, by following their gaze as they describe things. Share your sense of the scene, "So there's a window over here and a fireplace there...." Let your body reflect your sense of the scene. You might indicate objects with your hand, or follow the client's eye movements, looking in the direction of each feature as it is described. Experiment with talking in the present tense and including yourself in the scene, "so we are over by the dining table.."

For this kind of work, if you remain seated, you may find it more effective to literally move your chair so that you are sitting side by side with your client. Keep the questions simple and factual. Ask about sensory data. What colour are things? What temperature is the air? Can we smell anything?

Watch the client's face very carefully. Notice when he or she seems to be more deeply in the process. Notice whether some objects in the scene have particular emotional impact. You do not need to enquire into the emotion itself, but you may want to hesitate and let it develop or look a bit more closely at the thing which has evoked it.

Occasionally when you are doing this kind of work, someone may become very emotional. At this point you may feel it is time to gently leave the scene. You can ask the person if they have had enough. It is one of the strange features of this kind of work that a person can be immersed in the scene and yet able to respond to enquiries or instructions from the therapist without disrupting its trance. If you sense it is time to finish you can say, "I'm wondering if we have done enough for now. Do you want to leave it there?" the person will then be able to answer and then either end the scene or continue without disruption.

After you have finished, take a few minutes to give feedback whilst still in counselling roles. Encourage the client to share anything they wish to, but not to feel obliged to say more than they want.

If you are working in a group, take time for everyone to debrief. If the work has been effective, this will need sensitivity, as the client, and indeed the therapist, may have become quite deeply involved in the scene. Debriefing can include:
• personal sharing
• feedback on observations and technique

In particular it will be useful if the observer has noted facial expressions, gestures and eye movements which related to the scene setting process.

The Side by Side Viewpoint

Because the client is being encouraged to describe their world rather than their personal thoughts, the counsellor is privy to the significant features within the client's self-world, and is left to perceive the mentality and emotional script by inference and observation.

Just as we may watch a film and see a character portrayed in relationship with places and people, and, in watching it, may feel his deepest struggles without ever having to have these explained, so too in object-related work, the therapist does not have to hear the client's emotions described, but senses them in the flow of the unfolding drama, alongside the client.

This shared experience creates a particular style of

relationship. Object-related work can be both intimate and robust. As characteristics of the landscape of the client's world are described, the therapist gradually becomes familiar with the territory. The fact that this method uses questions to establish the scene means that the therapist can clarify and refine her picture until she has a good enough approximation of the client's world in her own view. This has two effects.

Firstly it means that the therapist develops a high level of empathy for the client's position. Viewing the world which the client describes, the therapist sees what the client sees, and is naturally drawn into the "as if" position. Looking at the client's world, albeit imperfectly understood, the therapist allows her mind to be conditioned by the same factors as the client is experiencing, and thus increases her level of empathy. Of course in the process of the describing his perceptual world, all sorts of nuances creep into the client's story which communicate his responses and feelings about the situation. The therapist hears these nuances and not only "sees" the client's world, allowing herself to be conditioned by it, but also feels its impact on the client and is able to deepen her empathy through contagion of those feelings.

Secondly, in viewing the client's world, rather than focusing her attention on the client, the therapist metaphorically stands alongside the client. The object world, consisting of both scene and characters, becomes an element in the therapeutic relationship. Both client and therapist look at the scene, creating a triangular relationship with it. This means that, instead of engaging in a dialogue, a face to face encounter, the therapist and client create a triad with the client's 'others' and join in a side by side investigation of the client's world.

The 'side by side' viewpoint has a significant effect upon the character of the helping relationship. Whilst face to face relationships may offer a compassionate, intense meeting, they can also variously create resistances or dependencies. The therapist becomes focus of all the client's expectations and habits of relating; of transferences and projections. Such phenomena, which are basically part of the defensive process, may be multiplied by the client's own feelings of vulnerability, which arise from the direct scrutiny he is experiencing from the therapist, whom he may well regard as expert and powerful. In the object focused relationship such phenomena are diminished.

EXERCISE SEVEN: DIFFERENT SITTING POSITIONS

Experiment with different positions for counselling. This may be easier to do if you are practising in a student group, but if not, there is no reason why you should not try out some new arrangements with your clients.

You can vary the positions as follows:
• Face to face
• Half facing, so that the two chairs are angled slightly
• Side by side
• Closer together or further away

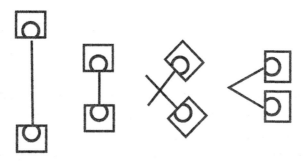

Try out counselling in all four positions and notice what effect they have on your relationship with the client.

In counselling work, there is no reason why you shouldn't sometimes move your chair during a session if it feels as if a different position would work better. Obviously this means having chairs which are light enough to slide around without inviting in the removal men!

In object-related work, even the projections and transferences, as well as the fantasies, and realities, of power differentials between therapist and client, can be explored in the more neutral arena of the created scene. Each figure can be represented imaginatively, perhaps using empty chairs, and the relationship can be examined from afar.

With so many possibilities for experimentation, the therapeutic space becomes a stage on which therapist and client can experiment with viewing the client's world from different angles or with rearranging its constituent elements. Switching to a more object-related style of therapy, with its side-by-side character, the therapeutic relationship can become more experimental as it develops a tone of cooperative enquiry.

The Self in Context

People exist within the contexts of their lives. The self is not separable from the conditions which create it. Although, as modern people, we may like to think of ourselves as separate, autonomous and authors of our own lives, even such thoughts are conditioned by the culture to which we are predominately exposed. To look into another's world is to be invited to share their psychic space, to experience the conditions which shape their thoughts and feelings, and to allow those same forces to operate upon us.

Of course the experience is not complete for we each bring with us other worlds and other conditioned patterns of view. But perhaps within those tangled influences, sometimes, if we can pay enough attention to the other's description of their world, we will glimpse them in their natural habitat.

Background References and Background Reading for This Session

There are many books which explore the use of story and myth in therapy, though most are not specifically focused on the topic of scene setting.

Gersie A 1991 *Storytelling in Bereavement* Jessica Kingsey Publishers UK

Watson (trans) 1991 *Saigyo: Poems of a Mountain Home* Columbia University Press, USA

Woolger, J & Woolger R 1990 *The Goddess Within* Rider UK

SESSION SIX

Closeness and Distance

In this session we will explore:
- Finding a working relationship with emotive material
- Common strategies for distancing material
- Flash-backs and under-distancing
- Triggers and flash-backs
- Amplification and containment methods
- Creating a working distance: comment on a counselling session

In modern society many people have learned to distance themselves from their emotions. As humans, we have many strategies for doing this. We have already noted some of these. They might include:

- A retreat into abstraction. As discussed in the last session, one way in which people distance their emotions is by theorising, generalising or intellectualising their experience.

- The expression of emotion which is distanced from the experience itself. The person weeps or protests loudly but, in doing so, does not really face the issue. Rather, such expression is a performance (though usually unconsciously so) made in a way which blocks out the more genuine emotion .

- Dulling experience through repeated exposure to emotive subjects. With our constant exposure to media coverage of trauma in news and drama, modern people can easily become desensitised. We watch news broadcasts and maybe hear of thousands of deaths in floods, famines, war and other disasters in the process. We see interviews with tear-stained or stoic relatives on daily basis. Our capacity to care is stretched and exhausted.

- Distraction with sensory experience which is pleasant or compelling.

EXERCISE ONE: LISTENING TO SADNESS

Listen to a news broadcast on the radio. You may like to record it so that you can listen a second time.

Notice what accounts it contains of deaths and injuries and other traumas.

Notice how these stories are presented. Do they invite emotion or not? Notice your own responses to the stories. Do some touch you and others not?

Imagine you were personally involved in the stories, perhaps as a relative or as an aid worker involved in a disaster. How would this affect your hearing of this news broadcast?

What effect do you think listening to the news has on your sensitivity to others?

Choose one item from the news and write about it, trying to bring out the reality of the experience being described in a way that does justice to it.

In the previous session we explored ways in which the therapist can help the client to explore a scene in which a significant incident took place. As the person is imaginatively taken back into the places where events happened or which have associations with particular people or periods of life, they experience the rupa elements in their object world more directly. Such techniques are *amplification* methods.

Many clients are over-distanced from their experience, and find the invitation to explore in this way helpful. It puts them in touch with the visceral experience of situations and the associations which underpin their thinking and reactions. Because the mind is conditioned by objects to which it gives attention, bringing the world of imaginative objects to the fore provides the conditions for memories to surface and become more vivid, and for patterns of thinking and behaviour to be explored.

Flashbacks and Insufficient Distancing of Material

For some clients, however, the rupa aspect of their experience is already too powerful. Memories and images flood into such a person's mind and threaten to overwhelm them. In this situation, sometimes the person may experience *flashbacks* in which they spontaneously slip into vivid memories or even hallucinations of past events. Such experiences tend to be linked to extreme trauma, whether from childhood abuse, often sexual, or from violent incidents. They may form part of a diagnosis of post-traumatic stress disorder.

Flashbacks and similar experiences are like waking nightmares. The person becomes terrified and often sees the abuser or the scene of a trauma vividly and may even believe themselves to be there. Though often visual, flashbacks can involve other senses, particularly those of hearing or touch. The difference between a flashback and an ordinary memory is that the person is so absorbed in the experience that they lose their ability to separate from it. They feel themselves to be in the situation again, rather than recalling it as something that happened in the past.

The degree to which the person is immersed in the memory during a flashback varies. In extreme examples, the person completely forgets where they are and believes they are back in the traumatic situation. Being with a person who has lost touch with reality in this way can be very frightening for you as the therapist, particularly if it is the first time you have experienced such a phenomenon.

For the person experiencing such a state, the experience is not therapeutically healthy. Although it is possible that naturally occurring flashbacks may be part of a person's healing process, so should be treated with a matter-of-fact calm when they are reported, in therapy it is better to help the person not to slip back into them. Deliberately evoking this kind of under-distanced experience is likely to re-traumatise the person. Therefore, when a person is experiencing this kind of traumatic resurgence of memory, far from amplifying the rupa quality of it, the therapist needs to offer ways of containing and distancing the experience. This often means being firm and directive with a client who is slipping into such a state in order to help them to create psychological distance from it. This session will focus primarily on methods for achieving enough containment so that therapeutic work can happen.

When a client experiences a flashback, it may seem that they are totally immersed in the memory, but it is good to be aware that even when the client seems completely dissociated from you and the reality of the room you are in, unless he is extremely mentally disturbed and in need of hospitalisation, part of him is almost always available to hear you. You may, however, need to speak strongly and assertively to catch its attention.

EXERCISE TWO: WORKING WITH FLASH-BACKS

Have you ever worked with someone who experienced flash-backs? Have you ever experienced them yourself or known other people who have?

Reflect on the experience, on how it affected you emotionally, and on how you worked with it. If you have no experience of this area, take some time to read any first hand accounts you can find.

Think of the experience of having a nightmare. Use a counselling exercise or free writing exercise to recount a nightmare you have experienced yourself as if it were currently unfolding. Flash-backs are a bit like waking nightmares.

How would you comfort a child who had just woken from a nightmare and still believed that monsters were pursuing them?

Terrifying Rupas and Terrified Selves

As we have already discussed, the self is conditioned by the object world, and we create a world of perceptual objects which supports our sense of self. This being the case, you may be wondering why flashbacks, and their more normal counterparts, nightmares, occur. Flashbacks and nightmares are clearly power-fully rupa. They are made up of objects which transfix the client, holding him in a state of re-living past or imagined terror. Could this be said to be a support to the self, or does it have some other derivation?

Experience has many layers, and so does our identity[53]. Old habitual ways of behaving, and the identities which they constellate into, may get over-written by more recent material, but they are not erased. The seeds of past actions lie dormant, waiting to be activated[54]. When a person has been exposed to an extreme situation, they develop an identity which is built up in association with that trauma. That identity is often very frightened and distressed. This frightened identity remains a significant part of the person because our predominating identities are those based on significant life events. Painful experiences etch strong traces on our sense of who we are. It is probably true to say that we are shaped more strongly by our painful experiences than by our pleasant ones. Certainly if you ask people to describe the formative events of their lives, these often include significant painful experiences.

In the case of flashbacks, however, the incident is one which the person has had difficulty in integrating into their story of who they are. It remains cut off from their day to day experience in a state which is often referred to in Western theory as *dissociation*. The memory, or aspects of it, is psychologically encapsulated. Related to this cut off memory, there is an identity which is also encapsulated and dissociated from the person's everyday life. This frightened self, which is often still in a childhood mindstate, is generally hidden by other, more ordinary selves, but it is easily evoked when emotional material relating to the traumatic experiences is stimulated. Its presence creates fragility in the person's everyday identity.

Reflecting on flashbacks in the light of object-related theory we can conclude:

- The terrifying rupa (such as occurs in flashbacks) is created by the mind, so in some sense is part of the self-world
- It is linked to an identity which is often a childish identity, and appears to be cut-off from 'adult'[55] mind states

- The terrifying rupa is based on what was originally a source of acute suffering. Since identities are an attempt to defend against suffering, it appears that a flash-back may occur when it was not possible, in the original instance, for the person to distract themself from the situation sufficiently. The identity associated with it therefore feels brittle and insubstantial.

- The flashback may be an attempt by the mind to complete a process of creating a defensive identity which did not happen properly at the time. It appears to have some function in rehearsing the frightening situation over and over, perhaps in the hope that, should the trauma happen again, the person will have a strategy to cope.[56]

Triggers to flashbacks

Flashbacks may seem to arise spontaneously, but really they are triggered by some perceptual experience. Commonly this is something which occurs in the ordinary process of the person's life, though sometimes it may come out of a thought process. Something reminds the person of the original incident, and this evokes not just an ordinary memory, but a re-living of the event. Thus, car headlights at night might take a person back to wartime searchlights or a helicopter overhead might bring back the terror of an air attack.

Because most childhood abuse happens in domestic environments, this can mean that ordinary household items may trigger this kind of unwanted association. The piano may be a reminder of the abusive music teacher, or the smell of tobacco may evoke a powerful memory of the elderly relative who touched inappropriately. Such triggers involve the senses, and it may be that the most powerful of these come through the less dominant senses such as taste, touch and smell.

In particular, some kinds of physical touch can bring back memories of sexual abuse. It follows that the therapist needs to be aware of the impact of physical touch on someone who has this sort of history, and to be wary of touching clients without their consent. For the same reason, flashback can create difficulties in people's sexual relationships, not just because the person is psychologically conflicted about their sexuality, but also because intimate contact acts as a trigger for flashbacks.

EXERCISE THREE: IDENTIFYING TRIGGERS

Think about the examples of flash-backs which you identified in exercise two.

What sort of things triggered those flash-backs? See if you can identify the detail of how the flash-back arose. What was the sequence of images and thoughts? How might you use this knowledge therapeutically?

Offering Containment

In the previous session we looked at methods for evoking a scene and thereby intensifying the rupa quality of experience. In the remainder of this session we will look at ways of creating distance and containment. I have previously discussed the use of methods of amplification and containment in my paper *Looking In, Looking Out* in the anthology *Beyond Carl Rogers*.[57]

Amplification and containment are in some senses opposite processes. Amplification brings the person closer to psychologically significant material, whereas containment creates distance from it. In fact, though, these are not so much opposites as complementary approaches. Providing containment enables amplification to take place. If containment is provided, the client will then feel safer and will be more able to explore distressing memories. Containing methods are about creating the psychological container in which exploration can take place without re-traumatising the client.

Sometimes such methods involve distancing the material which is being explored so that it is no longer overwhelming, other times they involve simply providing the normal forms and boundaries of therapy in a clear and authoritative way. Either way containing methods provide the client with a feeling of safety, which then allows exploration of significant material.

Amplification and containment operate a conjunction with one another. Containment activities create the therapeutic ground. Within this, amplification of rupa elements happens. The evocation of rupa energies may then involve strong feelings which need containment. In this way, a balance of the two processes provides the optimal conditions for therapy. It's a sort of 'nice guy, nasty guy' scenario, in which challenge and reassurance alternate to create a safe space in which increasing levels of disclosure can happen. Finding the right psychological distance is a matter of occupying the middle ground[58] where emotion can be engaged but will not become overwhelming.

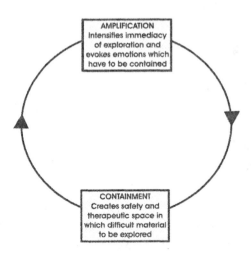

My husband, David, when he talks about finding the right distance, sometimes uses the analogy of telling a child a bed time story. If you make the story too distanced, avoiding the sort of detail which brings it to life, the child loses interest and gets bored. If it is under-distanced and the witch is too real, the child will have nightmares. Most parents discover how to offer the right level of arousal for a particular child, so that her interest is held but she is still able to go to sleep afterwards.

As therapists we need to develop a similar awareness of our clients' needs. Just as children have different tolerances in this respect, so too, in therapy different clients may have different capacities for re-experiencing emotion and different needs for support in the process. Some methods of distancing and containment are subtle, being variations of language and focus. Others are more active. Many of these methods are instinctively employed by experienced therapists, but it is nevertheless helpful to identify such techniques consciously, so that we can reflect on our work intelligently.

The following list is divided into distancing methods and grounding methods. *Distancing methods* place the client's material in a place which is psychologically separate from him. *Grounding methods* help the client to contact positive, calming rupas so that he may proceed with the work. They create *an anchor* in something which is reliable.

Distancing Methods

Shifts of subject matter

When someone is under distanced from psychological material, the most obvious way to create distance is to change the subject. People naturally do this in ordinary conversation.

In the normal course of counselling relationships, therapists usually counter this tendency and bring their clients gently back to topics which are being skimmed over. This is good practice in most circumstances, as clients often come into therapy because they are over-distanced from their experience and want to face it more directly in order to understand the issues which are handicapping their lives.

Sometimes, however, a person is under-distanced from an incident or memory, and it can be helpful to deliberately counter this and even sometimes change the subject. Responding to such under-distanced material is best done in a direct way which acknowledges the client's distress and then puts the matter on one side temporarily. One might say, "I can see this is really distressing, and we will probably need to look at it later, but perhaps we should talk about other aspects of your life for now."

This approach recognises the power of the topic, and allows it to be addressed at a rate which is comfortable for the client. More than this, it demonstrates to the client that it is not necessary to be constantly preoccupied with the gloomiest aspects of life. It cuts across any tendency the person has to compulsive rumination.

EXERCISE FOUR: OFFERING CONTAINMENT

Think about whether there have been times when you have drawn a client away from an emotive topic, or times when you felt that they were avoiding such a topic themselves. Did you bring this process into the open? What did you say? If you said nothing, what might you have said if you had commented on what was happening more directly?

If you are working in triads, notice the way that emotive material is approached, and maybe diffused, during a counselling exercise. This is not an exercise you can easily stage, as, by definition, you are likely to behave differently if you are expecting to look for instances of avoidance. It

---

may be easier to reflect back on exercises which you did in a previous session.

The observer may be particularly helpful in identifying points at which the client or counsellor backed away from something.

You do not need to identify what was being avoided, just explore when it happened. The client may also be aware of points where the session might have taken a different direction.

Was this to do with self-censorship or a subtle message from the counsellor?

Shifts of tense

We have already seen how a client's sense of being "in the scene" can be increased by changing the tense in which you are speaking so that you talk in the present tense. Conversely you can create distance by talking in the past tense, and even referring to the fact that the event happened a long time ago. Unlike the shift to using the present tense, which is often made subtly and is not brought to the client's attention, the shift to the past tense is often most effective if it is made assertively and overtly. "That all happened when you were a child..."; "You were four when she left..."

Shifting perspective from identification to observation

In order to take a person imaginatively out of a scene, you may wish to move from first person pronouns to using third person pronouns. This takes the person out of the scene and distances them psychologically from the 'self' who was involved in the incident. They can then view the scenario more objectively.

Notice the shift of intensity between the following three statements:

- "So you are very frightened.."
- "So you were really frightened…"
- "So little Susan must have been terrified." (Susan being the client's name)

Moving between present and past tense and between first person and third person pronouns, the client is shifted from a position of identification with the child to an observer position, looking at the child. This shift of perspective creates a stronger differentiation between the child of the story and the client in the present.

Another distinction, which you might use to provide a feeling of safety, is the shift from "you" to "we" used in the last session.

Many shifts of this kind occur naturally, and it is often best to follow your intuition, but, as you refine your skills, it is worth reflecting on your habits of speech more consciously and developing your flexibility.

Levels of evocative language

Different words carry different levels of emotionality. For example when talking about a death, people might talk about:

- The deceased
- The person who passed away
- The person who died
- The dead person
- Brenda

As you can see, each of these words is differently placed on a spectrum between distance and immediacy.

Most social conversation moderates the impact of emotive subjects by using euphemism. In therapy the counsellor often deliberately uses a more direct form of language to bring the focus of the person's grief into the open. Breaking such social taboos and talking directly about life events such as death is generally therapeutic. It means that subjects which are often hidden can be faced. In this way, the client might say "My aunt passed away," and typically the counsellor respond, "She died."

There may be times, however, when it is good to modify this tendency to intensify speech, and, instead, to use less emotive words. If a client is overwhelmed with grief we might feel it too intrusive to talk directly about the death yet. If we are empathic we will notice when a person cannot bear to speak of their grief directly and may feel it is right to respect this. In most instances it is best to pitch the response at a level which is slightly more emotive than that which the client is using.

Objective language instead of emotional language

As we have already seen, abstraction is something people commonly use as a way of avoiding emotion, and it is often something which the counsellor challenges. On occasion, however, abstraction can provide a tool which brings the person out of an extreme emotional state and re-establishes their adult identity and a working relationship.

When a person is becoming under-distanced from traumatic material, one strategy which can be helpful in creating distance is use less emotionally fluent language, and instead to talk in rather more technical, objective terms. Counsellors usually use vocabulary and turns of phrase which focus on the emotional aspect of what they are talking about. For the person who is beginning to feel overwhelmed, though, they may sometimes find it helpful to move discussion of the situation into a more theoretical perspective.

Projective techniques, sculpting and drawing

Although creative therapeutic methods are often thought of as emotionally expressive, some techniques can help a person to create distance from the material which is being talked about. In the last session we saw how it is possible to increase emotional impact by imaginatively reproducing the scene in the therapy room. Being able to look at, or even physically get inside, the space that is being set out, and explore the territory of past events amplifies their affective aspect.

On the other hand, other methods which are sometimes described as *projective* involve creating an image or physical representation of the client's world which is smaller and which is physically located outside the client's body space in a place where is can be observed but not psychologically entered. Such methods might include art work, sculpting[59], or sand-tray work[60].

In these methods, the creation of a scene or image consisting of emotionally charged material takes place on a small scale in a boundaried place: the sheet of paper, tray or table top. It places the material in a demarcated location, and allows the client to disentangle himself and find distance from it, moving from subjective identification to objective observation of it. Thus the memory or event becomes an interesting phenomenon, seen from afar. Of course the object world conditions the subjective, and therefore even the objective is still technically self-material, but by distancing it in this way, a working space is created.

These techniques also allow the therapist to create further degrees of separation between the client and the terrifying object by moving the piece of art or the sand-tray to a location which is further away from the client. Greater physical distance creates greater psychological distance. This method can be used to investigate what constitutes an optimal psychological distance. Thus a therapist might invite a client to place a picture of a frightening scene on the other side of the room, and then try moving towards it and away from it to discover the point at which it becomes too threatening.[61]

Imaginative methods of containment

Whilst the projective work we have discussed uses changes in the physical location of things to place images or objects at a safe distance, similar distancing techniques can be used when working with the imagination. A client may be invited to visualise the object or scene which is frightening and to place the image in a distance which feels far enough away to be safe. For example, the counsellor might suggest that the client imagines playing events through as if they were a programme on a television screen.

Using this imaginative technique, the images can be viewed as smaller and contained by the imaginary television set. The association with television itself creates a degree of distance since television programmes are, at best, seen as representations of reality rather than reality itself. This technique also has the advantage that the 'programme' may be stopped and even rewound or switched off, so that the client can gain control and understanding of the sequence of events and of his reactions to them.

EXERCISE FIVE: THE CINEMA SCREEN

Practice facilitating someone who is working with a scene by imagining that it is projected on a cinema screen or television. If you are in a training group and can work in triads, you can do this as a counselling exercise. If not, you may like to try it with a colleague or, if you feel confident to and it is appropriate, with a client in your regular work.

Invite your client to think of an incident which has recently troubled him. Invite him to imagine a cinema screen a distance away from him. Experiment with the size and position of the screen. Notice how the larger and closer the screen is, the more powerful the effect of the material becomes. Distance is achieved by reducing the image size and placing it further away, so be specific about the location of the screen.

Once the screen is established, invite your client to imagine that he is watching the incident unfold as a film projected on it. Ask him to tell you what he sees as it happens. Encourage him to actually view the story, rather than just talk about it in the abstract. If the process is taking some discussion, don't let this go on too long. You may need to be directive and say something like, "OK, well let's just go with the first thing which comes into your head and see what happens."

As the client runs the 'film' and tells you what he sees, remember if he is really 'seeing' it, he will see himself on the screen rather than being 'in the scene'. He will refer to this image of himself as 'me' or 'him'. Even if he describes the screen image as 'me', you will notice a difference of tone if he is watching 'himself' enact the scene, rather than 'being' in the scene. If he seems under-distanced, ask him to use the third-person form, 'him'.

Again, language is important. Notice the difference between:
- I'm doing it
- That's me doing it
- He is doing it

As the story unfolds, ask questions. As therapist, you need to know what the client is seeing. You can let the client stop, fast forward, or re-run bits of the story, just as he might with a film. Notice how this helps to develop control and allow deeper exploration. Notice the effect that 'watching' the scene has on the client.

Reflect on the process and discuss when you might find it useful.

Symbolic objects as containers for feelings

Sometimes the client will use a physical object as a container for painful feelings or a frightening rupa. This often happens naturally with projective work. For example, if someone uses sculpting methods, a stone might be used to represent someone who was abusive. This stone will then probably become associated with strong negative feelings. At the end of the work, it might be important to 'de-role' the stone and return it to its ordinary status, but alternatively it might sometimes be helpful not to do so, but to keep it as a container for the negative power of the rupa. In this case the therapist will need to notice what happens to the stone. She might invite the client to choose a safe place to put it in.

Since the stone is carrying strong negative energy for the client, it may psychologically contaminate whatever place it is left in. If it remains in the consulting room, its presence could, at the extreme, affect future therapy sessions, and create a bad association with the room. On the other hand it may be useful to have the object available for future work.[62] When we talk of negative energy in this sense, we are not, of course, referring to an actual force, but rather, to a perceptual overlay which has been activated in the client's mind, and possibly in your own.

EXERCISE SIX: SAFE-KEEPING FOR A
DANGEROUS RUPA

When a client creates an object which symbolises a frightening rupa, they might want to do a number of things with
it. Think about the implications of each of the following
possibilities. What benefits and pitfalls might be involved?

- Tell the person it is really just a picture/stone/cushion
- Throw it away
- Give it to the counsellor for safe-keeping
- Let the client take it home
- Put it somewhere out of sight in the therapy room
- Put it somewhere in sight where it can be watched
- Put it somewhere else

As you can see all of these might carry particular consequences, so there is no right answer, but reflecting on
implications may help you to consider different possibilities before a situation arises.

Creating a safe corner in the therapy room

When a person is doing action based work, and is investigating
situations which are emotionally charged, it can be helpful to
create a 'safe place' to which they can go, should the work
becomes too emotional. This is particularly the case if you are
doing any kind of dramatic work. The safe space should be
outside the physical space of any scene which has been created
so that the client can retreat there.

Having a space of this kind can allow the client to go in and
out of the emotionally charged material at choice. The 'safe
space' might be your usual sitting place if your working method

has taken you out of your seats, or it might be a different location in the room. Some clients like to create a nest of cushions and blankets which they can hide in.

Grounding Methods

We have already seen in session two how grounding methods can be used to create and maintain the therapeutic space. Grounding can be particularly important when a client is exploring frightening material, and particularly if the client is likely to experience flash-backs.

If a person actually experiences a flashback during a therapy session, you probably need to talk the person out of their state of terror and restore them to a more normal mental state. The following methods will help you to do this. In more ordinary circumstances they can provide a means to gain closure at the end of a piece of work. Knowing how to use grounding methods can give you confidence when you are working with particularly painful material.

Noticing the first signs of under-distancing

Clients who experience a lot of flash-backs are often acutely aware of the first signs that the emotional energy is rising. You can help the client to develop and use this awareness. Increasing awareness of these early warning signs can help to create a sense of control.

Often this means becoming more tuned into the details of body sensation and the feeling of panic as it first starts to surface. If you observe a client starting to become under-distanced, gently point it out and bring the client's attention to the earliest physical feelings associated with their reaction before moving on to other less emotive subjects.

Learning to interrupt the process

Once the client has learned to recognise the early body responses or has become aware of what triggers might initiate a flash-back, they can learn how to interrupt that process. Being able to put the brakes on may actually be more important for some people than exploring what the incident was about. Once the person has gained confidence in their ability to cope with the material, it often becomes less frightening and less pressing. It will then naturally settle. If a client is actually experiencing a flashback, however, you may have to intervene more decisively to interrupt the process for them. You will find suggestions for doing this below.

Learning to move in and out of emotive material

When a client frequently experiences flashbacks, it can be helpful to teach them how to move in and out of the emotive material in an intentional way. This involves learning to look at the emotive material in short bursts. Where someone has difficulties remaining distanced from a traumatic memory, you may want to agree a strategy in advance. For example, you might agree to talk about a memory for ten minutes, and then to move onto a different topic.

Working in this way the client develops confidence that it is possible to talk about the difficult feelings for a while, without having to deal with them all at one time and has the experience of not becoming overwhelmed by them. Once the client has learned that therapy does not always have to be taken at fever pitch, you can probably move to a more free-flowing way of working.

Creating anchors

In *Listening to the Other* we saw how it is possible to create an *anchor* which can act as a support in times of stress and a reminder to adopt calmer mind-states. An anchor is an object which is deliberately cultivated. This is done through the use of relaxation techniques.

The client is brought to a calm state of mind using a relaxation method, and then is given, or chooses, a small attractive object which he will be able to take away from the session with him. This might, for example, be a smooth pebble. The client holds the object whilst in the state of relaxation. By focusing on it, he builds a link between the object and the feeling of calm. He may also use positive affirmations or visualisations.

The object is then taken away by the client. It can be carried in a pocket and held at times of anxiety, or when he fears going into a flashback.

This kind of method involves creating positive rupa associations with the object. It has the advantage of taking attention away from the body centre where most emotion tends to be felt, whilst still grounding the person in physical contact.

In addition to those associations which have been deliberately created through visualisations or affirmations, the object also carries associations with the therapy process and with the therapist. It becomes a sort of transitional object[63], allowing the feeling of safety which is felt in the therapist's presence to be taken back into everyday life when the therapist cannot be present in person.

Sometimes this kind of anchor will naturally appear. The client might already have some object which they feel is protective or supportive. Many people carry lucky charms or religious objects. People often carry reminders of loved ones: photographs or gifts that remind them of family or friends. Where this is the case, the therapist may encourage the client to use the object either during therapy sessions, where its symbolic power can make it a good focus for projective work, provided this is sensitively done, or in between sessions where it can be consciously used as a source of support.

Talking a person through a grounding process

Sometimes a person will experience a flashback or become under-distanced from feelings during a therapy session. At such times, you will need to 'talk them down'. Draw their attention away from the terrifying memories or thoughts, and back to the everyday reality of the therapy room. Just as the mind is conditioned in fearful ways by the prospect of the abuser or the traumatic event, so too, it will be differently conditioned if the person pays attention to ordinary objects. Adopt a manner which is kind but firm. You may need to speak quite strongly if the person is very distressed.

In bringing someone out of an under-distanced state, you might:

- Use their name.
- Assert that the abuser, or other threatening figure, is not in the room.
- Remind them that you are here with them.
- Ask them questions about what they see in the therapy room. Direct the client to pay attention to their real surroundings.
- Tell them to focus their attention on something which they are holding, or on the sensation of sitting on the floor.
- Draw their attention to the present. Ask them if they can hear traffic outside.
- Ask them what they are going to do this afternoon or tomorrow.

All of these possibilities bring the client's attention back to ordinary things and help to banish thoughts of the threatening presence.

EXERCISE SEVEN: HELPING SOMEONE
WITH GROUNDING

If you are able to work with a partner: practice talking a person through a grounding exercise. You might use any of the suggestions above, or you might focus on awareness of the body as presented in session two of this book. Pay particular attention to your own level of authority, relaxation and groundedness. Afterwards get feedback.

If you are on your own: try making a relaxation tape. Although this is not quite the same as working with another person present, it will give you practice in talking someone through a process of becoming calmer and more relaxed. As you play the tape back, notice whether you pacing is right or whether you have rushed the instructions in some places (a common problem). Listen to professional relaxation tapes and compare their style.

Mindfulness methods

Mindfulness methods have become popular in therapeutic circles. These methods involve paying detailed attention to the active processes in which one is engaged, as they unfold. This sort of active engagement with the present activity can be valuable in two respects.

- Firstly it grounds attention away from the traumatic memories, usually anchoring it in physical experience.
- Secondly it helps a person to develop an observer mentality, which itself creates a distance from psychological material.

Mindfulness methods have their limitations, which largely arise from the fact that they are often taught as a method that is only containing. Whilst this may help to reduce immediate anxiety, unless they are used in conjunction with other therapies, in the longer term will not address the emotional turmoil which may underlie the client's problems. They can be used in more constructive ways if they are used to increase emotional literacy. In this case they can offer a similar methodology to focusing[64]. Mindfulness methods may also be used in an other-directed way, as we will explore in a future session.

Creating a Working Distance

In her paper *Creating a Workable Distance to Overwhelming Images*, Mia Leijssen[65] describes and analyses a therapy session in which she works with a client who has been experiencing overwhelming images and hallucinations. Mia helps her client to find a way of facing and working through these images using focusing[66] method. During this therapy session, Leijssen demonstrates a number of stages and methods which help the client to look at the experience which is terrifying her without being overwhelmed by it. If you have access to a copy of this article you will find it interesting to read her detailed account of the client session, which includes verbatim material, but if not, the following summary will highlight some of the key stages in the process.

Creating a safe place

In the session described, the therapist starts by helping the client to *"clear a space"* in which she can feel comfortable and safe enough to work. The client is ready to plunge into the material, but the therapist, knowing from previous experience that the client is likely to become highly distressed, prevents her by inviting her to *"start where you are now[67]"*. She brings the client's attention to the therapy room. This room provides a safe space.

In particular it alerts the client to Mia's own presence as therapist, which is reassuring.

Mia builds the connection between herself and the client both by commenting on it and by reaching out to the client, using touch to create a physical link. Of course, as we saw earlier, use of touch is a sensitive issue in therapy and should be avoided or used with great caution with any client who is prone to flashbacks, but Mia comments in her paper that making a strong connection at the sensory level was particularly relevant here, since she had not been able to catch the client's eye and connect visually.

As the client begins to talk, the first thing which the therapist helps her to identify is a feeling of peace. At this point the client seems to move in and out of the emotive material, for she says "I feel on the edge of something", but then, "I'm just feeling at peace now."[68]

Moving in and out of the material in this way the client seems to naturally discover the method of moving closer or further from emotive subjects which was described earlier. The client has found the edge. A little deeper, and she feels emotion, a little further away and she feels at peace. Given the space to explore, she naturally vacillates around it.

In her commentary on this section, Leijssen speaks of the importance of maintaining an attitude of open attention to the client's process and remaining present to what is not yet speakable. This is a basic attitude of focusing method, but it has echoes in the practice of meditation or in mindfulness methods. Quiet observation creates both the opportunity to relate to the feelings, and a workable distance. It allows the mind to adopt an observer position towards the process.

The therapist names the two 'parts' of the client's experience. These are the peaceful part and the scary part. She is aware that the peacefulness comes not from resolution, but from a temporary relief, resulting from her own presence as the therapist and from the distancing methods which they have used. Perhaps this realisation of the temporary nature of the calm is based on empathic intuition, for at this point the client again becomes overwhelmed and starts to experience hallucinatory phenomena.

We can understand this in an object-related way. Temporarily the client's attention was focused on the therapist. Whilst that was the case, her object of attention was in the room, and had associations of support and positive presence. This brought a peaceful mind state. The memories were temporarily forgotten. Then, as a frightening mind-object arises once more, the memories return. Now the focus of attention is on the terrifying rupa and the client becomes frightened once more.

Responding to this development, the therapist calls the client, asking her to *"listen to me... look at me."* This invitation to engage directly with the therapist involves two of the sense channels, hearing and sight. The therapist calls the client, inviting her to once again make her, the therapist, the object of her attention. Thus, the therapist again becomes the anchor, conditioning a calmer mental state. To reinforce this, the therapist calls the client by name, *"calling her back"*[69] from the scary place.

Creating a working distance

Feeling a need to make the separation between the client and the object of her terror more concrete, the therapist suggests that they create a place for the scary feeling in a specific location in the room, at some distance away from them. As we have seen, one can create psychological distance by physically locating a symbolic or imagined object at a distance.

The object is referred to as *"a scary place"*. You will notice that, in this, the frightening object is still quite abstract. Abstraction is a distancing method. For the client it is evident that this phrase is on the edge of what she can bear to voice. It is a way of communicating a potent meaning without actually naming the scene. The therapist does not know the detail, but the client, at least at some level, does. She may not have voiced this detail to herself yet, and is not ready to unpack it. The client finds a middle way. She expresses something of the frightening experience without having to face all of it.

The therapist now invites the client to experiment with finding a place at a safe distance and placing the *'scary place'* there. With this invitation she involves the client in a co-creative act. She invites her to function in a co-operative, adult to adult mode. This supports the client in remaining in touch with the stronger, adult, aspect of her identity. In this mode the therapist and client work together for some time, creating a safe distance between the client and the material.

Although the client repeatedly appears to be on the brink of being overwhelmed again, the therapist firmly repeats her instructions that she should place the frightening apparition at a safe distance. Eventually the client imaginatively places the image at a location some distance away.

Use of the therapist's self as a positive rupa

As one reads Leijssen's account of the therapy session, one is struck by the strength of her presence as the therapist in this early part of the session. The first stage of the work is primarily concerned with creating a working space and this is largely done through the working alliance. At one point, for example, the therapist says *"you stay at your safe place with me. Don't let that come in again[70]."* Here she explicitly introduces herself as an anchor, a positive rupa, and a safe refuge in a frightening situation. One can also imagine that the tone of her invitation is similar to that of a parent comforting a frightened child. It seems to say, "It's OK, Mummy's here".

There is probably, here, a subtle process creating a second, subsidiary rupa. In inviting the client to trust her, she becomes an embodiment of the loving parent comforting a child as it wakes from a nightmare. Being implicit, this rupa is never defined, and its exact nature is left for the client to receive in her own way, but the tone probably influences the development of trust and the progress of the therapeutic relationship.

Throughout this early section, the therapist refers to herself overtly in eight out of the first twenty interventions. Some are direct references to herself, such as *"Do you feel more comfortable when I am close to you?"*[71] Whilst others allude to the fact that they are engaged in a shared task by using the inclusive we: *"We together, we are trying to make a safe distance.*[72]*"* This repeated emphasis on her own presence no doubt creates the container in which the work of the session can be done. We might hypothesise that:

- These self-references create a strong image of the therapist, a positive rupa, so that the client can feel safe, knowing there is a secure presence to which she can return if she ventures into her fear.
- Some instances evoke a sense of shared task, of adult to adult interaction and co-operative task orientated activity, conditioning a more adult self in the client.
- Other instances create a parental or supportive presence, with resonances of archaic, childhood security.
- Some instances create an authoritarian presence, strong enough to fight the forces of darkness.
- All model confidence in the face of the terror.

Together these different therapist roles condition a place of safety from which the client can start to explore the material.

References and Background Reading for This Session

Berne, E 1961 *Transactional Analysis in Psychotherapy* Condor, New York (or other books by Berne)

Leijssen, M 1993 *Creating a Workable Distance to Overwhelming* in
Brazier, D 1993 *Beyond Carl Rogers*, Constable, London
Gendlin, E 1981, *Focusing*, Bantam, New York

SESSION SEVEN

Developing Exploration of Rupa

In this session we will explore:
- The way that the self-world is maintained through the cycle of identity
- The exploration of the rupa element in therapy
- Process in object-related therapy
- Deliberate and spontaneous shifts of mind-state.

In previous sessions we have explored the way that identity and perception are closely related and the way that our mental states depend upon the things, or objects, which we attend to. We have seen that an object-related way of working places its overt focus on the object world, rather than on the client's feeling reaction, and that, in doing so, it allows the therapist to achieve an empathic connection with the client by entering into his world and exploring it alongside him. By giving attention to those things which are significant to him, and by allowing herself to also be affected by them, the therapist gains a feel for the client's predicament. Meeting his world, she meets him and comes to know him, at least in as much as she is able to enter it.

This encounter with another's world is an honour which is both deeply human, for we all long for human connection and seek it out, and a rare privilege. In my work as a therapist I have often been moved by the gifts which my clients bring in allowing me to see through their eyes and hear through their ears and so to enter their cultures, which I otherwise would never have access to. At the same time I can never pretend that my level of empathy even remotely approaches a complete understanding, and I can only wonder at the inevitable gap between us, and the mystery of person to person communication.

In object-related work, the perceived object, or rupa, becomes the centre of attention and facilitation, whilst the felt reaction is largely left to rise and fall naturally as a result of this attention. As we have seen, the self and the self world are closely linked and mutually conditioning, so this emphasis on one side of the system allows the whole to be observed, without causing the level of defensiveness or self-preoccupation which direct focus on the self might arouse.

For the client the object of attention is the object world; significant others from his past and present life, ideas, dreams, possible futures or other phenomena that embody his life passions. For the therapist, these objects are also a focus, as, in side by side attention, she allows herself to experience her companion's world. In addition, however, the client himself is an object of attention. His responses and mental processes are also objects to which she attends.

The work of the object-related therapist centres around firstly achieving an empathic understanding of the client's world, and then facilitating the client's interaction with it. This may involve deepening the experience of the power which that world holds for the client and the way that it conditions his mental process, or it may involve bringing the rupa quality of that world into question.

Ultimately the aim will be to help the client to reach a point where his relationship with his perceptual world is healthier; where it no longer conditions extreme or limiting mental states, and where he starts to become less entangled in his own mental constructs and more aware that, behind that perceptual world, is a world of real others.

The world of others is hidden by layers of projection and interpretation, but, as rupa energy is dissipated, the veil becomes thinner and glimpses of the world of real 'others' become more likely. By changing the perceptual object, we change the reaction which a person has to it. Seeing something in a new way changes the perceptual object.

Exploring perception is therefore an essential part of therapeutic process. What we see is not the objective reality of things, but a world which has been painted with our personal colouration, or rupa-ness. This means that, since rupa is illusory, it can be changed without the need to alter real circumstances at all, though sometimes, seeing the world in a new light, a person will choose to make real environmental or relationship changes.

Identity and the perceived world of objects are related to one another. Each provides the conditions for the other. On the one hand we tend to seek out experiences and environments which support and confirm our world-view, and on the other hand we tend to respond to what presents itself in habitual ways and so reinforce that view and our own identity.

In this session we will look in a bit more detail at that process which maintains the identity and the self-world. During the last two sessions we have explored some of the conditions which a therapist might offer in the therapy situation, and which forms the context for her work. In session five we saw how creating a sense of place is a good first step, both because place is a powerful conditioning factor for mental states and provides a context for whatever therapeutic exploration follows, and because a sense of place can give stability and a feeling of a safe place to be returned to.

Often, in fact, setting the scene is all that is needed. As we recreate the familiar environment in which an incident took place, the objects of that imagined world transport the person back into that context and the identity which it supported. The client is five years old again, or ten or sixteen, so that, in that other self, they often immediately know what they need to know and a cathartic resolution follows.

Other times, the past, or the imagined world is too frightening to be encountered directly in this way. In the last session we saw how the method allows us to distance frightening objects and to create other objects which support positive or less frightened identities. In particular, we saw the importance of the therapist herself as a supportive object in the client's world.

This perception of the therapist as a supportive object is complemented by another aspect of this method which allows the therapist to work in a less authoritative way. Because the focus is on achieving shared view of the client's world, the therapist can remain out of the client's line of sight, metaphorically, and sometimes literally. The relationship is commonly co-creative, sharing a focus on the object world. In this 'side by side' relationship, the therapist and client form a strong therapeutic alliance.

Maintaining the Self World

The identity and the world-view are in relationship. This relationship is maintained in a cyclical way. Buddhist psychology offers a model which explains this process. This model derives from a number of Buddhist teachings. We have already referred to the teachings on conditions, and on dependence. Another key teachings which we have not yet addressed describes the model of self creation based on five stages or elements which as said to make up the person, or, we could say, the identity. This is the teaching of the *skandhas*.[73]

In *Buddhist Psychology*[74] I have described in detail how this teaching can be understood as a cycle and how other important Buddhist teachings can be mapped onto it. I have shown how it gives us greater insight into the way that people create a world view[75] and the way that they respond to the object world by using it as a platform for creating their identity. This process of self-construction is basically defensive. Indeed, it is interesting that in one text the metaphor of a tortoise is used to describe skandhas[76]. The self is a protective shell in which we hide when danger threatens us.

Since these theoretical points have been elaborated elsewhere and this book is primarily a book of method, I do not intend to revisit the arguments for these interpretations here[77]. It is, however, useful at this point to look at the basic structure of ideas which are presented in the model so that we can under-stand the way that object-related work can influence mental process and a person's sense of identity.

Here, then, is a brief summary of this cyclical model. In this summary I will take the form of the model which suggests that we can represent the relationship between identity and the perceived world by a six stage cycle[78]. This is the model which we most commonly use since it gives sufficient detail for most purposes without becoming overly complex. Other teachings, such as the teaching of Dependent Origination, allow the model to be elaborated by adding further stages at intervening points, but the overall implication remains the same.

Rupa[79]

Rupa is the perceptual object. We have already come across rupa. Rupa is what is perceived. It may be perceived by any sense. Rupa is not the object itself. What is being described by the term is the power that the object has to catch our attention, though in practice, because we tend to think of the object as existing in its own right, we may loosely talk of it as *being* a rupa. We are not usually aware that we are simply seeing our view of it, which is distorted or embellished by our mental configuration. Some therapeutic work can involve simply exploring this distinction between the perceived object and the real one.

Reaction[80]

The second stage of this model is *reaction*. When we perceive something, we react to it. Rupa conditions reaction. This stage in the process involves us with the object. Because when we see the object we have a personal agenda, we get hooked by it. This process of 'getting hooked' is sometimes referred to as 'attachment' and is the first building block of the self. You may hear Buddhists talk about being unattached. This does not mean disengaging from life, unless the person has misunderstood the teaching, it means trying not to get hooked into using our experience as a way of reinforcing our identity. In this sense it is really about engaging more fully with life.

Reaction, in this context, is defined as taking three forms. It is a technical term, describing the first impulse which a person has when they see or hear something. *Reaction* has no cognitive content, but is simply what we might think of as a gut response. It has a strong body connection. We grasp the thing, push it away or have a neutral or confused response to it.

One way of thinking about this stage is to see it as being about appropriating experiences of the world to reinforce our sense of self. We grasp or reject experience according to whether it supports or conflicts with our identity. We are initially drawn to things or images which we identify with, or which make us feel good about ourselves, and we reject those which we feel define what we are not or which undermine our sense of self. In this latter case our rejection is not simply disinterest, but rather a deliberate warding off of the thing. It establishes a clear differentiation between the object and our identity. 'I am this because I am not that'. It is a compulsive response. The attraction to or pulling away from the object is also compulsive. *Reaction* is a very physical process, rather like an amoeba engulfing some things which it experiences as food and shrinking away from other things which it sees as danger.

EXERCISE ONE: EXPLORING REACTION

Take an old magazine and tear out all the photos. Do this quickly without too much thought, and as you do so, throw them into two piles, one containing those which you like and the other containing those which you don't like. If there are ones which you cannot place on either pile, put them to the side.

When you have finished, take the two piles and look at what photos you were drawn to and which you rejected. How do these reflect your sense of self? It may be that some connections are obvious, but others are less so. Think about these and look for associations which you may have with them which are not obvious.

Notice which photos evoked particular energy for you. How did you experience this at a bodily level? Did you feel an impulse to do anything with the energy?

Talk or write about your observations.

Entrancement[81]

The third stage of the model is *entrancement* or *association*. Having reacted to the rupa, the mind is caught up in an old pattern of thought and behaviour. The energy tied up in the perception of the rupa brings up associations from our store of habitual responses.[82] We start to follow an old script and act according to our usual patterns of thinking and behaving.

In doing this we have become drawn into a mild trance state. As we have already seen, this is not something dramatic, for we spend most, if not all, of our time in one trance or another, following old ways of responding to situations rather than acting in a clear headed way. It is part of the natural laziness of the mind that most of the time we switch off and go about the world on automatic pilot.

You will recall that in session five we talked about the way in which the client enters a particular trance state in response to certain rupas. Those rupas which are powerful for us are likely to condition stronger reactions and throw us into more all encompassing patterns of association. On the other hand, everyday rupas condition other trances, and we do not escape the entrancement simply by living mundane lives.

EXERCISE TWO: EXPLORING ENTRANCEMENT

Look at the images which you reacted strongly to in the last exercise. Choose one which had a powerful effect on you. Place in front of you and look at it for five minutes, noticing thoughts and impulses which arise as you do so.

What associations does this image have for you? Do you feel any impulse to act in particular ways or engage with it or with elements in it in ways that you have done in the past? Does the image have a story associated with it?

Notice the way that different images may bring up quite different sets of associations. Perhaps one picture makes you want to travel, whilst another leaves you feeling troubled, a third leaves you wanting to do something about the state of the decoration in your house. Advertisers use images to persuade us to do things. Because some rupa elements are common in a culture they can rely on enough people sharing similar reactions to make it worth funding

---

an advertising campaign based on a particular image.

Write or talk about your own associations as they arose during this exercise.

Mental Formation[83]

The fourth element in the model is *mental formation*. This stage in the cycle involves the creation and proliferation of habit patterns in the mentality. In other words, having been drawn into a habitual response and an old script, that self-story is now reinforced by repetition. At this point whatever reaction we have had to the rupa has been acted upon. Having acted, we create the likelihood that we will respond to similar situations in the future in a similar way[84], and will once again act in accordance with our habits.

There are some parallels between the idea of mental formations and the Western idea of personal constructs, but mental formations are seen as less cognitive and more action-based. They are also thought of as seeds[85] which are created by those actions which we carry out intentionally. Our mentality is said to be full of such seeds, which are the dormant traces of things we have done in the past. Some seeds are positive and have the potential to be activated in the future as positive actions. Other seeds are less benign and are likely to grow into harmful responses.

So, on the one hand, we are already carrying a store of possibilities which may be acted upon if we get hooked by the particular rupa with which they are associated, and on the other, as we react and become caught in old habit patterns, we create new seeds which lay down the foundations of future reactions and responses. In this way the cycle is self-perpetuating, but can be viewed as a constant discharging and renewal of habit energies, rather than a fixed entity. It is conceptualised as the seeding of the mentality with behavioural possibilities and the subsequent flourishing of these propensities as actions, like the growth of weeds in a previously cleared flowerbed.

Some spiritual practices are seen as practices of cultivation; pulling up the troublesome invasive elements and watering and nurturing the benign seeds so that they grow into a pleasant garden rather than an inhospitable jungle.[86] This style of practice has obvious parallels with ideas of behavioural therapies. It relies upon supporting and reinforcing positive reactions, whilst avoiding reacting in negative ways. Intentional action is seen as having more power to condition our minds than thoughts have, although thoughts also have conditioning effect since they also create action traces.

Behind this approach is an understanding that the seeds of actions, which are found in the mentality, will ripen when the right rupa triggers them, but that if the cycle of response is interrupted and the person does not follow their habitual impulse, the seed will not proliferate and lay down new seeds for the next time. Thus gradually the old store of negative seeds will be used up and not replaced. Such a view provides a model of working, but its value is limited in two ways. Firstly it relies on the person achieving self-restraint at the point when they are becoming most entranced, and most likely to simply react in an old way. Secondly it requires that the quantities of weed seeds are small enough that their reduction will have a noticeable effect.

Self-Building Mentality[87]

The last element in the *skandha* cycle is *self-building mentality*. This term describes the way that we approach the world. Our experience, built up through our *reactions* and *associations*, is of being separate. We see ourselves as a special case. We view the world from a distance, cut off by our sense of 'I', seeing ourselves as separate from 'the rest of the world'. This sense of being a special case leads us to look for experience which supports our particular interests. It leaves us looking for a world that reflects our expectations and we find this in the self-world. So it is that the self-building mentality leads us back to rupa.

Expanding the Skandha Model

As we have already discussed, the process of self-building is described in a number of different Buddhist teachings, which can all be seen as mapping onto one another. Comparing these teachings can give us a better understanding of the process being described. In particular, the stage of *self-building mentality* can be better understood by adding other elements to the *skandha* model which are taken from one of the other models of mental process[88]. This leads us to divide the *self-building mentality* into two aspects:

Intentionality[89]

Intentionality is the element in the cycle which describes the orientation of the mind towards the world. This element is seen as the driving force in the mentality. It goes about the world with an aim of grasping at experience for its own ends. *Intentionality* is a key aspect of mental process. It is essential for the creation of mental seeds. If we do something accidentally or without intending to do it, Buddhist psychology suggests that the action is far less likely to create a propensity for the future. Intention creates the channels which persist in the mind.

EXERCISE THREE: INTENTIONALITY

Think about an occasion in the last twenty-four hours when you set out to do something intentional. Choose a time when you felt purposeful, and acted on your own

---

initiative rather than simply responding to someone else's request.

Try to identify what preceded the intention. What were you doing when the thought came into your mind? What had led to that train of action?

Directed Attention[90]

The ordinary human mind is self-directed, and so the attention which we give to things is always subtly, or not so subtly, conditioned by our need to build identity. We look for objects which will fit with our expectations. If we are in a good mood, we notice that the sun is shining. If we are in a bad mood, we notice the litter and dog dirt on the pavement. Our minds seek out things which are confirmatory both of our current transient mind states and of our enduring sense of identity. In this way they tend to reinforce both our immediate mentality and our predominating self-image by finding objects which are significant rupas.

Note on terminology: In this book, apart from the term *rupa*, which, as I have already suggested, is an easier word than its English equivalent, and *skandha*, which does not really have an adequate English translation, I am using English words to translate technical Buddhist terms. This has potential pitfalls in that the meanings are quite specific and do not necessarily follow common usages and associations.

Since some of the words which are used here technically are in common English usage and may occur in ordinary usage without the technical meaning in the rest of the book, when I am using one of these terms to mean a specific stage in the cycle, I will put the term in italics. If the word is not in italics it may be taken to be being used in the common way. Of course some instances are ambiguous.

If you are interested in knowing the Sanskrit terms which I am referring to, you will find them in the notes at the end of the book. You will find fuller explanations of the derivations of these translations in *Buddhist Psychology*[91].

The cycle which is referred to in the teaching of the *skandhas* describes how perception is coloured by personal agendas, and then becomes the basis for creating the self-referenced mentality. This mentality conditions our perception, making it into a mechanism for reinforcing self.

The model describes how we see something in a distorted or selective way, and, in doing so, put our personal slant on it (*rupa*). We then immediately react to what we have perceived (*reaction*) and either grasp at the object because we identify with it, "that's my sort of thing," or reject it "I don't like that," or have a confused response. With this *reaction* we are drawn into a personal story or script, either about the object, or in some way sparked off by it (*entrancement*).

The script which we are drawn into involves us in habitual patterns of thought and action, which in turn sow seeds in our minds (*mental formations*) which will form the basis for our future behaviour and our *intentionality*. This *intentionality* then leads us to approach the world with certain expectations which lead our *attention* to be focused in such a way that we will encounter more *rupas* which fit with our world view.

We go round this cycle repeatedly, building up many layers of mental conditioning. It is a complex process, and hard to identify as neatly as the model might suggest because it unfolds both in big ways and at the micro-level, moment by moment, in relation to everything we see, hear or perceive. We cannot possibly follow every instance of it, but we can get a general sense of the process that is going on and spot more significant instances.

Our whole experience of life is coloured and shaped by skandha process. Our experience of the world is filtered through like-me/not-like-me *reactions* which divide things which we identify with from things which we define ourselves as different from. Our behaviour is shaped by these responses and by the stories and habits which we carry over from the past.

This process is one of attachment. The habits create a sort of stickiness[92] in our minds so that we resist change and cling on to old ideas. We are attached to our ways of doing things and to our expectations and ideas. In this way the whole cycle conditions both our sense of self and our attitude to the world and so creates a semblance of permanence and stability.

EXERCISE FOUR: THE CYCLE OF SELF-BUILDING

Think about the cycle that has been described. Does it make sense to you in terms of your own experience? Try to identify instances of your own behaviour following this cycle and spot the different elements which occurred. It is often easiest to notice when you reacted to something strongly and then trace back to the rupa which triggered the reaction and then to the mentality which led you to "tune in" to that sort of experience, and so, perhaps, back to earlier events.

In session three we saw how the human predicament in which unpleasant occurrences are an unpredictable and ever-present possibility leads us to seek out distractions. As you will remember, the initial response to unpleasant experience is to escape into sensory distractions. Something pleasant or compelling takes our mind off everyday discomforts. This pattern of distraction is enacted many times and becomes established so that we start to identify with it. At this point we move into the second level of distraction which is self-creation or identity formation.

The cycle which we have been exploring in this session is really concerned with this second level of self-formation, but you can see that this process grows out of our repeated involvement with sensory distractions. The rupa appears before us and catches our senses in the first instance, and we move into *reaction* with a visceral response, a physiological impulse towards or away from the rupa. This bodily involvement predisposes us to sense-based distraction, but it also leads us to use those sense-based responses to build habits and identity. We perceive the object through our senses, and then we respond to it in a physical way. Having had our *attention* caught and our impulse to find a way of incorporating the experience into our world-view activated, we slip into habitual patterns of activity which lead us to seek out more objects to distract ourselves with.

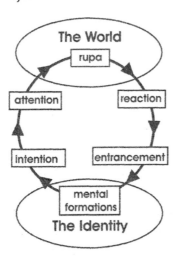

The cyclical model shows a number of possibilities for intervention. One of its strengths is that it offers a means of integrating approaches which in the West are seen as the province of different therapeutic schools. It unites those who attempt to understand the dynamics of the process with those which focus on changing behaviour; those which focus on awareness and sharp observation of detailed reactions with those which delve into the implicit life philosophy and intentionality of the person. In an other-centred approach all of these possibilities have validity, not least because the cycle is an integrated process, but the emphasis of an other-centred approach is on the client's relationship with the world. For this reason we tend to work more commonly with the area of perception, and in particular the experience of rupa.

The model which has been presented in this session gives us an understanding of how rupa is conditioned by past experiences and by expectations and *intentionality*. Things which are powerfully rupa catch our attention in positive or negative ways. We have a *reaction* to them. We either want them, crave them and cling to them, or else we reject them. The world is full of things that catch us, and create psychological traps for us. It is on fire[93] and in response to the heat we thirst[94] for the familiar and the distracting.

Deepening the Experience of Rupa

In session five we left Susan and her therapist exploring the scene in the classroom with Miss Richards. Susan's therapist has spent some time helping Susan to re-create the experience of being back in the class using the scene setting methods discussed in that chapter. At this point she senses that Susan is ready to move on.

"So what happens now?" asks the therapist. "Where is Miss Richards?"

We have already seen how important the sense of place is in

object-related work. We have also seen the importance of following the client and allowing her to get a feel for the situation herself.

Susan points to the far wall. "She's standing there, at the front of the class. Laurie's just come in late."

The therapist follows Susan's gaze. She hesitates for a moment to see if Susan will say more spontaneously, but, as she doesn't, her therapist proceeds.

"What does she look like? Can you describe her?"

Again, appearance is important in making the scene real. If Susan can recall apparently trivial details about Miss Richards' clothing, hairstyle and facial expression, her image of Miss Richards will become more vivid. Of course the details which she remembers may or may not be accurate. Recalling a teacher after several decades Susan's memory will probably have distorted the image. Indeed, her perception as a young girl looking at her teacher would already have been distorted by all the associations which a teenager would have about a member of staff at their school.

This does not matter. What is important at this stage is that what Susan experiences is true to her present psychological reality, not to historical fact. There is a place for revisiting earlier perceptions and re-evaluating them in the light of an adult view in object-related work, and we will explore this in later sessions, but for now, in exploring rupa, we will look at the colouration which history and our present conditioning gives to objects and the way that amplifying this experience of rupa-ness can be therapeutic. Indeed, it is often helpful to this kind of work if the colouration is slightly exaggerated, so long as the exaggeration does not take the scene into pantomime. This exaggeration is an aspect of amplification process.

EXERCISE FIVE: INTRODUCING THE RUPA

If you are working in a group you can use this exercise as the basis for counselling. The counsellor should facilitate using the present tense and questioning details to bring the image to life. If you are on your own, use it as a writing exercise.

Think of a person who was a powerful influence in your teens. Imagine them in the room which you are currently working in. Where would they choose to go? Would they sit or stand?

What would the person be doing? What would they wear? What expression would they have on their face? What sort of shoes would they have on?

Hold the image of the person for about five minutes, trying to intensify your experience of them. Try to visualise them in a particular location, sitting or standing, or perhaps moving about. Notice the incidental details. Try to make these as vivid in your mind as possible. Use your imagination to recall sensory data, not just visual but auditory and from the other senses. What is the person's voice like? Is there a smell which you associate with them or with their common activities? (For example you might associate them with baking or fresh coffee or a particular perfume or the smell of a science lab or a changing room)

At the end, ask yourself whether the person had a message for you. Why did you recall them at this point in your life?

Now say goodbye to the person and let the image fade.

Reflect on the experience both in terms of what you learned from the exercise about the significance of this person as a rupa for you, and also about the method of facilitation.

Whether you have been working in a group or on your own, after you have finished, take time to clear the space in which you have been working of associations with the person you imagined. You can do this by moving furniture, deliberately telling yourself or your partner that the person is no longer there, or by talking about something in your present life. This kind of imaginative work can be powerful and sometimes it takes deliberate action to bring oneself back to the present.

As Susan describes her teacher, the therapist notices that as she mentions that Miss Richards had very small piercing eyes, Susan's own face screws up as if in mimicry of this.

"Tell me more about those eyes," the therapist invites.

"They look... sort of mean... like she's angry"

"Like she's angry?"

"Yes, sort of all pinched up... she's often angry."

"And this time... she's angry?"

The therapist holds Susan's attention on Miss Richard's eyes. When Susan's attention wanders off this focus, making a generalised comment about Miss Richard's anger, the therapist brings her back to the scene. She picks up Susan's interest in the anger, but brings her back to this occasion by asking 'and this time?'

"She's angry... I don't know... because Laurie's late..."

"And her eyes look narrow and angry,"

Susan was searching around for meanings, but her therapist once more brings her attention back to Miss Richards' eyes. This was where Susan's energy was last engaged.

There is a pause during which the therapist notices that Susan is continuing to alternately screw up her eyes and then release them, as if she is trying out the feeling that this induces. After a few moments she stops and looks intently at the other side of the room.

"Yes, she looks like she's going to wring Laurie's... like she's going to really get even..." Susan stops. Her voice fades away. She is staring at the space now.

"What are you seeing?"

Susan hesitates. "I'm not sure why, I've suddenly got this feeling she's frightened. She's not angry at all, she's frightened."

The therapist says nothing, but waits for Susan to continue.

"It's odd. Now I have two sets of feelings. I can still remember the feeling of terror I had when I thought she was angry. She could be really scary. I can see how I used to react by getting into a panic and just kind of shut down but be very angry myself inside... but now I can also see that she probably wasn't nearly as scary as she looked to me as a child. She was scared herself."

Understanding Susan's Insight

Susan's response is interesting. Re-entering the scene has given her an opportunity to re-visit her childhood experience in a strong and experiential way. She has felt once again the anxiety of being a school girl in a classroom, at the mercy of the teacher who was so frightening to her, who she saw as unpredictably giving out punishments, unjustly imposing them upon innocent and guilty alike.

The experience of 'seeing' Miss Richards within the scene means that Susan not only remembers her feelings of the time, but also experiences a feeling reaction in the present, evoked by that image of Miss Richards. Details of the classroom appear before her and condition a response, which itself belongs with that school-age self which is conditioned by the rupa-ness of the scene. She is effectively once again experiencing being twelve or thirteen years old. She feels the fear again. In this, the re-creation of the scene amplifies the rupa energy. It gives her a taste of her past whilst still retaining an element of her adult self as observer of the process. She can revisit the scene in a feeling way and yet is not overwhelmed. Her child-self is held alongside the adult one.

In many explorations of this kind, Susan would simply have continued to explore the child-self's experience. As she focused on Miss Richards, she might have experienced fear that was intensified to the point of catharsis. She might have become extremely emotional, or equally might have become angry and expressed her rage in a way that she had not been able to do at the time when she was actually in Miss Richard's class. She might have recognised feelings of powerlessness, of victim-hood, of wanting others to take the blame instead of her.

In this particular scene, Susan's re-entry into the childhood environment brings a new insight. This insight surprises both to Susan and her therapist.

EXERCISE SIX: INSIGHT AND DIRECTION

Think about the insight which Susan had at the end of this piece of work. What do you think provoked it?

Can you think of examples from your own client work when someone had such a turn around in their perception of a significant person? If so, what precipitated it?

If Susan had not had this insight, what direction do you think the session would have taken next?

The direction which object-related work may take varies greatly. The therapist simply helps the client to amplify the rupa world and to stay present with the responses which arise. She does not actively draw attention to the feelings, so the affective responses are able to flow and change, rather than being concretised, judged or suppressed. If the client voices this process and names feelings, the therapist may follow that lead and join in trying to clarify and acknowledge the response, but this is secondary to maintaining the client's experience of the rupa world.

For example, when Susan says, "Yes, she looks like she could wring Laurie's... like she's going to really get even," if Susan had continued "I'm really frightened..." her therapist might have responded with a reflection, "You feel really frightened, sitting here in the classroom, seeing Miss Richard's face." This would acknowledge the feeling which Susan has voiced, but re-establish the context as well. Notice that the wording of the response holds the scene in place by keeping the interaction in the present tense. It gently brings Susan back to the image of Miss Richards.

In the case which we are discussing, however, Susan herself spontaneously makes a shift. First of all she recognises that she has two distinct sets of feelings. This level of self-awareness is not surprising. We have already seen that Susan identified that her feelings relating to her supervisor were echoes of her earlier feelings at school. She has the ability to step back from her own stream of thought and move into the observer mentality. There is part of her that is able to watch her process and make a more theoretical interpretation of her reactions, whilst another part is fully immersed in the emotions of the scene. This is a normal healthy response to memory, and shows that she is appropriately distanced from it.

We can see the shift of perspective between immersion and observer states in Susan's use of language. When she says that she remembers the feeling she is speaking in the voice of her adult self. Observing the feeling makes that feeling into the object of attention, and this in turn conditions a different mind-state. It evokes her adult curiosity. In effect, the feeling becomes rupa. Susan is now telling the story of the feeling. She is no longer immersed in the scene with Miss Richards. She says 'I thought she *was* angry' and 'I can see how I *used* to react.' Her shift of attention from the scene to the feelings has conditioned a change of mind-state.

This shift of object spontaneously brings Susan back to the present and the therapy room. She brings with her insights. Back in her adult mind-state, she can now describe more fully the feelings which were apparent in varying degrees whilst she was re-experiencing them in her school-girl identity. She can tell how she felt panicked, how she shut down, and how she was angry but did not express it. The recognition of these patterns of response will no doubt have relevance to her responses to her supervisor, and may help her to reassess her reactions to her.

In particular, Susan shares her realisation that her childhood interpretation of Miss Richard's appearance may have been wrong. She now sees Miss Richard's in a new way. This second vision of Miss Richards as a frightened person rather than an angry one seemed to emerge of its own accord during the exploration. At some point, perhaps when she was trying to determine the exact expression in Miss Richard's eyes, a perceptual shift occurred. Susan had two images: the one she had been seeing, which conditioned her child-mind, and the new one, viewed by her adult self; that of a frightened woman.

This second view was probably at least partly conditioned by Susan's attempt to understand the expression on Miss Richard's face. As we have already seen, the client is never totally immersed in the scene which is being re-created, but has the capacity to view it from present-day, adult eyes a well as through those of the earlier self. It is not surprising either that Susan's adult, enquiring mind is present alongside that of the school-girl.

Her capacity to step into the observer mind, which is a more adult mind-state, is supported by the style of therapeutic interaction; the therapist's presence, and their shared intention to understand. It is probably partly under the influence of this adult to adult aspect of the therapy relationship that Susan sees Miss Richards in a new light. She sees her as a woman who has fears, faced with a class of rebellious, unruly girls. The fellow feeling which she has been receiving from the therapist perhaps allows her to feel fellow feeling with Miss Richards. Now Susan has new feelings. Perhaps she feels sympathetic or recognises other pressures her teacher might have felt. Whatever the new reaction is, she clearly no longer feels scared of her.

It is interesting to reflect on other aspects of the process which might have led to this change. When Susan was 'looking at' Miss Richards, her therapist noticed her screwing up her own eyes in the attempt to recapture, and perhaps understand, the exact expression on the teacher's face. She seemed to be experimenting with *being* Miss Richards.

It is perhaps this attempt to embody Miss Richards which brought insight. Whilst looking at the image of Miss Richards, Susan saw what she expected to see. Miss Richards carried rupa energy associated with harshness, anger and injustice. This image conditioned Susan's experience of herself as frightened and angry, which in turn led her to continue to see Miss Richards as a tyrant. Now as she tried to understand the expression, Susan effectively moved from looking at Miss Richards, to feeling how it was to be her. This shift of experience took her out of the fixed position and led her to question her perception.

In fact what Susan was doing spontaneously was effectively to use a technique which we will explore in a later session; that of *role reversal*. She mentally moved out of her own position and experimented with being in Miss Richards'. Her attempt to understand took her into experimentation and investigation and this threw up a new way of seeing the situation.

Much of therapy method is to notice what happens spontaneously. When clients are investigating their experience they will often naturally use ways of viewing it which might be thought of techniques. This is therapy at its best. The therapist has no need to introduce methods or tools if the client if finding his own. Providing the container is sufficient. At the same time, sometimes, the deliberate introduction of a method of working can be helpful, if only in offering guidance about what is possible. Without such offers, most clients will be reluctant to move beyond the usual forms of discourse. In most cases they will not reach the kind of intensity which is required for object-related work.

Integrating the Learning

So far, Susan has spent most of the session exploring her perception of Miss Richards. This exploration, however, originally came about because she was distressed by her supervisor's behaviour. When she arrived for her counselling session she was very upset by an encounter with her superior at work, whom she described as overbearing and critical.

Whilst at the outset the therapist accepted this description without comment, the characteristics attributed to third parties are always best regarded as provisional. The therapist does not know the supervisor, and even if she did, she would have her own experience of the woman. It is not that she needs to voice doubt about Susan's experience, for to do so at this stage might well jeopardise the therapeutic relationship. (Sometimes, as we will see late, a direct challenge in this sort of situation is appropriate, but more commonly it is best to wait and see what develops.) Holding the information provisionally means that the therapist recognises that Susan's experience is conditioned and liable to change. Indeed changing Susan's perception and experience of the world might be seen as the aim of therapy.

Having re-visited the earlier scene in the schoolroom and reached new insight, the new therapeutic need is to integrate this learning into the current situation at work. Susan might well do this for herself. As someone with a good level of self-awareness and fluency in the therapy process, she may well start to wonder if her supervisor also feels frightened and might explore this in the therapy session. If she does not, her therapist may invite her to reflect on possible links, perhaps simply by reminding her that this was how they started to explore the topic. For example, she might say, "I remember we got into this because you were upset about your supervisor at work. When you walk into the office tomorrow morning, I wonder what is going to happen when you see her."

Whether the final stage in the enquiry is spontaneous or is prompted by a question from the therapist, its conclusion is not to be assumed. It may be that Susan does indeed realise that her supervisor has more complex feelings than she is allowing and that she has her reasons for behaving as she does, which have nothing to do with Susan. She might even realise that she had been misinterpreting the supervisor's remarks because she expected her, as someone with authority, to be like her image of Miss Richards. On the other hand she may also conclude that the resemblance between Miss Richards and the supervisor is less strong than she had thought. She may conclude that the supervisor is critical and unpleasant and that she needs to look at how she can respond to this without feeling like a child again.

Whatever the reality, Susan's experience of exploring the scene with Miss Richards will have helped her to disentangle her responses and to unhook from some of the reactions which draw her into the child-self trance.

References and Background Reading for This Session

Brazier C 2001 *Buddhist Psychology* Constable Robinson UK (for theory on skandhas)

Brazier, D 1997 *The Feeling Buddha* Constable Robinson UK

Hanh, N & Neumann, R 2006, *Understanding Our Mind* Parallax Press US (for material on karmic seeds)

SESSION EIGHT

Moving into Action

In this session we will explore:
- Moving into action work in counselling
- Dialogue in action work in counselling
- Psychodramatic techniques and their role in object-related work
- Director and double roles in psychodrama as therapist options
- De-roling objects

In ordinary counselling, object-related work, is commonly done sitting in chairs, with the counsellor encouraging the client to talk about important objects in his life. We have already seen how the positioning of chairs can affect the sort of relationship which evolves and how, frequently it is more appropriate to adopt chair positions which are not directly opposite each other.

This is because everything in the environment of the counselling relationship conveys some sort of message about what is being undertaken and creates conditions for the process to unfold. In this arrangement the environment is ideally brought into line with the ambient quality of the process, the co-creative attitude of this kind of work being replicated in a 'shoulder to shoulder', or at least obliquely angled, relationship of the seating.

The arrangement that is adopted needs to allow the therapist to observe the client closely but not intrusively, for, as we have discussed, observation of the minutiae of facial expression and body posture is important if the therapist is going to spot shifts of mental state and identification.

At the same time, it is the object world and the scene which are the primary focus of both therapist and client's attention. For this to unfold, creating an empty space in the physical space of the room, rather as a stage before a performance, waiting for players to appear, invites reflection. If both chairs look towards this space at least in some degree, and the amount will be a matter of personal preference and particular circumstances, the conditions give the message of 'let the play begin'. It will offer an invitation to explore and improvise together.

As we have seen, this implicit invitation may be enough. The creation of psychological and physical space can condition work in which imaginative unpacking of the client's world unfolds without the need for anyone to leave their seat. The method does, however, lend itself to more active approaches, and, if you become skilled in it, you may sometimes find it helpful to move out of your chairs and into using the whole space of the room. Psychological material is given new life as it is given territory and as aspects of the story are played out in spatial relationship.

Facilitating work in this way can be very similar to the work you do sitting in a chair, except that its scope is greater. You can, for example, experiment with moving around within the projected psychological space, taking different viewpoints, and looking at the scene from different angles. Investigations of different aspects of the scene can happen sequentially, and different characters be highlighted in different ways. It even becomes possible to hold several scenes simultaneously, or to create a 'safe place' to which the client can go if material becomes too distressing.

We have already looked at some possibilities for this kind of work, particularly in our discussion of creating safe spaces, but in this session we will focus more directly on adopting active methods. We will look at how a verbal interaction can be transformed into a piece of action work, and at some of the different possibilities that emerge once this is done. In this, we will focus particularly on how these methods might be employed in one to one sessions and we will look at some common pitfalls, so that if you are experimenting with this kind of approach you are not caught in these.

Dramatic enactment is a useful and powerful form of therapy, and it is generally practiced by people with specialist training. Taking on a full-blown drama can have its complications, and this book does not intend to equip you to handle these. Should the methods interest you, you would be well advised to take further training in them. The intention here is to give you some basic skills which naturally follow from the other object-related skills discussed in this book, and to show you how, in small steps, you can start to be more adventurous in your use of the space of the therapy room.

Working in this way we are particularly drawing on some of the methods of *psychodrama*, the therapeutic approach developed by Jacob Moreno[95]. As an approach, psychodrama combines well with an other-centred perspective. Its methodology is adaptable to different psychological models. It offers flexibility and, in particular, it accommodates a perspective which is not grounded in investigating the self directly. In this it has much in common with our methods. It uses the spatial dimension, and it offers opportunities to move between roles, to explore other positions which are not the self one[96], and even to view the self from afar through the eyes of a third party[97].

Understanding some of the basic mechanisms of psychodramatic method is not only useful in providing therapeutic tools to the other-centred therapist. It also gives clear demonstration of some of the psychological structuring of human relationships and particularly of therapeutic methods. By seeing these played out physically, the trainee counsellor becomes familiar with concepts which describe the different styles of relating in a very concrete way. For this reason, in our own training courses, psychodrama is a regular feature. Not all our students will go on to use dramatic methods, but all will learn to think about their behaviour as therapists in more concrete ways.

EXERCISE ONE: THINKING ABOUT SPACE

Think about the room in which you generally work. How is it arranged? Do you ever change the arrangement of it?

When you have time to experiment, try making changes. Re-arrange the furniture. Introduce something brightly coloured, perhaps a blanket or large cushions or a coloured throw. Create a large empty space. Take out the chairs.

With each change, sit in the chair or place where your client would normally sit and see how the room feels. What does it invite? What sort of work might you expect to do here?

Arrange your space in a way which feels comfortable to you as therapist (would this be the same if you were the client?) and then ask yourself: "In this room, where is the stage?"

Reflect on your answer. Does your room invite action work? Would you want it to?

The Power of Action

Action has a greater power to condition mental process than thought. What we do creates mental formations by laying the seeds for future action. Thought has the power to condition the mind in as much as it too is action, but its influence is far less potent. The actions of thought are small scale, micro-impulses of muscles, repeated over and over; the tensing of body as anger surfaces, the forward rush of anticipation, the relaxation of love.

The body-mind finds its habitual stances and so reinforces its position. Action is fundamental to mind.

For action to be effective in conditioning the mind it mostly requires intention. If mind and body are both committed, then the new course is etched in our mentality as a future possibility to be revisited. Once there, the seeds of that activity lie dormant in our psyche, awaiting the opportunity to spring into life when circumstances come again. We cycle through old tracks. We repeat.

This being so, there is argument for the power of action-based methods to be employed therapeutically. If clients can not only talk about change, but also rehearse it, they are far more likely to go through with it. The person who wants to speak to a friend about a difficult topic will have more confidence to do so if she has played out the scene in advance. The person who wants to take up a sport, but keeps putting it off, is more likely to actually start it if he can be persuaded to visit the sports club, even if it is just to introduce himself to other members or staff. The person who wants to change her job is much more likely to do something about it if she has taken a first step and sent off some applications or visited a job centre.

Action can be important in helping someone to face and explore the past too. A dramatic re-enactment of a past event may provide an opportunity for a person to express things in words which were not said at the time, or to experience doing something which was left undone, or to choose a different direction and then explore its consequences. Although such work is, in one sense, fantasy, in another way, it is often cathartic, insightful and has the potential to change the person's sense of things *as if* the reality had been so.

Psychodrama is a therapy of action. It carries with it the opportunity for this kind of work, which takes people out of their habitual ways of thinking and acting and gives them an experience of being a different way. Other dramatic therapies also offer this possibility. For the purposes of this book, we will look at simple applications and limited ways of borrowing from these methods, but even these, in as much as they are active techniques, offer the benefits of an action-based approach.

EXERCISE TWO: CONDITIONING ACTION IN
THERAPY SESSIONS

Think about your own therapy practice. What sort of emotions have clients expressed in the last week? What proportion of client time is spent expressing:

Sadness
Interest
Anger
Confusion
Resentment
Joy
Worry

What effect do you think the act of expressing these emotions has on your clients?

What mental states are conditioned by what your clients do in therapy sessions?

Moving Into Action Work

Creating a scene within the therapy room in an active way, as opposed to talking imaginatively about that same scene, is a skill which offers many therapeutic possibilities. If you feel you would like to try working in this way, some experience of psychodrama, role play or drama therapy is useful in giving confidence, but if you have colleagues willing to join you in experimenting, you can start to introduce action into your work in small degrees, and develop experience in that way. Let us look at how you might start.

There are many different ways of introducing action work, but usually it is best if the move into action arises spontaneously out of the therapeutic discourse. If you look back at the dialogue between Susan and her therapist, you can see that it wouldn't take a big step to move from sitting together, imaginatively talking about the classroom, to standing up and talking about it, and then maybe to walk around it. The classroom was clearly 'there' for Susan, and her teacher, Miss Richards, evidently had a presence in the room that was located in a particular place. Susan 'saw' her. The therapist observed that Susan looked at the place where she 'saw' Miss Richards standing at the front of the class; she saw that her eyes were fixed on that location as Susan described her.

We can imagine that, had her therapist suggested it, Susan could have stood up and walked over to stand by the 'classroom window' or might have been induced to move nearer or further from where 'Miss Richards' was standing. She might have experimented with finding a safe distance, as Mia Leijssen's client did, or she might have been invited to think about what she would like to say to Miss Richards, or even to try out actually saying it. All these possibilities would not have taken a big step on from the work which was described. They would have just meant capitalising on what was already happening and pushing it into dramatic enactment.

If you are starting by setting up a scene, one of the simplest ways to move this into action work might be for you, as the therapist, to invite the client to his change mode of working by simply saying, "Show me".

If the client is already talking about a place in which an incident happened, in order to create the space imaginatively in the room one can begin with the small steps we have already discussed, shifting the tense into the present and inviting the client to imagine being in the space. This is likely to lead to a verbal exploration of the type we have been describing in previous sessions.

On the other hand, if the therapist stands up and says "OK so what is it like?" gesturing around the room, the invitation to shift gear and move into a new form of exploration is far more powerful. The client will then probably be willing to join the therapist on his feet and to indicate where he imagines the door, window, furniture and other features of the scene to be.

Other times, the shift might come spontaneously out of an observation by the therapist that the client is already 'seeing' the scene around him. Watching the client's eye movements and reactions, you may sense that a significant feature of the scene is imaginatively located at a certain place within the room. When you observe this, you may choose to continue to facilitate the process from your seat, as we saw in the last session, but alternatively you could get up and go to a place from which you can indicate the feature, and thus use this as a jumping off point. You might say "so the table was over here and where were you standing?" or even, "so the table is over here, and where are you standing?"

Notice here the difference in tone which a shift of tense can bring, as illustrated by these two statements. As we have already seen, a shift to the present tense can be effective in drawing the client into the action of the story. At this scene setting stage, the use of present tense may be helpful if the client is already well 'warmed up' to the material. On the other hand, sometimes it can feel too artificial if the client is still talking about the event in a more abstract way. In such circumstances, it can actually have the opposite effect, shutting the client down because it seems contrived and artificial, and raises self-consciousness.

Timing is important when making such a shift. With

experience you will gain a feel for when it is helpful to bring the scene to life, and when it will simply create confusion and defensiveness. It is often a matter of close observation and having a way of inviting the action which does not cut across the grain of the therapeutic process, but rather seems to flow naturally from it. Confidence helps, for if you are hesitant, this will not inspire the client to trust this new way of working. Experience and intuition will guide you in finding the right level of immediacy in this work. Experiment with making shifts of tense, or gesturing to locations which seem to be associated with elements of the story as you develop your skills. Let us look at an example of how this might work.

Tom has been talking about his relationship with his girlfriend, Marie. Marie lives with her parents and Tom reports that he always feels difficult about visiting her at home because her parents are around and he feels under scrutiny.

"As soon as I walk into the living room, there is her mother sitting in front of the television, and her father in his arm chair and I feel as if I'm being watched the whole time. If I sit next to her on the sofa I feel they are watching to see what we do, and if I don't... well, where else do I sit?"

"Sounds really uncomfortable... as you're talking, I'm seeing this room... big television... is it?"

"Yes, a huge screen... I don't even watch telly a home..."

"So if we were in the room now, where would the telly be?"

Tom hesitates. The invitation has slightly shaken his story. Probably without it he would have talked about his feelings about television, and how it was a waste of time, as he had in a previous session. Jolted out of this script, he looks up. His therapist looks questioningly round the space of the consulting room and repeats her question.

"So if we were in the room now, where would the telly be?"

Tom thinks for a minute, then responds, "Over there in the corner probably, to the side of the fireplace. There's a hideous artificial stone fireplace too. You know, one of those pink and grey and yellow ones. And china ornaments... lots of them... all along the mantelpiece."

Tom's therapist notices that he is looking across the room. It is not clear from his manner if he is really 'seeing' the fireplace or simply telling her more facts. She gets up out of her chair and crosses to stand beside where she thinks the fireplace is.

"Is it about here?"

Tom nods.

"All those ornaments..."

"Yes, and she is sitting here..." Tom gets up quickly and darts over to point out where Marie's mother's chair is. "And he is over there..." now animated, he points to the other side of the room. "And the sofa is here in the middle..."

"I see what you mean, sort of hemmed in..." the therapist comments.

So in a short space of time, Tom has moved from his chair and is imaginatively showing his therapist round his girl friend's living room. The initial resistance is quickly forgotten because his therapist has the confidence to carry on encouraging him into action.

From here the scene might progress in a number of ways. Tom might explore memories of similar scenes from his past. He might explore in more detail his feelings about either of the parents. He might try explaining to Marie, imaginatively, how it feels sitting in the room. If they are to continue the scene and the course of action is not clear, it is possible the therapist might simply ask him "What do we need to do next?"

On the other hand, as a first move, this scene setting may be enough for now. He has shown his therapist this part of his inner world and she has understood an aspect of how it impacts upon him. They have already moved a step beyond his habitual script.

Whatever option they follow is likely to come out of his therapist's observation of his behaviour. She notices where his attention is being drawn, and how that is influencing his reactions and mood. She notices when he has energy for action work and when this seems to decline into discussion.

EXERCISE THREE: SETTING THE SCENE USING ACTION

In session five you practiced scene setting using imaginative work. Now repeat the exercise, this time using the space of the room. Get up and walk around the scene with your client and encourage them to explore it from different angles. Do not use props at this stage, unless you client strongly wants to. Just use your imagination to 'see' where things are. Notice whether particular 'objects' which are identified as being in the room carry rupa energy and whether you can see your client's *reaction* to them.

After you have created the scene, finish and debrief. Discuss how you invited your partner into the activity. Did it feel natural or did it cut across his or her pattern. What effect did this have?

How easy was it to facilitate the scene setting process? Did you 'see' the room correctly? Were there any points where you got it wrong in ways that interfered with your client's experience, for example by standing on a 'piece of furniture' or even on an imaginary person if there was anyone in the room?

Getting used to recalling and respecting the space, and to relating to it as if it were furnished or landscaped in a particular way, takes skill. Take opportunities to practice.

If you decide to try moving into action in your regular work and want develop ways of working in which you and the client 'walk around the room' or set up scenes, you may like to bear the following points in mind:

The imagination is powerful

Keep things simple. In this sort of work, less is often more. Do not get side-tracked into using elaborate props. Often you do not need to mark items in the object world at all. You can simply indicate that a window is here, or a table there with a gesture. Where you do use objects, simple cushions, chairs or boxes will work better than more complicated items, as they are blank canvases for the client's imagination.

Speak in the appropriate tense

As we have already seen, tense is important in any imaginative work, but in action work it is vital that you respect the client's temporal experience of the scene. Often he will be 'in' the scene, even if it occurred in reality many years ago, and you will need to use the present tense to support this psychological reality. Once the scene is established, try to enter into the object world yourself, and in doing so speak in ways that honour it. Frequently this means using the present tense unless, as in the example given earlier, there is a therapeutic reason not to, for example, when a client is still tentatively moving from the 'talking about' mode into experiencing the scene more fully. Sometimes this is a transitionary phase, but other times use of the past tense occurs in a situation where the client wishes to show the therapist, within a 'here and now' mode of relationship, how a scene was.

In addition to reflecting on your use of tenses, you can also reflect on whether or not to include yourself in the scene. You might ask, "So, what can you see through the window?" or "So what can we see through the window?" for example.

Be guided by the client

As far as possible, allow the client to choose any props. Ask 'What could represent the chair?' or 'Do we need something over there for her bed?' Let the client pick something from the furnishings which you have available. Don't try to organise him too much. Even if a choice seems odd, go with it unless you have reason to think the item chosen might be dangerous. There will be a reason for the choice. You may find out later what that reason is, but for the present, trust the process. This may mean that you do not want to have items in your therapy room which have particular sentimental value to you. If you move into doing action work, you need to be willing for items to be used. You may also wish to avoid having items to hand which could be dangerous if thrown or misused, especially if you are working with volatile client groups.

Respect the space

At the beginning, try to stand well back, outside the space which will become the stage on which the scene will unfold so that it can remain an empty canvas. Once they are established, do not walk through walls or stand on pieces of furniture. Remember objects and spaces which have been significant to the drama and treat them respectfully until they have been 'taken out of role'[98].

Invite exploration of the scene from different angles

Use the space to explore new vantage points. Walk around it. You might say to the client "So shall we wander over and look out at the view?" or "I wonder what this room looks like if we go over and sit in father's chair?"

Respect the power of the method

Do not attempt to take someone into a scene in this way unless you are confident that you can offer them grounding and containment if they should become overly emotional. Evoking a scene, particularly from childhood, may occasionally trigger under-distanced reactions or flashbacks. Whilst this is rare and the possibility should not put you off working in this way, it is good to know what to do if it does happen.

Do not take on roles of characters in the scene

There is always a danger in action work, as with any therapy, that you attract counter-part or transference roles. Sometimes this happens inadvertently in the course of the work, but where it does, it is best to avoid playing into the role. Where possible, actively distance yourself from it.

Enactment can offer ways of deliberately separating yourself from roles which the client is imposing on you. For example, if you feel that the client is seeing you in a strongly coloured way, perhaps as the perfect therapist, or, conversely, in overly negative ways, as 'never getting it right', you can deliberately move out of your chair in order to separate yourself from the projections. You can then invite the client to look with you at the image which he has of 'the therapist' sitting on the chair and to talk about the person he sees. I have found this technique very effective on occasions, and have even occasionally asked the client to *role reverse*[99] with his 'therapist' so that she can 'tell him what to do'.

Avoiding getting swept into the drama yourself is also important when it comes to role-playing third parties. Don't do it. Imaginative work is very powerful and taking on a role in someone else's drama can have many problems. In a group, dramatic enactment in which significant people from a client's past are played by other group members can be useful, but, in one to one therapy, taking on a third party role is potentially disastrous. It is best to adopt a golden rule: **never act an auxiliary role for a client in a counselling situation**. If you do so you can potentially destroy your neutrality and leave the client in a vulnerable position with no therapeutic support.

Stay out of the client's line of sight during dramatic work:
Although not always appropriate, it is often more helpful to keep out of the client's line of sight. A good position for this sort of work is by the client's side, or even slightly behind him. This works well for two reasons.

- Firstly your support and interventions will be more neutral. For the client it will feel either as if you are like a travelling companion, offering assistance from a friendly space, or you may even seem like the "voice in the head" of the *psychodramatic double*[100]. In this way you will provoke minimal resistance and assume a low profile in the scene. The client will feel more able to accept or reject your invitations.
- Secondly, if you are out of the line of sight you will not contaminate the scene with our presence, nor will you attract to yourself roles in the scene. You will avoid getting overly embroiled in transferences.

In both these ways you will also remain a relatively neutral source of support.

Dialogue and Empty Chairs

If you are using action work in a counselling setting, you will probably discover that situations arise where you feel that it would be useful for the client to get into dialogue with a character they have been talking about. It is not hard to imagine that Susan might have wanted to say something to Miss Richards, or that Tom might want to speak to Marie's parents. Having imagined these figures in the scene, it is a small step for the counsellor to ask the client "And what would you like to say to him?"

Let us imagine how this might work. There are a number of

ways that Susan might have responded had this question been addressed to her. For example, she might have said:

- I wanted to tell her I was frightened
- I want to tell her how frightened I am
- I want to say 'I'm frightened of you'
- "I'm frightened of you!"

These responses reveal different degrees of immersion in the scene. If Susan responds, "I want to say 'I'm frightened of you'" this includes a phrase which is direct speech 'I'm frightened of you' within her answer. This suggests that Susan is very close to enacting the dialogue with the imagined Miss Richards. It would only be a small step at this point for Susan's counsellor to say "Well, you tell her then!" to which Susan would probably respond by doing so.

In the last instance, however, where the response is simply "I'm frightened of you", there is no need for the therapist to offer an invitation because the client is already enacting the scene. Here any invitation would tend to take Susan out of the action. This is a mistake which beginning therapists often make. They do not recognise and capitalise on what is already happening, but, instead, they interrupt the client's process. Do not tell a client to do what he is already doing. It is a bit like waking up someone who is suffering from insomnia to find out if they are sleeping well.

Many clients, however, need some help in moving into dialogue, but with good facilitation, the process need not feel too strange. Addressing words to an empty space may sound bizarre but, as we have seen, the imagination is potent and, once immersed in the scene, it becomes logical to act in this way. The third party who is being addressed may already be represented by a space in the room. This sort of work can also be facilitated by using a chair to represent the person. This method is often called *empty chair work* for obvious reasons.

An empty chair can hold a space which has already been spontaneously created. In the case we are discussing, for example, the therapist might deliberately take a chair or cushion and place it where 'Miss Richards' was located. While doing this she might give some explanation, for example saying, "So suppose we put this chair here to represent Miss Richards..."

This action is often sufficient. Once the scene is in play, Susan will probably see Miss Richards on the chair without any need to develop the image. If, on the other hand, one were doing a similar piece of work from 'cold', then the therapist would probably need to spend a little time helping the client to 'see' the character, using questions about things such as the body position in which the person would sit, their facial expression, their clothing and so on. You have already worked with creating this sort of image in exercise five in the last session. This sort of work may feel slightly artificial at first, but once the dialogue starts, the person being imagined will generally become more real.

Facilitating dialogue requires some initial encouragement and permission giving. People may feel a little inhibited about speaking to an empty space, even though, if they are immersed in the scene, it is not a big step to move into verbal action. The presence of a counsellor who embodies confidence, and who takes the process in a matter of fact way, will implicitly allow the client to follow his natural flow and speak. Once the presence of the third party is established, however, as with most object-related work, the therapist will follow the client's process and allow space for him to explore. Simple questions like, "and what happens next?" or, "What do you really want to say?" can invite the client into dialogue. Once the dialogue is underway, you may wish to check with the client how he imagines the other person reacting. This again can be done with simple questions. "How is she reacting?" "Is she hearing you?"

Often in one to one therapy a short interaction is enough.

Occasionally there will be merit in letting the conversation run on, inviting the client to tell you the imagined responses of the other person. The use of dialogue can be particularly helpful in voicing unspoken thoughts, wishes and regrets. Sometimes it can help when a person previously felt silenced or felt that they expressed things which they did not feel to be true. Then revisiting the scene may allow the person to experience 'getting it right this time'.

Sometimes you may alternate between getting the client to talk to the person on the chair, and discussing the process. If you do this, the transition from one mode of conversation to the other needs to be clearly defined so that the two modes of relating do not merge into one another. This may involve a shift of position from one in which you are by the client's side, looking at the third party, to one in which you turn to face the client, with the third party to your side.

In a future session we will look at ways in which the use of dialogue can be extended and the perspective of the recipient can be explored through a method called *'role reversal'*

In this sort of dialogue there are a number of points and pitfalls to watch out for. Some we have already mentioned:

Under-distancing

Voicing thoughts and feelings to an imagined figure from one's past can be powerful, and takes the drama one step closer to reality. If you have moved slowly into action and know your client, you will probably have a sense of whether introducing dialogue is going to be problematic. On the other hand, there is always the possibility that something unforeseen may happen and the client may become more distressed than you anticipated, or may recall incidents or details which had not previously been voiced which lead him to become under-distanced. In this case you may need to use containing methods and, in the extreme, reassure your client that the other person in the dialogue is not really in the room.

Becoming the focus of role play

As we have already suggested, taking a part in the drama if you are sole therapist is potentially very problematic and not something to be done. I have seen student therapists offer to play the part of various 'others' in their client's lives in training sessions, but this is just not wise. Even if the situation seems innocuous, like, for example, role-playing a job interview, it can leave a taint in the therapeutic relationship.

Be aware of what behaviour you are conditioning

As we have seen action sows seeds for future behaviour. For this reason behaviour which might reinforce negative patterns, such as for example expressing excessive amounts of anger or complaining and blaming others, is not helpful. Be aware of the patterns you might be encouraging your client to act out in this kind of work and whether they are setting a healthy precedent for future action.

This does not mean you should never let your client express anger. Repressing feelings is not healthy either, and taking an honest view of ones emotions gives a solid foundation for relating with others. What is likely to be problematic is if the predominant patterns of thought and action being expressed are negative or harmful to others. The bias towards negativity which evident in the work of some therapists is likely to breed will create conditions which are conducive to continuing negativity in their clients.

Take care how chairs or other objects are used later

Even if you de-role the chair which has been used in this kind of work, the power of action work can persist. It is not a good idea if you then sit in that same chair which earlier was representing the vindictive employer or the much loved mother or the footloose daughter. If you do, there is a fair chance you will attract associations with that person. It is a good idea, if you are interested in doing this kind of work, to have an extra chair or two (folding ones will do) in your consulting room.

EXERCISE FOUR: INTRODUCING DIALOGUE

If you are working in triads, experiment with dialogue, using an empty chair. When you are the counsellor, place the chair at a small distance from yourself and your client and invite them to imagine someone whom they know well in their current life sitting on it. (Choosing a current figure should make it less likely that they will 'see' someone with whom they had a traumatic relationship in childhood. It is probably as well not to choose someone with whom one has a particularly painful relationship the first time that you try this.)

First of all, take time to facilitate the client so that they can 'see' the person. Invite them to describe their appearance. Work in the present tense.

When you sense that the client is ready, if it feels right, invite them to speak to the person. You might simply say, "What do you want to say to him/her?"

Encourage the client to continue the dialogue by asking about how they see the person responding.

When the dialogue reaches a natural end, carry on counselling for a few minutes to explore with the client the

---

meaning of what has taken place.

Now de-role the chair. Tell your client that the person is no longer present. Ask them to move the chair so that it is no longer in the same place.

Discuss your experience. What seemed to work, and what didn't? How did the client experience the work?

If you are working on your own, reflect on the value of this sort of work and whether you might want to try it. Experiment on your own with visualising a person and thinking about what you might say to them. Try saying it.

Write a letter to someone you know or used to know which you do not intend to post, expressing things which you have felt too difficult to say in the past.

Different Positions in Action Work

Psychodrama offers a model of working which allows the therapist to work in two distinct positions.

The double

The first of these positions we have already mentioned. This is the position of the *double*. The double is generally a closely empathic position. When used in a psychodrama, the double expresses the thoughts and feelings which the client might be experiencing, but is not voicing. She stands just to the side and rear of the person whose drama is being played out,[101] with her hand on that person's shoulder, following him and echoing his body language and gestures, voicing whatever she imagines might be going through his head. She is a bit like the 'thinks bubble' which one finds in cartoon strips. In psychodrama the double may be played by a member of the group or may be a co-therapist. Psychodramatic doubles have sometimes been used therapeutically with disturbed patients as the role offers a supportive presence without being overly intrusive.

We have already seen how, in object-related work, the therapist accompanies the client closely and may often choose to sit in a side by side position to reflect this. This position is one of accompaniment and fellow feeling, an unobtrusive, but active presence. Similarly, the psychodramatic double, in the position by the client's side, may sometimes be quite vocal, and, being in close empathy, can even risk trying out hunches which seem off-beam. It is a position which has a quality to it which is more akin to a peer relationship. It contrasts with the other psychodrama position; that of the director.

The director

Whilst the psychodramatic double represents the client's "voice in the head", the psychodramatic director provides the external authority and facilitation for the work. The director, as the title suggests, keeps more of an over-view on the direction of the work. She stands outside the scene, often against one of the walls of the room, at some distance from the person whose drama is being enacted, and usually faces him. From this position she can talk directly to the person and, if necessary, take control of the action or tell him to act in a particular way.

In a full psychodrama, the director may make decisions about the way an issue will be explored and the scenes to be enacted, and may be quite forceful in pushing the person to do things. Directors vary in how authoritative they are, and some are more consultative, whilst others are highly proscriptive, but there is always a price to pay for indulging in too much negotiation, as this tends to pull the person back into discussion and out of the action.

Because the director is outside the scene, she can have some discussion with that part of the client which is also observing what is happening, without disrupting the action too much. As we have already seen, a person who is immersed in the object world is also capable of interacting with the therapist in a direct, adult, everyday way, as long as that negotiation is brief and clearly outside the scene. In director mode it is possible to negotiate decisions with the client about how to proceed with the work, and then allow them to be able to return fully into the scene afterwards.

In this situation, it is to the everyday self that the director speaks. This everyday self co-exists with the self who is immersed in the drama. Indeed, it is when a person starts to lose their capacity to step in and out of the scene that it is time to bring the person out of the situation, for at that point they have become under-distanced and too deeply enmeshed with the material.

Whilst the director makes some decisions on behalf of the person who is exploring their life through the drama, these decisions are the ones which are peripheral to the psychological work. Some decisions need to be made by the person himself. For example, the choice of locations of objects, of props where they are used, and of people to play characters in the drama should all be made by the client. These are the significant rupas in the scene, and it is important that the person chooses ones which feel believable to him in order for the scene to work.

The director on the other hand may make decisions about the way to tackle the storyline or may suggest starting points. Occasionally she may direct the client to action, for example telling him to speak or to stop. In making her decisions, the director needs a high degree of empathy for the client, for, if she is not empathically connected with him, she will not choose the right scenes or intervene at appropriate moments. She also needs acute observation skills as she has to read the person's facial expression in order to watch the changes of emotion and levels of involvement in the drama. She needs to see whether a particular intervention has worked, and whether a new tack is needed.

The use of the director role in object-related work is rare. The director's position really comes into its own when psychodrama moves into dramatic enactment and involves a number of participants, since then the director has to keep order and make sure that the drama centres round the client or protagonist's scene and does not get high-jacked by another group member. Much of her role is as gatekeeper for other group members' contributions. In one to one work, it is more common, as we have seen, for the counsellor to take on a role similar to that of the double.

Occasionally, however, it is useful to become like the director. In particular, if you are working with scene setting, you might move to a distance. This is particularly the case if the client is very disturbed or overwhelmed by feelings of helplessness. This may feel counter-intuitive, but in such a situation there is a danger of you becoming caught up in the same helpless feelings as the client through psychological contagion. Preserving some psychological distance can be important. If a client seems overwhelmed by feelings, your instinct may be to rush towards him to give support, however, if the client is able and willing to carry on with the work, keeping a distance may help you to support him more effectively. Also on such occasions you may need to exercise some authority in order to interrupt the flow of the session if the person is becoming too under-distanced. It is easier and more powerful to do this from a director position.

In general if you move away from the client into a director position when working on your own, it is good to remain mobile and alternate between this distant position and the usual side-by-side position of object-related work. This way you can retain close empathy and fellow feeling, but moderate it by preserving your capacity for objectivity.

EXERCISE FIVE: ACTION METHODS
IN COUNSELLING

Reflect on the use of action methods in counselling. Do you
ever move out of your chair during a counselling session?
If not, can you imagine doing so? Think about your current
clients. Who might be amenable to working in this way?
Think about your recent sessions. Were there points when
you could have invited exploration of a scene?

Think about the ways in which you respond to your clients
when you are doing regular counselling. Do you think that
your style has more in common with the double's or the
director's roles? Are you a quiet empathic presence staying
out of sight, or do you speak more directly to your client's
rational side? Do you reflect their mood or do you
negotiate the therapeutic process with them?

Discuss these issues or write about them in your journal

De-Roling Objects and Spaces

When we have been working in an object-related way, if spaces or
physical objects have been involved in the work, these may well
have taken on powerful associations, which could persist and
cause problems in later work. At the end of a piece of work it is
therefore important to return the objects, as far as possible, to a
neutral state. This is called *de-roling*. In psychodrama people as
well as objects need to be de-roled. This is not the case in one to
one work, but if you are in a training group you may need to
think about this. In particular you need to watch that people do
not get type-cast, playing the same role repeatedly.

At some times de-roling is more important than at others. It is not always necessary. Sometimes you may even feel that it is not a good idea to do it because the process would be too disruptive or would feel disrespectful of work which has been done. Sometimes objects can remain a repository for associations over a period of time and in this way provide an ongoing source of support and a tool which can be returned to in future sessions. Of course, whilst this can work for small items, which can be placed in a safe place and be returned to later, larger things, like pieces of furniture or areas of the room, or things which are in constant use probably do need to be restored to something approaching psychological neutrality

Taking things 'out of role' involves cutting through the rupa element which has been attributed to them and returning them to normal status (which of course will still be perceived with some level of rupa-ness, but will not be contaminated by the strong emotional energies which have been evoked in the session.) This process is often one of simply stating in an author-itative way that this is now just a chair or just a table or just John. Sometimes you may ask the client to tell you what the item really is in their own words. "This is not Grandma, it is a sofa cushion."

If the item can be moved, it may be good to move it to a different location in the room. If a person is involved they should speak for themselves and say a few things about the ways in which they differ from the part they were playing.

Even when such a process has been undertaken, it is still likely that some psychological contamination of the space remains. Powerful work of this kind can leave a lingering presence for people, and you may need to be aware of this in future sessions. Watch out for signs that a scene from a previous session is being thought about or that it has been reactivated. When this happens, it is often fruitful to do further work with the situation, but sometimes it may be an indication that there is more need to ground the work in reality by trying to get beyond the rupa elements.

EXERCISE SIX: DE-ROLING THE SCENE

Practice methods of de-roling the scene. If you have undertaken the scene setting activity in exercise four, take time at the end to see whether there are places in the room which need to be de-roled. Discuss whether any residual elements from the original scene remain.

Practice setting up scenes and then dismantling them and de-roling the objects and spaces which have been used. Experiment with different methods until you feel comfortable in being able to do this.

References and Background Reading for This Session

Blatner A 1998 *Foundations of Psychodrama: History, Theory and Practice* Springer Publishing US

Holmes P and Karp, M, 1991 *Psychodrama; Inspiration and Technique*, Routledge, London

Scheff T.J. 1979 *Catharsis In Healing Ritual and Drama.* University Of California Press

SESSION NINE

Working with Physical Objects

In this session we will explore:
- Definitions of rupa
- The power of the object world
- Providing objects in the therapy room
- Evocative objects
- Holding objects in the spaces between sessions
- Letting go of objects

Whilst so far we have understood rupa to be the perceptual object, and have defined this meaning in terms of its role in the creation and maintenance of the self, more properly the word rupa is simply used to describe the power associated with the object. In the way that we have used the term up until now, this implies the power which the object holds to draw our attention; a power which we give it through our desire to inhabit a world which is constant, safe and reflective of our identity.

Often the power is one of fascination and positive *entrancement*. We have seen that also sometimes it can hold negative associations. At such times, when its power seems threatening to us, the terrifying rupa is still a function of the self-world, and has its place in maintaining the self. The rupa may be an apparition which frightens us or fills us with pain or dread, perhaps associated with an abusive experience in the past or some unresolved loss, but even here the rupa is inextricably linked with our sense of who we are, supporting those 'selves' which we might prefer to eradicate, but which, nevertheless, are part of our identity.

This insubstantial fabric of delusion stands between us and the inevitable existential pain of life. It is in one sense artificial; a protective barrier, like a curtain, which hides uncomfortable prospects from us. Whilst enmeshed in the selective view which it gives to us, we can believe, at least in part, that we are safe and special, but such belief is founded on shaky evidence.

In the West, therapeutic work is mostly concerned with exploration of the nature of this artificial territory. Its aim is often to ease the process which we might describe as self-formation and to help clients to integrate experiences from the past into acceptable stories about themselves. From an other-centred perspective, we might see such integration as a process of changing the qualities of powerful rupas so that they cease to condition a helpless or frightened mind-state and personality, and become the foundation for a more functional sense of self. Such concepts are compatible with the Buddhist notion of rupa as a part of the self and a mechanism of its maintenance.

As a step in the cycle of self-creation, rupa is the colouration which we give to the world in order to make it our own. The word rupa, which is a Sanskrit term, is also used in other ways. Even in Buddhist terminology, the word is not always used to name an aspect of self. The statue placed upon a shrine is called a Buddha Rupa. This use of the word is not a reference to the process of identity formation. It draws on the more general meaning of the word. It describes the colouration or phenomenal quality of the object, and particularly refers to the object's power, however this may be construed. In the case of the Buddha Rupa, it describes the numinous, spiritual energy of the figure, and its spiritual power.

Everyday rupas have the power to catch us. They inflame our passions and draw us into relationship with themselves because we are looking to them to support our sense of identity. We feel a hunger or lack,[102] which draws us to these objects because of their capacity to provide us with affirmation of our identity. It drives the cycle of craving which leads to the accumulation of self-building habits.

Sometimes, however, an everyday object is perceived as

having power which is not so much self-orientated, as representative of something other. The religious object has powerful associations which are not primarily to do with self-building, but to do with a bigger truth. The power of the Buddha Rupa is not that of the practitioner, but of the teaching and teacher which it represents. It originates from a source beyond the self. It is other-focused. Other-focused objects are not only religious. They may hold associations with other significant figures from our lives, people who have inspired us, and who live with us in our aspirations and dreams.

Of course, in making a link between a symbolic object and a source of religious or secular inspiration, one is aware that it is always possible to bring to question whether the process is genuinely other-inspired. In reality, it is impossible for us to completely escape from such processes, so the other-focus will inevitably be mixed with reflections of self. For many people, a religious rupa is used, to some extent, as a support for identity. It can be subverted into self-serving ends in all manner of ways.

This does not, however, prevent other-focused aspects rupa also being present in objects which we venerate. The human preoccupation with self is strong, and, as we have seen, everything is on fire with the flames of our passions and desires for safety and escape and self-aggrandisement. We use experience wherever we go to reinforce identity. On the other hand, objects have a reality which is not dependent upon our view, and the universe is not simply a projected plaything of our minds. Objects can represent this universe of others in powerful ways.

So, whilst the rupa generally owes its quality to our desire to create identity, it also contains a representation of that reality which we intuit beyond our projections. It symbolises for us the important and real existence of something which is not self.

In working with the object world, we can not only explore our personal agendas and mental functions, but also open to the possibility of encountering objects which are not self-objects, but real others. Imperfectly glimpsed, and overlaid with the self-building faculties, the real others in which our perceptions are grounded offer the possibility for us to encounter the world.

A World of Objects

In most of the examples of object-related work so far, we have worked with objects which, strictly speaking, are mind-objects. Although we have talked about Susan 'seeing' Miss Richards, in fact we have described a process where Susan imagined Miss Richards as a figure who appeared to her mind's eye[103].

Some therapeutic work, however, may involve working with objects which are actually in the therapy room. These objects can be perceived with other senses. They can be seen and touched primarily (though in principle they could be heard, smelt or tasted). They are real others, and as such have the potential to remind us that our delusions are not all that there is. Sometimes they will be useful because they have the potential to be containers onto which we can project our world view; they will become deliberate focuses for us to explore rupa. Sometimes they already hold important associations.

Other times they may offer a presence which is significant in its own right, which conveys an experience of their own power. Sometimes they are other-invested and have the potential to awaken us to the world of others in new ways. In practice, to some degree, they are always a bridge between these two worlds, the world of self, and the world of other. Working with objects can be helpful for a number of reasons:

Involving physical senses concretises the work

Objects can be helpful in mapping concepts or relationships. Using objects allows important psychological phenomena to be placed in particular locations. They can be talked about, looked at from different angles or returned to later in a session. They can provide an over-view. There is no need to rely upon memory.

Using object to map situations can be very helpful both to the therapist and to the client when the therapeutic exploration relies on complicated groupings or has a number of aspects or scenes. The objects can be used to create a diagrammatic representation and so hold the facts of the story, keeping track of the details and allowing them to be explored more systematically.

Use of objects involves bodily contact

The sense of touch can be particularly powerful in conditioning mind-states. Being able to physically hold an object in your hand can be grounding, or alternatively may evoke strong emotions. Even when this function is not explicit, the handling of objects may have a subliminal influence on the client's process, as it literally puts them in touch with something solid and satisfying. For this reason, the choice of natural or aesthetically rich objects for therapeutic work can bring additional benefits.

Objects can be used to hold emotional experience

When associated with a painful or emotionally potent experience, an object can come to represent that experience. As such it can become a container for the emotions. The emotion which is contained by the object may be positive or negative, making it a source of support or a repository for difficult feelings. This phenomenon is particularly useful in:

- **Creating anchors:** As we have already discussed in session six, *anchors* are objects which hold positive energy and become a source of support or calming for the person.[104] A small object such as a pebble is used for this purpose. It is usually held by the client during the creation process, since touch is valuable in building a bodily connection with it. Relaxation and visualisation techniques are used to form the association between the object and the desired positive feelings. Anchors help the client to maintain a more peaceful mind state, or to feel of the continued support of the therapy in between sessions.

- **Creating memorials:** it is common for people to use objects to feel close to those they have lost. They may visit a grave or place which they associate with the person, or they may value a personal reminder such as a piece of jewellery or a letter. Memorials give a place for the emotions to be expressed, but they also 'hold' the emotion sat other times so that the bereaved person feels that they can get on with other aspects of their life, knowing that the memory of the loved one is being honoured and that they can return to it when they feel the need. Sometimes it may be useful to encourage a client to create a memorial as part of the grieving process. This might be done in the therapy room, but would more likely be something which the client would plan in therapy, and then create in their own home or some other special place.

- **Holding the therapeutic space between sessions:** Objects which have been significant in a therapy session may be left with the therapist or in some other 'safe place' so that issues being explored may be put to rest between sessions. This phenomenon sometimes happens accidentally, but may sometimes be something a client asks for, or even that the therapist invites. We will return to this phenomenon later in this session.

Objects can represent significant others or non-material phenomena

An object can offer a means of bringing significant others into the therapy room with a vividness that an imagined object may not offer. Although the imagination is powerful, and as a rule it is better to work with few props, if someone has an object which already has strong associations, perhaps with an important person in their life, a place or circumstance, or a belief system, this may provide a focus for work.

EXERCISE ONE: SIGNIFICANT OBJECTS

Go into a room in your own home. Look around you at the objects in the room and make a list of any objects which you think have symbolic significance for you. Against each object, write three words about what that object means to you.

Now look around the room and make a list of other objects which you see. Include whatever catches your eye – ornaments, furniture, pictures, utensils and so on. Include at least twenty items.

Against each of these items, write three words which describe something which it might symbolise. Try to do this quickly and spontaneously.

Afterwards look at your list and reflect on whether any of these turned out to be significant for you. Some may feel contrived, but perhaps some of the symbolic resonances turned out to be important either in representing an aspect of yourself, or in pointing towards a significant person or thing in your life.

Sculpting and Projective Work Using Objects

The technique called sculpting involves using objects, stones, small toys, buttons or similar small items, to create a diagrammatic representation of a system. They might be used to represent a group of people, elements in a situation, or even a set of ideas[105]. For example, a common subject for a sculpt might involve representing members of a family group. When making such a sculpt, the client is invited to place stones or other items on a surface such as the floor or a table, so that they represent the relationships within the family. Those who are considered to have a close relationship are placed close together, whilst those who are hostile or more distant from one another are placed further apart.

A sculpt represents a psychological reality, and as such it is a transient artefact, being a glimpse of the client's perceptions of a system at a specific moment in time. Its form will be conditioned not only by factors connected with the group being sculpted, but also with the client's agenda in making the sculpt. It will be coloured by his mood and by the issues which he is discussing in the counselling relationship. So, for example, if he is exploring issues of conflict, those members of the family with whom he has difficulties may be more prominently represented in the sculpt. The sculpt therefore represents a reflection of the client's own mental formations, as much as it represents the family he is describing.

The technique is useful in setting out a dynamic which can be discussed and worked with in various ways. Sculpting can be used to:

- Keep track of complicated relationships within large groups (an aid to the therapist as well as the client.)
- Explore patterns within the family, and particularly the repeating or mirroring of such dynamics between sub-groups. Some families seem to fall into pairings, others into triads for example.
- Spot cross generational patterns. Exploring the dynamics of a family over several generations, perhaps using a family tree or genogram[106], can reveal repetitions of events or behaviours between people of these different genera-

tions. In this kind of work a client may well identify a common feature with a grandparent or great grandparent which he was previously unaware of. He may come to see how family stories or roles have repeated down the years.

- Discover unexpected insights arising from the choice of objects. Unconscious connections and nuances are especially likely to occur if the choice of objects has been made spontaneously and quickly without reasoned thinking.

From an object-related point of view, sculpting can be a useful technique, in that it allows the client to place a conceptual frame, such as his view of the family, into an external physical space. The use of objects creates distance and containment and, in one sense, renders the mental construct 'other'. Something which was previously held in the mind is placed at sufficient distance that it can not only be looked at, but also walked around, manipulated and dialogued with. It becomes the focus of both client and counsellor's attention, allowing discussion and co-creative exploration.

Creating this distance can allow the material to have its own voice. The client, previously enmeshed with his habitual conceptualisation of people and events, can now take a step back, and may see things differently. He is released from his thought structure and it is released from him. In seeing it displayed before him, he may find it changed.

Seeing objects from new angles is fundamental to much object-related work. We have our habitual angles of view, and follow our well worn perceptual grooves, but with this kind of work, the holding offered by the physical placement of the mind-object in the external world allows us to step out of them and see them.

EXERCISE TWO: FAMILY SCULPTS

Collect together some small objects suitable for sculpting. These might be stones, toys, ornaments, coins or buttons.

On a suitable surface, sculpt your family. You may like to sculpt your family of origin, or your present day family, or both. Do the exercise quickly, picking objects and placing them without a long deliberation. If you are working in a group, you can do this exercise in pairs, taking it in turns to facilitate one another. When you are facilitator, encourage your partner to add as many family members to the sculpt as possible until he or she thinks the sculpt is finished.

Now look at your sculpt and describe what you see, If you are working in a pair you can do this by talking with your partner. If you are on your own, write about what you notice.

In particular, look at:

What object have you chosen to represent each family member? Are any similar to one another? Do any 'go together', like for example a knife and fork might?

Which objects are biggest? smallest? brightest?

Which members are closest to which? Who is furthest apart?

Do you notice any repeating patterns?

Are there any surprises?

Did you miss anyone out?

Reflect on what you have learned from the process of doing the sculpt. How might this experience inform work which you might invite a client to do?

Providing Objects in the Therapy Room

We have already seen that a variety of possibilities exist for working with objects therapeutically. Object-related work lends itself to this kind of exploration, so having some suitable materials to hand can be useful. Things which you might want to have on display in your therapy room might include:

- Art materials: paints, crayons, paper, clay, plasticine
- Small toys: suitable for projective work, sand tray-work and other exploration involving setting up miniature scenes
- Pictures: postcards and prints of images which might spark responses
- Soft toys and dolls: which can be cuddled, used as props, or to represent people
- Stones, counters, buttons or other objects for sculpting[107]
- Cushions and blankets for comfort and creating safe spaces
- Objects with spiritual or religious association
- Extra chairs for empty chair work
- Growing plants and natural objects

As you will see from this list, some of the objects which are included are likely to be used for projective work, but others might be more suggestive of other-focused rupa energy. Notice that some objects are likely to be used by clients in an active way, whilst others, such as pictures, plants or ornaments, are present more as stimulus material which will be visible in the room and may or may not be directly referred to.

As well as the objects themselves, the way in which objects are displayed will also communicate a message to clients about your style of working. For example, in some situations, clients may feel invited to help themselves to art materials or sculpting objects as a result of the way that those items are set out. In other circumstances, they may feel inhibited from taking initiative and only use them if specifically invited to by the therapist.

It is worth reflecting on what is made easily accessible in your consulting room and how suitable the provision is for your regular client group. An art therapy room, with 'messy areas' and paints in a central place will be more likely to encourage creative work than a small basket of paints and paper discreetly tucked into the end of a book case, for example.

Some choices preclude others. A warm, welcoming carpet may give a message of comfort and support, but will probably also discourage more expressive art work. An uncluttered room, decorated in pale colours, may suggest tranquillity, whilst a more cluttered room may suggest action.

EXERCISE THREE: WHAT DO YOU OFFER?

Reflect on your own consulting room. What objects are available for clients to use during sessions?

How accessible are they? What message does your therapy room give about your approach to therapy and what a client might expect to do during sessions?

Religious and Inspirational Objects in the Therapy Room

The presence in the consulting room of objects which have religious or spiritual significance is controversial. Having generally worked in rooms where there is an unobtrusive, but evident, religious element, often a Buddha Rupa or small shrine, I find that such a presence introduces a positive element to the therapy process. Those clients who have no conscious interest in the spiritual dimension tend to ignore such artefacts, and probably regard them as ornaments if they see them at all. The mind, after all, is very good at construing the world according to its own agendas. For others I sense that the presence of religious symbols holds open the possibility for spiritual dialogue, honouring that universal dimension of life which is so often excluded from the therapeutic process in Western approaches.

Natural objects too can provide a focus for spiritual reflection. For some people they may touch a dimension of life which, even if it is not voiced, is healing or challenging. The plant or flowers may convey a sense of growth and natural processes unfolding. A basket of stones may give a sense of the enduring qualities of the planet, and its solid presence beneath our feet. A window onto a garden or parkland may offer a view of time passing with the changing seasons. Such objects may bring a more universal, and therefore more accessible, spiritual presence into the space. On the other hand, they may be so commonplace as to lose impact and fail to provide much direct stimulus.

Objects which are perceived as having spiritual meaning tend to be viewed as introducing calm and peacefulness into the therapeutic space, but some objects which you include in the room might be disturbing. You might, for example, think about the effect of having an object in your room which is a reminder of death or impermanence. This might be an actual part of a dead animal, say a skull picked up on the moors, or it might be an image, a painting or photograph.

Choices of this kind are not straightforward, and they

impinge on debates about how much of oneself, as therapist, one should reveal. Our surroundings, as other personal choices such as dress or style of working, reveal things which will affect the client's experience of us. Giving personal messages is unavoidable, however. A completely plain room carries a message just as strongly as a full one.

Sometimes too the interpretation which a client makes may be erroneous. The therapist who has a crystal hanging in the window may have New Age leanings, or simply have been given it by a previous client and hung it there as a reminder of work done together. Often more is read into items than they warrant. I have been amazed sometimes at things clients have construed about me from small clues, which in fact were complete fabrications based on minimal evidence. Such interpretations happen all the time but only come to light occasionally.

Often the objects in the room do not provoke direct comment, and may not be consciously 'registered', but they create an ambiance which will influence the course of your work. Imagine for yourself the difference between sitting in a conservatory full of a rich abundance of foliage and sitting in a white walled room with fluorescent lighting and vinyl chairs. How might these two environments influence different themes in your therapeutic process or the way you felt about the work?

EXERCISE FOUR: SPIRITUAL OBJECTS

In the past physicians and priests might well have kept a skull at hand as a *memento mori* but such a practice today would probably be thought of as morbid. What effect do you think it would have to include an object which would act as a reminder of death in this way in your consulting room? What object might you choose?

> Having thought about this question in the general case, think about particular clients you are working with, or have worked with, and what impact such an artefact might have on them, if any.

Reflecting on these matters, you may choose to include things in your working space which have the potential to inspire but also to challenge. Whether religious, spiritual or human, the various objects and images which you include in your working environment will influence the quality of healing which you provide. Variety is probably important. You might include in the room objects from different spiritual traditions, for example. Not everyone is drawn to the same things or touched by the same associations.

Freud was a collector of archaeological artefacts and had many items from his collection in his study where he saw his clients. These often became a source of illustration for their work together. Some such objects might have strong, sometimes negative, associations for some clients. Looking at negative reactions could be as valuable as looking at positive ones. They should all be open to discussion in the therapy.

If you are going to have religious symbols in your room, it is important that, although you, as therapist, will have your personal associations with these artefacts, you are able to put these associations aside sufficiently to see the religious rupa as 'just a piece of wood or stone' so that you can be in empathy with your client's response to it and facilitate their exploration. As with any object in your consulting room you will have limits on what you would allow them to do to it – few therapists would be happy for a client to destroy their chairs or throw paint on their carpets – but beyond this, your attitude needs to be robust enough to give space for exploration.

Evocative Objects

Whilst much objected related work takes place in imaginative spaces and concerns important people who are not present, physical objects too can be highly significant for people. Sometimes a real object will evoke memories or personal connections because it has associations with a person who has been important in the past or because it is a reminder of an event or even a belief.

This occasionally happens inadvertently in a therapy session. A particular chair reminds a client of his grandmother's rocking chair. The painting conjures up memories of the abusive art teacher. The photograph takes a client back to a holiday in which some dreadful event occurred.

The reaction to such objects can be strong. One needs to be wary of amplifying the scene associated with an object of this kind, without enquiring into the association and knowing what it may involve. However, if the object has triggered an under-distanced reaction or flashback, the client may well already be caught in a strong *entrancement* when they comment on it. Your first observation may be the person's bodily reaction as they start to fall under the object's power. In such cases, you may need to offer containment.

More commonly, though, when a client spontaneously comments on, or reacts to, something in your room, focusing attention on the object can provide a useful way to begin exploring the client's world.

In *Listening to the Other* there is a section about how personal objects could be used as stimulus for conversations about significant events and personal stories[108]. For example, the listener might bring attention to an object which the person is carrying with them.

Sometimes, in the case of professionals whose brief takes them into the person's home, they may have the opportunity to comment on something which is on display in the person's living space, say a photograph or ornament.

Counsellors are probably less likely to initiate conversations about objects in this way, but occasionally this sort of approach may prove useful if a client arrives with some object, for example a piece of unusual jewellery or a book or an interesting purchase they have just made. Occasionally a client will bring an object to therapy in order to show it to the therapist and talk about it. In this case we can think about the meaning of the act of bringing the object, as well as the object itself.

When an object seems significant, it can be talked about, or it can be used as the basis for inviting the client to create a scene. If the object is one which the client spontaneously reacted to, the scenes may be highly emotionally charged. The client who commented on the chair might be invited to imagine his grandmother sitting in it. This might lead to him expressing grief, and the scene might be very tender.

On the other hand, the client who identified the painting with a person who abused her may not even feel safe working in the room where the art is on the wall. To suggest dramatic enactment in this case would be inappropriate, and initially the picture might need to be taken down and even removed from the room. Later it might be used to explore finding a safe distance with the material and experimenting with levels of containment.

As with other enactment, the client might be invited to work with a question such as "Where do you see this object?" or "Who might use this?" or, in the specific instance of the rocking chair, "Who is sitting in the chair? What room is it standing in?" In this way, the client would be encouraged to expand his felt sense of the object and its associations.

EXERCISE FIVE: EVOCATIVE OBJECTS

If you are in a group, work in triads. Ask the person who is in client role to choose an object which has personal meaning for them. It might be something which they have on their person, like a piece of jewellery or a photograph, or it might be something they choose from a selection of objects on offer in the room.

Invite the person to set up a scene around the object.

Ask them to think of the first a place which they associate with the object. This place might simply be empty of people or might have people in it. Spend some time setting this scene up, either imaginatively or using the space in the room. If this process of scene-setting seems to naturally lead into some sort of dramatic action, allow this to happen. If not, use the scene to explore reactions and associations.

Afterwards discuss how useful this process has been. Would it have been more or less effective to simply talk about the significance of the object?

If you are working on your own, choose an object from around your home that interests you. Sit with the object in front of you. Imagine that the object is in a different place. Let associations develop, and from these create a scene. Notice the features of the scene, and if people are involved. If there are, what are your reactions to them? Notice if there are things you want to say or do relating to these people or the object.

> When you are ready, take some time to write freely about
> the object and your associations with it. You might create
> a short story about the object. Afterwards reflect on what
> you learned from this process and what personal meaning
> might lie behind your imaginative work.

In her book, *The Revealing Image*[109], Joy Schaverien writes about
the ways in which pictures and other art work created in the
therapy context takes on a powerful set of associations for the
client. Coming from an analytical tradition, she refers to this
power as transference, but we might talk of it as having particularly strong rupa energy. We might also extend the concepts
which she explores in the book in relation to clients' art work to
other objects which are used or encountered in the therapy room.

Schaverien emphasises the power of the object, both as a
repository for psychic energy and as a source of protection. This
power is evident and influential on people's psychological states.
To take an example, let us look at her description of her own
experience of the power of a particular object. This description is
interesting to us as it is rather similar to the kind of response
which you might have discovered in the last exercise or in
similar exercises in *Listening to the Other*.

It shows what could be seen as a commonplace example; a
family heirloom which had particular associations. Of course
such examples are highly personal too. The description is of a
particular brooch which was given to her by her grandmother. In
it we see how the brooch was especially significant for her. We
might say it had powerful rupa energy.

*The brooch is… not a valuable piece of jewellery in monetary terms, but
for me it has quite a different type of value. It was my grandmother's
good luck charm; she rarely wore it when I knew her, but she always*

carried it in her handbag or pocket. If she didn't have it with her she needed to know that it was safe at home in the drawer. This was because she feared that if it were lost ill-luck would ensue. When she grew old, my grandmother used to worry because she frequently feared that she had lost her brooch and would enlist help to search for it. Eventually she gave it to me and so relieved herself of the responsibility of caring for it; she knew that it was the one possession of hers that I wanted to inherit. The reason that I wanted it was because she had invested so much in it; this brooch was no mere decoration, it was an object of great significance to her... I value it differently, not for its good luck or protective powers, but because it is an object which meant so much to my grandmother. [110]

From this account, we see that the brooch carried strong associations for both women. In each case, though, these associations were different. For Joy, the brooch was symbolic a person whom she loved dearly, her grandmother. For her grandmother, although she had inherited the brooch from her own mother, the personal connection was not overtly significant. For her, the brooch's main function seemed to be as a protective power, which, as far as we are told, had no connection to its origins.

Of course one can speculate on whether such associations were present but unrecognised, and if a client brought a similar brooch to therapy one might indeed explore such questions. What is evident from this account is that the brooch had symbolic meaning which impacted upon each of its owners' mental states in different ways.

For Joy's grandmother, the brooch was an object which was perceived as lucky. It offered protection. But, as time went on, the brooch also became a source of anxiety and obligation. With increasing frailty, the anxiety increased. This combination of feeling the object's protectiveness and fear related to it, is interesting in the light of a Buddhist interpretation. The process of self-creation and of rupa-investment is a response to the inevitability of life's uncertainties: sickness, old age and death. It is our attempt to protect ourselves from recognising the precarious reality of our lives. As her old age and death approach, the symbolic token which had supported the woman's 'safe' identity, and which had become her defence against her fear, became of great importance. At the same time, as she had to recognise the inevitable prospect of that reality, the impermanence of the object itself seemed to begin to haunt her. She feared its loss. Probably this was symbolic of her fear of the loss of the self which it supported. She guarded it with all that same energy with which most of us cling to life, but in doing so she felt the burden of the responsibility of trying to hang onto control when change is inevitable. Eventually she was glad to pass it on and find peace.

We often feel duty bound to hold back the tide of the inevitable. The struggle to maintain out of date structures of ideas and identities becomes increasingly untenable. In the end, people are often grateful to hand on the baton to the next generation and accept their defencelessness.

Holding the Rupa Qualities of the Spaces and Objects

Any space in which emotional energy is expended is likely to become highly charged for us. It becomes associated with the emotions we have felt. The place where we met the person we fell in love with, where a tragic accident happened, where we were jilted, where we had an unhappy work experience, all take on a colouration which is persistent and which affects us when we return in later years. So too, the therapy room can take on emotional shadows.

Gradually, as you work with a client over time, the room in which you work starts to collect associations. These may be positive. The client may feel the atmosphere warm and embracing, even womb-like, linked with your presence as a supportive, caring figure. It may feel like a place of clarity and release where good insights emerged during your work together. On the other hand, it may feel clouded with negative associations, connected with painful issues which have been explored there, and with dark figures from the past, who have been re-visited there. Sometimes clients will talk about such things. Often they remain silent until some chance remark reveals their private thoughts.

"I really hate this room!" one client burst out, after several years of therapy. For her, the space had become redolent with associations with the painful subjects which she had explored there.

Objects too may become significant. Things which have been used as props or tools in therapeutic work, or perhaps items which the client has noticed and made some mental association with take on rupa energy. These things may remain significant for session after session. I can recall times when I have had to remember to leave all sorts of small items untouched in various locations in the room because they had personal meaning for particular clients: a pebble here, an old tissue box there, a note tucked under the cushions out of sight. With these items, clients left their 'others' behind when they went home at the end of a session. They felt the relief of not having to carry home whatever it was that those items symbolically held.

Such items were often associated with particular experiences or feelings. Often they held some association which was painful but hazy in the memory, a haunting sense of sadness and hurt long passed and yet remaining. In keeping care of them between the sessions I became the guardian of the memories which they represented, which could be re-visited in future meetings. For the clients in question, this provided an emotional link to our shared work, and support through the intervening week, for as long as it was needed. Their pain was safe, contained, and they could get on with life.

EXERCISE SIX: OBJECTS IN TRUST

Have you have ever experienced a client leaving an object with you for safekeeping? If so, did they make a request to leave it, or did it happen inadvertently or without negotiation? What meaning might this have had in terms of entrustment?

Would you ever invite a client to leave something with you between sessions?

What effect might this have on your relationship?

Letting Go of the Object

The relationships between images and their creators which are described in Schaverien's book are complex. They demonstrate a range of different types of psychological dynamic, personal investment, power and symbolism. Always the image takes its place in the therapeutic relationship as a shadowy third element, into which various dynamics are placed. This understanding is similar to that explored in this book. It reflects the triangular relationship seen in much object-related work, in which the scene, a third party, or the client's self-world, forms a point of focus for therapist and client.

Sometimes the images created in therapeutic artwork are direct expressions of the relationship between therapist and client. More often they overtly depict factors in the client's life. Always the image has some transformative function. Its representations and associations are worked upon in the process of the therapy. At the end of the therapy the perception of the image is changed. Among other things, the image has been a tool of the therapeutic relationship and so it has taken on a second level of potency associated with the therapeutic relationship itself. Now as the work comes to an end, this extra association must be relinquished along with the piece of work and the object must be given a final destination. Shaverien takes particular interest in what the client does with the image when a piece of work is finished. How is the picture disposed of? Is it given away, retained, worked on in subsequent sessions, handed to the therapist, given to a third party, or screwed up and thrown in the bin? Or is it taken away, retained and even treasured?

A similar process will unfold when other objects are used in therapeutic work, such as those used in sculpting or projective work. The object is a representation or a symbol of both the issue worked on and the therapist-client relationship. In addition to its intended meaning, it carries a quality derived from the psychological context in which it arose. The action of disposal throws light on the client's relationship with that image or object and the things which it symbolises. It also reveals the client's mentality and his attitude to the work you have done together and to you as the therapist too.

When you have been working with creative media, it can be useful to observe such processes. Sometimes an inadvertent action reveals an unspoken dynamic left over from the therapy work. The client's behaviour in clearing the space after any piece of active work, whether it involves putting away props or objects or tidying up after doing art work, is often less mediated by conscious process than executing the piece of work itself was. He may throw a stone which has been part of a sculpt into a basket with more force than necessary, or hold a cushion to his heart as he ponders where to put it. Such unguarded moments can bring fresh insight into the meaning of the piece of work.

For this reason, it is best to allow clients to take the initiative in putting a room straight after a session or in deciding what they would like to do with a piece of art work. In dismantling a scene, allow the client to return any items that have been used to their usual places. Notice how this is done. In what order are things put away? Is anything left out, or mis-placed? What sort of handling are things given? Whilst one can over-interpret these things, sometimes something significant happens. If you are using art methods you can also notice what the client does with their picture. Once more, this is an opportunity to observe unguarded moments, and sometimes to make reflective comment on the process which you see unfolding.

References and Background Reading for This Session

Schaverien, J 1992, *The Revealing Image: Analytical Art Therapy in Theory and Practice*, Routledge UK

Schutzenberger, A 1998, *The Ancestor Syndrome: Transgenerational Psychotherapy and the hidden links in the family tree.* London: Routledge

SESSION TEN

Rupa, Mindfulness and Reality

In this session we will explore:
- Rupa and reality
- Differing interpretations of mindfulness
- Mindfulness as remembering
- The spiritual dimension of mindfulness
- Bringing the spiritual into therapy

If rupa is the object which we perceive, overshadowed by our personal agendas and inflections, then what is the real object which lies behind the perceived one? If we inhabit a self-world which is delusory in as much as it is a highly edited and re-touched version of reality, how can we reach a less biased view point? This question has troubled philosophers and religious practitioners down the years. It troubles ordinary people too. Can we know reality? Can we know one another?

Buddhist practice and doctrine point towards a search for that knowledge. The self-world is a trap and a prison which ensnares us with false promises of security, but real security come through knowledge and experience of something beyond it. It comes from taking a step out of that embroiled state, into a space where we do not rely upon our own energies to maintain an illusion of omnipotence, but allow ourselves to be in the flow of experience.

As we saw in Rogers' description of the fully functioning person,[111] the vision of Western therapy is not tied to building a rigid self-structure, but looks toward a flexible, confident self which is at ease in different life circumstances. In seeking this goal, most Western therapies place their focus on mental processes and actions with a view to raising a person's awareness of these and thereby developing and changing them. Other-centred theory goes beyond this and focuses on taking attention away from the self altogether and into an investigation of the world which we inhabit; the world of rupa and the world beyond rupa. It is an approach which above all emphasises engagement.

So far in this book we have explored the way that the self-world is created and maintained, and ways of diminishing its intrusion into our activities or mediating its effects on our thinking. We have focused on the delusion, the rupa quality of perception, and in doing so have explored the person's relationship with their object world.

This is legitimate and useful work, since the self is not something which is likely to be eradicated, at least in ordinary human arenas. We can water good karmic seeds[112] and transform negative energies into more benign ones if we are lucky, or watch good humouredly as we catch our old patterns of deluded behaviour playing out again for the rest of the time.

Other-centred work, however, is also concerned with investigating our experience of the world, and within it trying to discern the glimpses of others which lie behind the filters of self. It approaches that ultimate question, 'what is real?' but does not cling to the pretension that we can find a definitive answer. We might think of this as a venture into the dark of the unknown, torch in hand, to track down experience, but perhaps it is more accurate to think of the otherness of the world approaching us and offering us a way out of our seclusion.

Although we endlessly try to control our experience and adapt the data provided by our senses to fit our expectations, still the world surprises us. The shock of reality can bring us up short, or soften our defences by offering a kindly presence. It offers us the gift of real contact.

EXERCISE ONE: SURPRISED BY EXPERIENCE

Think of an occasion when you experienced something unexpected which shocked you out of a train of thought or assumption. Try to recall the process in detail. What was your thinking before the incident happened? What actually happened? What did you experience in that moment? What happened subsequently?

Having reflected in this way, connect your thoughts with a more theoretical understanding. Where did the incident come from? Was it completely 'out of the blue' or did you in some way create it? When it happened, what was the momentary experience of unsettlement like? What happened next?

How much do you think the unsettlement put you in touch with something outside your usual world-view, and how did you return to familiar ground, re-creating the previous self-view? The experience of such unsettlement can be startling, exhilarating, spiritually uplifting or frightening. What sort of charge did it have for you?

Rupa and Mindfulness

In Buddhist teaching, rupa is associated with the way in which we *contact*[113] the world through our senses. This contact is generally grasping and concerned with the self-perspective. The opposite of this grasping involvement is what is called *mindfulness*.[114]

Mindfulness has become a popular approach amongst therapies influenced by Buddhism. Before looking at its applications, however, let us first look at what is actually meant by the term in the Buddhist context. Mindfulness[115] means 'to keep in mind'. This is similar to the old-fashioned usage of the verb 'to be mindful' in common English. In the past, we were reminded as we ran out to play to be mindful of the time, or as we went up the lane, to be mindful of the mud.

As it has become popularised in Western therapeutic contexts, in many interpretations the term has lost some of the flavour of this original meaning, so it is useful to go back and discover its origins, as well as looking at the writings of its main current proponents. In modern mindfulness practices, the practitioner's attention is usually concentrated on the activity which is being undertaken. The focus is on being present with that activity, rather than distracted by thoughts of the past or future.

As Jon Kabat-Zinn points out in his well known book, *Full Catastrophe Living*,[116] we spend a lot of our time on 'automatic pilot' caught in our own cloud of distracted thoughts. In his view, mindfulness means bringing our awareness into line with what we are currently doing.

... much of the time our mind is more in the past or the future than it is in the present. We can miss many of the moments we have to live because we are not fully here for them. This is true not just while we are meditating. Unawareness can dominate the mind in any moment and consequently, it can affect everything we do. We may find that much of the time we are really on "automatic pilot," functioning mechanically, without being fully aware of what we are doing or experiencing. It's as if we are not really at home a lot of the time, or, put anther way, only half awake.[117]

Some mindfulness therapies, as developed by Kabat-Zinn and the many others who have followed his lead, teach people to slow down and engage with the activities of their lives in a focused way, bringing awareness to the moment by moment detail of experience.

The Vietnamese Buddhist teacher Thich Nhat Hanh, who has become widely known for his emphasis on mindfulness as a spiritual practice, also stresses the importance mindfulness as a practice of awareness. He breaks this awareness down into the two elements of concentration[118] and wisdom[119]. In his book *The Sun My Heart*[120] Hanh talks of mindfulness as *'"being in the process of being conscious of" or "being in the process of remembering"'* and stresses that the awareness involved incorporates *'both the intensity of awareness and the fruit of awareness.'* It arises from *'the transformation of forgetfulness into remembrance'*[121].

Whilst these examples seem to emphasise the element of moment by moment awareness in mindfulness, this only partly reflects the intent of the word. The real meaning of mindfulness is, as Hanh says, remembering. In religious terms, this means remembering, or being aware of, Buddha. In more general terms we can understand it to mean remembering to be open to the reality of experience. It is about allowing our mind to open to the other. Grasping reality for our own ends, our senses are constantly seeking fodder for building identification. By contrast, mindfulness is about having a respectful relationship with reality, which appreciates its otherness and the fact that it is not under our control or a function of our desires.

Of course, these two meanings are not exclusive of one another, and as Kabat-Zinn says, the adoption of a mindfulness practice is about unhooking from the sort of mindless absorption which most of us engage in most of the time as we follow habitual thought loops and distractions. In this aspect it offers a route which may lead the practitioner to open their attention to reality. This more focused attention, like a sort of active meditation, forces the mind to observe the impulses towards *reaction*, but not to act upon them. In this way, it may help the person to reduce the habit-driven process of self-creation, though it will not eliminate it.

At the same time, more traditional interpretations of the term *mindfulness* do not require the focus to be so rooted in the present. Instead they suggest that the key activity is awareness of the spiritual dimension. They are closely linked to ideas of respect and appreciation. Developing such respect will probably draw the practitioner into a deep appreciation of what is encountered in the present moment, but may also incorporate appreciation of that other's context, with a history and a future. Remembering, after all, usually means recalling the past. There is a timeless weaving together of past, present and future in the appreciation of the depth of each experience of life.

Such remembrance puts us in touch with the sacred. In describing mindfulness, Hanh writes about an occasion when he was washing dishes.

One day, while washing a bowl, I felt that my movements were as sacred and respectful as bathing a newborn Buddha... Each thought, each action in the sunlight of awareness becomes sacred[122].

Mindfulness traditionally means mindfulness of Buddha, so we may ask ourselves what Buddha means. Of course there are many possible interpretations. Literally Buddha means 'awake' or 'enlightened'. The Buddha[123] became awake to the truth through the spiritual experience called his enlightenment. As Kabat-Zinn suggests, mindfulness can be taken to mean being fully awake to life. For some people mindfulness is the embodiment of the teachings of the Buddha, including his injunctions to vigilance and the quest for spiritual clarity. For other people, remembering Buddha means a recollection of the love and wisdom and the compassionate enduring presence of those qualities in the universe. In my own Buddhist tradition, remembering and calling on the Buddha is our central practice[124]. Transcending the endless self-building activity, the ever present quality of measureless love which the Buddha represents

241

becomes a source of release which reaches out to us[125].

So there are different possibilities in the detail of these different interpretations, but all suggest that mindfulness is a quality of involvement. We might even say encounter. Whilst rupa is the self-reflecting aspect of vision, which is conditioned by expectations and *selective attention*, mindfulness is the attempt to see beyond the self and be in relationship with the world.

EXERCISE TWO: EXPLORING MINDFULNESS

Introduce a mindfulness practice into your day. Choose a practical task which you do regularly. For this example, we will think about washing up, but you can adapt this approach to other activities.

Before you start take a few moments to become calm and quiet in your mind. Breathe out slowly and cast your eye around the room. Notice things which give you a pleasant reaction and also if anything disturbs you. Notice your body feeling and deliberately relax any parts which are particularly tense.

Now start the task. As you do so, consciously feel the physical objects which you come into contact with. If you are washing up, feel the water running through your fingers and the smooth surfaces of the china. As you lift each item, enjoy its shape, colour and texture. Notice how, with the washing, the surface becomes bright and clean.

As you hold each item, try to know it. Feel its solidity. Be curious about it. Notice how it feels in your fingers.

Reflect on who has used the item. Perhaps it was you, but maybe some else did too. Maybe different people have used that cup or plate over the months and years. How many hands have curled around it? Who has eaten or drunk from it?

Reflect on who created the item. How many people were involved in its manufacture? What did each do? If you do not know, and probably you don't, think about the implications of this. How often do we rely upon others without even appreciating what they have done?

Reflect on the gifts which you received in the meal, the crockery, the hot water, the light and all that has enabled this process of washing up.

Return to the process of handling the dishes and washing them. Allow yourself to feel reverence and gratitude for them.

As you finish the task, pause for a minute to enjoy looking at the clean dishes. Be still in the moment and enjoy the stillness.

Reflect back over the practice and write about your impressions of it.

Working with Mindfulness in Other-Centred Ways

Mindfulness-based approaches have already made substantial inroads into therapeutic practice in Britain and North America. This interest is heartening, for it demonstrates the willingness of the therapeutic and psychological professions to experiment and adopt new pathways. Since our business is in encouraging clients to do likewise, this is good modelling. We can find other common ground. Mindfulness-based methods foster attention to detail and emphasis upon awareness in daily activity. In other-centred work this attention to detail is also central, and is particularly applied in our exploration of the object world.

Let us look at the way that the sort of mindfulness exercise might be used in conjunction with an other-centred approach.

Slowing down and taking an outward focus of attention

For a client who is suffering from anxiety and is particularly tense, the first point to be emphasised may be that the exercise can be done slowly. Bringing awareness to the fine detail of the process is bound to have a slowing effect. This may help the person to relax. On the other hand, for some people who suffer from anxiety, slowing down could be counter-productive as some people are in the habit of keeping active as a way of distracting themselves from their worries or fears. With the sort of mindfulness exercise which we have just seen, however, the attention is actively directed towards the physical objects which the task involves – in this case the crockery and the water. This outward focus of attention occupies the mind with objects which are perceived through the physical senses. This may help the person develop a less frantic way of doing the activity and will also keep the attention off tangled thought processes which feed the anxiety state.

Focusing on grounding and physical contact

The physical nature of the exercise itself provides a second potential area of therapeutic focus. Bringing the person's attention to the tactile sense whilst they are handling cups and plates naturally encourages grounding. The client might be taught to start such an activity with a brief grounding exercise, focusing attention on the floor beneath his feet and on his breathing. From this, the person may move on to the task, transferring the attention from awareness of contact through the feet, to similar awareness of contact through the hands.

As we have seen, grounding can be very helpful to a person who suffers from anxiety. It may, on the one hand, be slightly more challenging to the client, since it may make him more aware of unpleasant body sensations, but, on the other hand, learning to pay attention to body sensation, and particularly the felt-sense, is a significant factor in positive outcomes in therapy[126].

Focus on the objects as 'other'

In this exercise, the client might be particularly encouraged to explore the physical nature of the object. This can have a number of effects.

- It may make him aware of just how little he looks at the commonplace things around him.
- He may find that he notices the aesthetics of the objects, or notices chips and cracks which come from previous careless handling.
- He may find that he becomes aware of feelings which he has related to the objects, such as appreciation, regret, or curiosity.
- It might be he even feels confused and uncertain, realising he does not know how to really discover what the object is.

Looking at the ordinary in new ways is a method which is common in the Japanese approach of *Morita Therapy*[127]. In Morita therapy a person is given exercises to do which will switch his awareness into new directions. For example he might be instructed to walk down the street observing everything which is blue, or to notice what sort of shoes each person has on. Such observation exercises deliberately disrupt the person's habitual ways of looking, and so introduce the possibility that they see the world in a less self-invested way.

Of course in looking at objects in a new way, some of the observations which come to the client will be about his own habits of thought. In this he will become more aware of the self element in his process. Does he look on the positive or negative side, seeing the flaws or the beauty? Does he feel regret or blame, appreciation or dissatisfaction? Such learning can be sobering and may give rise to further reflection.

Honouring the roots of the objects

Another focus which might emerge from this sort of work might be to think about the origins of the objects. Where did the cup or plate come from? Does it have a history that he knows of? Does it remind him of other cups and plates? This sort of contemplation might take the client in a number of directions. It might be that some objects indeed have a history, perhaps as things handed down in the family, or perhaps have been bought on a particular occasion, perhaps associated with someone whom he feels close to, or has even lost.

In such cases, the object is likely to hold a natural symbolism, and he may want to explore its associations in a similar way to our earlier work with significant objects[128]. Other times, though, the object's history will be more a matter of speculation. Here an enquiry into the origins is likely initially to evoke a combination of bafflement and brevity. "Well it came from the shop, didn't it!" Once past such initial responses, however, in making an estimation of all the people involved in the manufacture and sale of a cup soon reaches staggering proportions. Such reflection helps a person to develop a sense of perspective about their place in the world, their dependence upon others, and the role they play in the process.

Discovering appreciation

When undertaken with the sort of reverence which comes from recognition of the history and associations which the object carries, a mindfulness exercise can create a space in which a person discovers appreciation. This might happen as a result of any of the previous reflections. The client might feel appreciative of the physical process of washing dishes, of the people with whom they were associated, of the way that products are available for our consumption in modern society.

In a culture which places a lot of emphasis on entitlement and personal gain, it is easy for people to become unappreciative and to expect their desires to be met at first asking. People expect higher standards than previous generations, and the tea sets which were prised over the years by our grandmothers, and only brought out for best, may be shunned in favour of a series of newer replacements, each chosen to suit a new colour scheme or occasion. Utensils lasted for years in the old days, but now we pick up replacements with the groceries just because a handle got scorched or a knife was lost from a set, or because we simply feel like a change. Yet such marks carried family histories and gave character to the artefacts. Many of us recall such household items with affection. We recall grandmother's wooden spoon, its handle shortened by wear or marked by an accidental burn, and in doing so recall the love with which it was handled.

Finding spiritual meaning

In Thich Nhat Hanh's description of his experience of washing dishes, he tells of a moment of insight when the mundane task became suddenly transformed into something precious. It was a moment when he touched the sacred. Such experiences come spontaneously. We cannot anticipate or control them. If they arrive, we are blessed. At the same time, being willing to receive such experiences and creating a receptive quietness in our hearts can provide the opportunity for the surprising to occur. So, in offering such activities to our clients, we may open the way for them to discover a deeper meaning in their lives.

Mindfulness based activities are generally practised in between therapy sessions as a sort of 'homework'. This means that, as therapist, you might explain the method and perhaps demonstrate it during one session, and then invite the client to go away and experiment and then report back during the following session. Sometimes this sort of work can usefully be combined with journaling so that the client is invited to reflect on his process by writing daily on a theme. It is even possible to develop a series of different reflections to be carried out on different days.

This sort of practical approach, of course, has its impact upon the therapeutic relationship. As we have already seen, the other-centred style of working tends towards that of co-operative researchers and the structured investigation of a mindfulness task may be offered in this spirit. On the other hand, people frequently associate homework with school, and it could be all too easy for a client to become sucked into a negative view of the whole enterprise on that count, or else to fall into a child-like pattern of dependence. Inviting a process which is truly co-creative may work better if you share basic principles and then invite discussion of working possibilities. In that way the client can feel involved in the investigation, and gain skills in developing his own learning process.

EXERCISE THREE: FACILITATING OTHERS IN
MINDFULNESS EXERCISES

Reflect on the mindfulness exercise which you did and on the different aspects of the exercise which are highlighted in this section. How do these emphases compare with your experience of working with this form of practice?

Imagine that you were going to offer these exercises to a client.

How might you make the suggestion? What instructions would you give? What sort of feedback would you expect to receive the following session?

If you were going to introduce a client to mindfulness work during a therapy session, and wanted to get them to carry out an exercise during the session, how would you go about it?

Mindful of the Measureless

The concept of mindfulness is primarily one of remembering. In particular, it refers to our remembering, or holding in mind of the spiritual dimension. We can think of this as *the measureless*[129].

When we look from the self perspective, our view is limited and small. We reduce experience to palatable portions by interpreting what we see in terms of the familiar concepts and views which we already have, and we fail to notice the dimensions which do not fit with this schema. On the other hand, the real world, which exists in its own frameworks, is infinite in its possibilities and facets. We may inhabit a tiny existence, but we are surrounded by an immeasurable otherness.

The spiritual life concerns our relationship with this otherness. As an other which we mostly intuit and experience through limited glimpses and side-long glances, reality is infinitely mysterious, and the wider we think, the more so it becomes. Each of us has our own way of framing what we experience of this measureless quality, albeit in ways heavily coloured by our personal frame of thought. We each have our explanations and beliefs about the ultimate nature of things, but whatever these are, we can be pretty sure they fall short of reality.

Even in the therapeutic relationship each person is mysterious to the other. The therapist works to empathise with the client and see the world as through his eyes, and perhaps to fit it against a theoretical model, a diagnosis or a treatment plan, but this empathic connection is never completely successful. The client also probably tries to understand what the therapist is thinking, maybe as a way of working out whether she is trustworthy, maybe to gain her approval, maybe even to catch her out and prove her wrong. Such attempts are commonplace human strategies and they happen in therapy relationships just as much as in any other. They are about trying to understand, but, as must be evident, they are also inter-woven with self-interested motives. In addition, these strategies have more to do with observing than connecting. Each person watches the other in a way that is ultimately defensive of him or herself.

To connect is riskier, and, in some aspects, impossible in the therapy relationship, where to know one another in a multi-dimensional way would be inappropriate. The relationship is functional and has boundaries which prevent certain types of inter-personal exchange. But still there may be moments of meeting within the therapy process when we do feel an under-standing or common emotion flow between us. Such times are precious moments, remembered as the highpoints of the shared journey.

But then, even knowing another in a more rounded way, how much do we really see? After ten or twenty or thirty years of marriage do husband and wife know one another? After years of friendship, can we not sometimes be surprised to discover aspects of a relationship which do not fit our conception of it? Do we not experience shocks and delights in the unexpected responses of our children or parents?

People often experience the encounters of therapy as more intimate and open than their relationships with friends or family.

The intensity of the relating and the focus on personal subject matter can create a special kind of meeting which we just may not manage in many of our other relationships. But does this mean we really see each other better? Or does it simply mean that we *feel* seen? Does it mean that we encounter the real person with whom we share the therapy hour? Or is this another illusion, brought about by an exchange of affirmations – I will play the appreciative client for you if you will play my perfect mother or confidante or wise-woman?

Beyond ordinary encounters, we are each very much unknown to one another. The facts of our lives are certainly only disclosed in limited portion, but even our current thoughts and responses within the therapy relationship are still mostly unseen or uncomprehended. Much is misinterpreted, or at least read with a personal agenda.

Whilst I am writing this book, I am staying at our centre in France with Susthama. We have known each other for more than five years, living in the same community and experiencing its changes and perambulations. We have an easy going relationship and can relax over breakfast, or share religious practice, joke together, or get on with our various tasks in silence. But do we really know each other? Sometimes she will do something and I smile and think 'Oh yes, that's very Susthama!' but I have no doubt that she has the capacity to surprise me completely. I am sure she has the capacity to surprise herself. The point is, does this matter? And, if it did, could it be otherwise?

We live with mystery. Each comprehension brings more questions. If the universe began with The Big Bang, what came before that? Where did the primeval atom come from? Or if all was simply raw energy, what was its source? If, on the other hand, we live in a constant ebb and flow of matter that has been, is, and always will be, does that ease our uncertainty?

We cannot ultimately answer how or why, but only that

something is. Whilst our minds struggle to frame the enormity of existence with science, that discipline too begins to sound metaphysical in its speculation. Pushed to the edge, human curiosity seems always bound to end up standing before the abyss of unknown forces, only able to make sense of it by vague allusion and mythic imagery.

In the face of unknowing, a new sort of knowledge emerges. In the wind of confusion, our minds and hearts engage with something else. When the panicked attempt to control and define subsides, we start to trust our glimpses of the other. We start to allow the mystery to reach us and speak to us.

This is the encounter which takes us towards the spiritual dimension. The undefined inexorably leads us into questions which, though they may begin in the material and the mundane, quickly bring us into the fundamental questions and intuitions of humankind. The wordless territory beyond our definitions is welcoming.

I often say that everyone has a spiritual sense. When I talk with people about their experience of life, invariably we reach a point at which the other person shares some feeling or experience which points beyond the mundane. Sometimes this sense is clearly framed in traditional and religious concepts, other times it is vested in a vision of human possibility. Sometimes it is a belief in a personal God or spirit-guide, other times it is expressed in the person's relationship with the natural world. Often it involves a sense of connection with some greater being or phenomena; a sense perhaps of having touched the mystery, not just in ideas, but in a heart way. Sometimes it is a sense of having been touched, a certainty that beyond the ordinary boundaries, a presence has reached out and welcomed them.

We each experience these things in our own way, but common to us all is our ignorance[130]. Whether we use religious or secular language, the mystery of the measureless dimensions of experience, which are beyond our view, remains. More than this, though, these unknown others are the foundations for our being. At every level, in every way, our existence is conditioned by others. The mystery is benign. The measureless quality is generous. The fundamental principle is love[131]. It is this which we are reaching towards in being mindful.

EXERCISE FOUR: THE SPIRITUAL DIMENSION

Everyone has a spiritual sense.

This statement raises questions. What do we mean by a spiritual sense? What is spiritual? How is spirituality experienced? How can something beyond words be described in words?

How much does the spiritual have to do with particular experiences? How much has it to do with ideas and concepts? What is your own experience of it?

Make notes on these questions, and then reflect on what relevance, if any, you see in this for therapeutic work.

How would you respond to a client who had very different views on these matters from your own? If you were a client, how would you respond if you discovered that your therapist thought differently from you on these matters?

A Benign Universe

The exploration of our conditioned nature is something which is common in Buddhist practice. How are our minds and actions formed out of the seeds of past activity, and, ultimately, out of the legacies of other people and traditions with whom we are associated?

In *The Other Buddhism*[132] I wrote about the way that we tend to assume a false view of our independence and how, in Western society, the ideal of self-sufficiency has led to a pernicious struggle towards an illusion that we can achieve perfection.

As humans, we can have a rather over-inflated view of our own uniqueness. We are fascinated with ourselves and devote much time and energy to refining our credentials. Who doesn't in his heart of hearts see himself as a special case and an exceptional human being? But we do not function alone. We do not create from originality. We are the containers of a heritage that continues from before our birth and into an undetermined future. We are collectors and re-assemblers, reprocessing ideas and passing them on. We contribute to the spiral of ideas that unfold over generations to mark the development of cultures and civilisations, but each of us individually is simply a cog in a bigger process. We are less important than we think[133].

The illusion of perfection is a problem in Western society because it not only creates a situation in which people feel they have to be constantly striving to be better than they are and thus become stressed and anxious, but also because it tends to breed a sort of dishonesty at the heart of our interactions with one another. Although we may pay lip- service to the idea that we are all 'only human' there is still an undercurrent to much of our thinking which suggests that being less than perfect is in some ways a failure, and something to be avoided at all costs.

With this idea of perfection, we receive a closely allied ideal of self-sufficiency. The Western achievement-orientated dream is one of personal prowess and independence. 'I Did it My Way'[134] becomes our anthem, as we strive to actualise our individuality, oblivious of the fact that it is dependent upon so many factors human and natural, to keep us alive and functioning.

If we reflect on the ways that we are supported in our day-today existence we become much more aware of the complex web of things which allows us to live. Whether we look at the human dimension or the material world or the spiritual realm, we discover that in each thing we do, we receive the fruits of many people's efforts, and we use the precious resources of the planet.

EXERCISE FIVE: SUPPORTING CONDITIONS

Takes a large sheet of paper.

On the top of the paper, draw a circle and in it write down something practical that you have done in the past day. For example you might think of a meal which you have eaten, a visit you have made, or a piece of work you have done.

Identify a number of factors which made this activity possible and represent them with a row of circles, smaller than the first one, connected to your first circle with lines. In each write down what that factor is. You can make this row as long as you like. Probably the more that you think about it, the more will occur to you.

Now look at each of the factors you have listed and identify factors for each which made that condition possible. Draw these as smaller circles linked to the circle which they support with lines. These will create a further row or group of factors.

Clearly you can go on drawing more factors on which each factor depends indefinitely, but when you have used all the space and exhausted your ideas, draw a representation at the bottom of the page of all the other infinite number of

---

factors which condition even something quite simple like you dinner. You may want to give this a name or just to leave it open.

When you have finished, reflect upon your diagram.

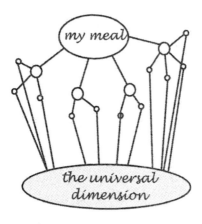

Bringing Awareness of the Spiritual into Therapy

Our spiritual sense is fundamental to our experience of life. How we construe the underlying principles of life affects our mental attitudes and our emotional well-being. It colours our interpretations of both the ordinary every day events of our lives and the bigger issues to which we are exposed.

When people do not trust life they tend to cling more tightly to things and be less flexible. In terms of the model which we have been exploring, they are more enmeshed in the processes of self-building. A person who is spiritually at ease is probably less tense and less keen to control their mental environment. This means that they will be less critical of others, less demanding, and more appreciative. Ultimately they will be happier.

Moving out of this cycle is not something which is easy to do of one's own volition. Often the attempt to free oneself is counter-productive, and simply creates the anxiety which sends a person rushing back into the behaviours which, as we have seen, reinforce identity. We can see this happening particularly clearly in the patterns which many people get into with trying to give up an addictive or compulsive behaviour. Let's imagine an example:

Sarah wants to lose weight. She has had a long term problem with being overweight, and has tried to diet many times. On Monday Sarah starts a new diet. The first couple of days go well, and Sarah manages to control her impulses to snack between meals. She notices that she craves sweet things whenever she feels a bit low or has to face a new task. She also notices that she tends to eat when she gets bored.

Sarah is delighted to step onto the scales a week later and find that she has lost a couple of pounds. She feels happy and confident and decides to go out and buy herself a new dress to celebrate. This perhaps a little premature, for when she goes to the dress shop after work, Sarah discovers that she is still the same size as she was before she started. Moreover, the sight of her body under the florescent lighting of the changing room reminds her that she still has a long way to go. She feels defeated and depressed, and on the way home she buys herself a bar of chocolate. "Well, if I'm going to be fat, I might as well enjoy it," she says to herself.

Sarah's experience is one that many of us go through. She tries to improve her life, and initially feels happiness and liberation. She becomes more aware of the ways in which her habit patterns tend to circle around food, and the way that she copes with small discomforts by eating. She notices that when space opens up in her busy life, she fills it by snacking. Perhaps in those times uncomfortable thoughts and fears come nearer to the surface, but she has become skilled at diverting them before she has to acknowledge their presence.

Food has become both a sensory distraction and a source of identity. She is a fat person. With the diet, Susan's protection from the world is diminished. She no longer 'medicates' herself with eating, a process which not only feeds her psychological structures but also keeps her blood sugar levels high. To a degree, Sarah begins to experience life a little more directly, but this is potentially threatening so, in order to manage the gap which opens up, she puts her energy into creating a new identity, with new supports. Her habit of acquisitiveness was previously satisfied by food, but now, instead, she supports her new fantasy self by going to buy a dress.

The experience, however, backfires and Susan is suddenly confronted with her old identity, seeing her body in the mirror as fat. She immediately feels despairing of becoming the person she had envisaged, who was thin and did not live her life surrounded by food. She falls back into the old patterns of comfort eating, buying herself the chocolate on her way home.

Such stories are common and illustrate how we often try to improve our lives by achieving a neat transfer from one (problematic) identity to another (new improved) one. As many slimming books suggest, one answer is to 'think thin'. Don't accept what you are, but 'fake it till you make it'.

Sarah's problem, though, is that her anxieties and fears a bout life are driving her to build ego-fortresses around herself. She keeps the scary thoughts at bay through her compulsive behaviours. At some level in her psyche she does not trust that, without these behaviours, her life would be viable. She feels she has to ward off experience. She lacks faith to face what might come along.

Mindfulness-based techniques offer a way to slow down and be with the moment-by- moment experience of life. Perhaps Sarah might use such a method to become more systematically aware of what happened when she felt the impulse to snack. This awareness could even be extended by using our understanding of skandha process elaborated in session seven. She might become more aware of the body responses she had; of the *reaction* which came up in her when she experienced stress, which led her into the old habits[135] that centred on eating. She could observe what rupa energy triggered these patterns, and how the patterns led her into situations where more triggers, or rupa objects, presented themselves. This awareness might help her to become more able to live with a level of emotional unease, and perhaps more able to face any larger life issues which were being masked by the eating behaviour.

To really change things, however, Sarah needs to develop more confidence that life is not a hostile experience and that, if she lets go of her shell-like self-structures, everything will not fall apart or destroy her. Her problem is basically spiritual. The real need is for her to increase her *faith*.

The problem with this analysis is that it is not generally the counsellor's role to introduce discussion of the spiritual aspect of life. At the same time, many, if not all, problems can be seen as spiritual crises of one kind or another. Sarah is not asking for spiritual guidance. She would probably prefer a behavioural solution which could change her problem with as little personal pain as possible, as if she were under general anaesthetic. She is not even concerned to look at the psychological factors which may be contributing to her eating and has no concept of the existential or spiritual difficulties which might be impacting on it.

One challenge in working with Susan is to find language in which to communicate about the roots of her problem and the way that it relates to a basic distrust of life. This means learning to listen to the ways in which the client expresses their spiritual sense. The therapist does not have the brief to turn the discussion onto spiritual matters without invitation, nor, in all probability, would it be helpful to do that. On the other hand, if the therapist listens with an awareness of this aspect of experience, she may hear within Sarah's story, the faint glimmerings of awareness and curiosity which can be supported. To do this means having faith in Sarah's spiritual sense.

In this, the therapist's own attitude and faith is one significant conditioning factor. Even if this is never expressed directly, as we discussed earlier, our values and beliefs transmit themselves into the counselling process. If we have confidence in the life and see the universe as a beneficent place, if we have a sense of the spiritual underpinnings of human existence and find them trustworthy, this faith will be communicated. We may say nothing of our own faith and beliefs, but somehow our clients will be influenced by our own ability to be mindful of these elements which support our existence.

EXERCISE SIX: FAITH OF THE COUNSELLOR

Discussion points:
What role do you think spirituality has in therapy? How can the spiritual dimension become part of the therapeutic process? What dangers do you see in this?

Reflecting on Sarah's story, do you agree with the analysis that the underlying problem is spiritually based? Do you agree that all psychological problems have a spiritual dimension? If so, how is this addressed?

Think of these questions in relation to specific people you are working with. What impact do they have in practice?

References and Background Reading for This Session

Brazier C 2007 *The Other Buddhism* O-Books UK
Brazier, D 2009 *Love and Its Disappointment* O-Books UK
Hanh N 1988 *The Sun My Heart*, Parallax US
Kabat-Zinn, J, 1991 *Full Catastrophe Living: Using the Wisdom of*

Your Body and Mind to Face Stress, Pain, and Illness Delta USA
Reynolds, D 1980 *The Quiet Therapies* University of Hawaii Press,
  Honolulu

SESSION ELEVEN

Real Others

In this session we will explore:
- Facilitating exploration of the experience of *others*
- Empathy for others in a client's world
- Beyond the frame of reference
- The person in the street attitude
- Role reversal and other focus

The world we perceive may be heavily coloured by our habits of view and our personal agendas, but the fact that we add this colouration to the things and people around us does not diminish their reality as people and things. Our perception may be distorted or falsified but the world exists in its own reality behind this mirage.

So far much of the focus of this book has been upon exploring the rupa aspect of the object world. We have explored how clients may be encouraged to *amplify* their view of these perceptual objects and so to understand both the power of those objects which preoccupy them, and the ways in which they uphold the mental structures and behavioural scripts which cause trouble in their lives. This exploration is concerned with understanding the process of the self-structure and its maintenance.

Other-centred approach, however, goes beyond this interest in the perceived other. The real focus of this work is in exploring our relationship with what is not self. Primarily, we are interested in finding ways to relate to real others.

If the rupa is the perceived object, then the real *other* lies beyond that perception. As we have already seen, philosophically, to talk of reaching such an experience of naked vision may be hypothetically interesting, but impractical in actuality. Therapy is not an exact science, if indeed it is a science at all, however, and we need not be too pedantic in our interpretation of terms. We can hypothesise that the real other exists, even though we know we will always see it through some degree of interpretation, and we can try to move with our clients, in the direction of a clearer relationship with reality and of reducing the imposition of personal agendas upon it. This is the work which we will start to explore in this session.

Beyond the Rupa

Mary is talking about her relationship with Tony. Tony came in last night from work and was irritable and sullen. He spent the evening sitting on the sofa watching television and wouldn't talk to her.

At this point, many Western trained therapists would ask Mary how she felt during the evening. What was it like for her when Tony was so withdrawn? By contrast, as we have already seen, a therapist who was working from an object-related way would probably be more interested in knowing more about the 'objects' in the situation. Typically, then, this other-centred therapist asks Mary "So tell me more about Tony".

In response, Mary describes Tony coming in from work and flopping down on the sofa, his hand reaching for the remote control of the television. She has been cooking all afternoon preparing dinner and she was looking forward to a pleasant evening with him, but now, looking at Tony sprawled out in front of the television, she feels angry and irritated.

"So he is just sitting there, flopped in front of the television..." the therapist reflects.

"Yes, and I'm stood there with dinner in the oven, feeling like I just don't want to serve it if that's all he can do.."

"Dinner's in the oven, and you are looking at him stretched out there, not speaking to you..."

"Yes... the so and so... can't he see I've been working all day too?"

> ### EXERCISE ONE: WORKING WITH MARY
>
> If you were Mary's therapist, what could you say at this point?
>
> What would your thinking be?

So far, the therapist has encouraged Mary to explore her view of Tony. She has echoed and amplified Mary's description of the scene, picking up the aspects which seem to have most roused Mary's reaction: Tony's silence, his attention on the television, his 'couldn't care less' posture.

This amplification of the rupa element has held Mary in the cycle of perception, and reaction which she was already in, keeping her on her familiar script. Her response is one which expresses the emotions associated with that script. It evokes emotions which she has probably felt many times in relation to Tony. The value in amplifying the rupa aspect of the scene is in tracing the pattern of reaction. This might have different applications:

Firstly, Mary might want to identify and circumvent her reaction. By becoming aware of the first bodily impulse, in this case to anger, she might wish to stop herself from speaking out and so avert a cycle of arguments. Conversely, she might notice her impulse to suppress the feeling of irritation and instead find a way to voice it. The suppression of irritation in small day-to-day situations may be building a backlog of anger which is poisoning her relationship. It may be healthier to tell Tony how she feels. This is not the only possible response, and, as we will see, questioning her perception of Tony may disperse the irritation, but there are still times when it is better to voice, and explore, negative emotions rather than letting them build up.

Secondly, Mary might want to explore the origins of the pattern of reaction. Did Tony remind her of someone else in her life who was sullen and uncommunicative? Was there another earlier figure, whose rupa energy is lurking behind her perception of Tony, and is leading her to interpret his tiredness at the end of the day as deriving from hostility towards her?

Either of these possibilities might lead Mary to look more closely at her pattern of reactions and how they were activated in this particular instance. They might give her tools to identify the specific triggers or to understand erroneous connections which she was making between Tony and other significant people from her past. This could help her to let go of these connections, improving their relationship.

Both these explorations involve the rupa aspect of Mary's response to Tony. On the other hand, an other-centred therapist might well decide not to work with the rupa aspect of what Mary was saying. Instead she might help Mary to investigate the truth of the situation. She might invite Mary to try to see beyond her habitual view.

When Mary talked about Tony lying on the sofa, her therapist might have responded:

"So what do you think is going on for Tony?"

This question invites Mary to stop. Her story so far has been concerned with her own view and feeling responses. She has not mentioned Tony's experience other than in a critical way.

Mary hesitates. "I guess he's had a bad day at work. I don't know. I didn't ask him. We had such a row, we weren't speaking."

"He'd had a bad day?"

"Yes, they are pretty stressed at his office at the moment. They lost two people in the recent redundancies, and they don't know who is going to be next."

"I guess that must feel pretty bad for him."

"Yes, I guess he is really upset about it. He's put a lot into that job."

"Like he's invested a lot."

"Yes."

"And now it's not working out. In fact he could just be out in the cold..."

EXERCISE TWO: A DIFFERENT RESPONSE

Reading this second possible response, what do you think the intention of the therapist is?

What effect do you think the responses have on Mary? Can you imagine counselling in this way yourself?

These interventions from the therapist have taken Mary onto a completely different track. Instead of focusing on her own feelings and effectively making Tony the cause for her distress, Mary is now thinking about Tony's situation and feelings. Her own responses to Tony are now in the background, temporarily out of view, though as her view of Tony develops and changes, they too will inevitably change.

As we have seen, changing the view of the object changes the conditions which shape the identity into a particular form. This line of enquiry, which focuses on discovering as much as possible about the real experience of the other, is distinctive of other-centred work. Most therapists would see Tony's situation as of marginal concern to the therapy process and, if they did enquire into it, would only do so briefly, wanting to understand Mary's situation and her feelings about it. They would only be interested to hear what aspect of his situation was directly impinging on her.

In an other-centred process, Mary is still of great concern to the therapist, but the therapist also appreciates the way that Mary's mental state is conditioned by her view of Tony, and particularly her ability to see him more clearly. Helping Mary to learn to empathise is seen as a therapeutic process in its own right.

Mary's therapist is interested to help Mary discover the truth of Tony's feelings. She wants to help her to understand how it really is for Tony. As we look more closely at the experience of those who are significant to us, we start to understand how they see life, and to stop seeing all their actions and thoughts in ways that are self-referential. We start to see them as real people who are not just part of our personal world, but who act as they do for their own reasons. We start to gain empathy for them.

The development of empathy brings us closer to a real view of the other person. Walking in their shoes for a while, we understand what might be going on in their minds. We start to see the world through their eyes.

In his paper *The Necessary Condition is Love*[136] my husband David Brazier argued that if the development of empathy was a positive, healthy activity for the counsellor to be engaged in, then it followed that the client too would benefit from developing empathy. In developing the other-centred approach he and I have taken this argument a stage further. We have found that it is health promoting for the client to be encouraged to develop empathy for the other. Indeed, we no longer see the client's part of the endeavour as being *'by contrast, to focus upon self'*[137] or that therapeutic effectiveness can be measured in terms of *'whether or not the client's perception of and attitude toward self changes.'*[138]

Now our measure of therapeutic success would far more commonly be whether or not the client's perception of and attitude to *others* changes.

Empathy for the Other

There are a number of things which we can say theoretically

about the focus which other-centred approaches place upon developing empathy for the other people and elements in the client's story. Some of these will already be obvious. Other points perhaps need some elaboration. We might think of the following factors:

Mary is not isolated from Tony:

Reaching an understanding for Tony's position brings with it an understanding of the conditions which are operating in the relationship between him and Mary, and in Mary herself. Because an other-centred approach does not place as strong an emphasis on the individuality of the self, and places more weight on the way that confluences of conditions create particular mind-states or behaviours, the exploration of Mary's mentality includes the exploration of Mary's world, and this in turn includes exploration of those real other factors which influence her experience.

Whilst Mary experiences inhabiting a world of objects, which she perceives through the mediating influence of her mental formations and karmic tendencies, she is also subject to the push and pull of real events, and to the effects of the behaviour of others. These other forces are outside her control, except in as much as she makes choices about how to place herself in relation to them, or tries to impose her will upon them.

More than this, whilst many psychological models are presented as centring on the individual, in this approach, one might equally view the processes which we have been describing as operating within a system, of which Mary is just a part. A couple relationship is not just two individuals living separate paths under the same roof. It is a system, and in this context, the two people involved in it create a shared identity, which is formed and maintained by just the same processes of distorted perception, *reaction*, *entrancement* and *mental formation* as the individual self is. This couple identity serves a similar process to the individual one, providing a protective sense of permanence around the pair.

Sometimes the couple identity and an individual identity will be at odds with one another, and one member of the pair will struggle to reconcile the two, creating tensions for the partner.[139] Other times, the couple identity becomes a powerful conditioning factor on each person's individual sense of self, but this may be at the cost of other relationships. In order to maintain their shared identity, a couple may have to agree that their shared view is right and the views of others are wrong.

EXERCISE THREE: COUPLE IDENTITIES

What is your experience of couple identities forming, both in your own case and in that of other people you have known?

How far can the therapy relationship itself be seen as a couple relationship?

Do you have a sense of what sort of shared identity you might be forming with particular clients?

If Mary develops empathy for Tony, their relationship will improve:

Since Mary's mental process is closely connected with the conditions which her relationship provides, her perception of Tony's behaviour as in some way hostile to her creates a problem for her, whether or not her perception is true.

If Tony is hostile, she needs to do something to find out why, and so try to address the causes of his hostility and improve the relationship. If he is not hostile, realising this will improve the way that Mary relates to him. In either case, at quite a simple level, the health of Mary and Tony's relationship is an important condition for Mary's mental health. Conversely, if Mary is happier, this will probably have a positive effect on the relationship.

More generally, developing the ability to empathise creates a condition for better relationships. If Mary has better empathy skills, she will be more understanding and responsive to Tony, and their communication will improve. In all probability, in this ambiance, his empathy for her will also improve. They will listen to one another better.

The relationship between Mary and Tony may be conditioned by a mental formation which she already had before the relationship began:
Each of us carries a set of blueprints or scripts which come from our experience of previous relationships. These lead us, firstly, to seek out others who have complementary scripts, and will play supporting role in our habitual dramas, and secondly, to coerce those with whom we live or have close relationships into playing the roles which form counter-parts to our own.

For example, if we have been in the habit of being subservient, we may look for people who are authoritarian in their manner, and we may behave in ways that encourage those around us, to be more domineering in their behaviour towards us, even if they are not usually like this.

In this way, people not only find people who are 'just like Daddy' or 'another Mummy' to marry, but also gradually convert relationships which began on quite different terms into replicas of past ones. Looking at the current situation and the reality of the other person's thinking, feelings and action can help to clarify the real similarities, and the differences, between them and other people from the past.

Mary may be falsely seeing her relationship with Tony as following old tracks:

Whilst sometimes the dynamics of a relationship closely mirror those of past relationships, other times it is not so much the reality of the dynamic, as our perception of it, which is conditioned by the past.

Our history leads us to interpret present experience as repetition of patterns which are familiar from the past. This can be reassuring, since we know how to act in such situations. On the other hand, it can be anxiety provoking, and we may react to behaviour which seems as if it might be beginning to follow a familiar pattern with irritation, withdrawal, or even anger. A person who has experienced violence in the past may react very strongly if her partner raises his voice in an argument. A person whose parent is alcoholic may watch his partner's drinking and become very anxious if he believes it is increasing, even if, to other people, it seems quite moderate.

In such instances, gaining objectivity about the partner's behaviour can be very helpful. This may involve looking for evidence to support or contradict the perception which the client is holding. Identifying the reality of a situation, or at least getting a different perspective on it, can be reassuring and demonstrate that the fear of falling into an old script is actually ill-founded.

EXERCISE FOUR: OLD TRACKS

If you are working in a group, use in counselling triads for this exercise. If you are on your own make notes in your journal.

Explore the ways in which your current relationships reflect relationships in the past. (You can look at relation-

---

ships with friends as well as with your partner)

How much do you think that you have been drawn to people who have similar temperaments or characteristics to people you have known previously?

How much do you think you may have behaved in ways that invited those people to become like parents, previous partners or other significant figures from the past?

How much do you think you have seen the people in your current life in distorted ways as a result of past experience?

Reflect on these questions. If you have undertaken this exercise in a counselling relationship, have you imported any of the dynamic you are exploring into the way you see, or behave, towards the person you are working with?

Mary is not being encouraged to be self-preoccupied:

Therapy can have the effect of taking us deeper and deeper into our own experience to the extent that we become completely self-obsessed. For some people, a process of inward reflection may be a necessary stage, in which they discover more about their thoughts and reactions and the conceptual and felt structures in the psyche which inform these. They may journey into their past and present experience, searching for meaning and volitions, and reaching new insight into these personal constellations.

On the other hand, such a process has its cost, and if the result is that the person becomes more self-centred and comes to believe in a sort of special personal entitlement or status, this is not mentally healthy, and is not likely to help their relationships. A healthy mental state is one in which we are interested in the world and in others.

As we have seen, what we do, whether in therapy or in other fields of experience, conditions our future actions, so at a straightforward, behavioural level, encouraging Mary to be interested in the process Tony may be going through, rather than only seeing her own part in it, may condition her to adopt a more outward orientation in the future, which is likely to improve her relationships with others as well as enriching her life.

As Mary's ability to empathise improves, she will be happier in general:

Since our basic nature is to be sociable, our ability to relate to others is important to our emotional well-being. Whilst most of us enjoy occasional periods of solitary time, there is much evidence that the quality of our connection with others is a powerful conditioning factor for happiness and psychological well-being.

A recent report by the UK government thinktank Foresight, suggested that ordinary people could follow a five-a-day programme of social and personal activities in order to increase their mental health[140]. The activities it identified were:

- Connecting with friends and family
- Learning something new
- Being active
- Taking notice
- Helping friends and strangers

This list is interesting from an other-centred perspective, in that all the activities which it suggests are concerned with outwardly orientated engagement, either with people or with other aspects of the object world. Two out of the five specifically refer to our relationships with other people.

This awareness of the importance of relationship is not new. It has long been established that people who have good relationships live longer, are mentally healthier, and are less likely to be suicidal.

EXERCISE FIVE: ROUTES TO WELLBEING

Reflect on the five activities listed as leading to mental wellbeing:
• Connecting with friends and family
• Learning something new
• Being active
• Taking notice
• Helping friends and strangers

Do you think this report has relevance for counsellors and therapists? If so, how do you think a therapist can support a client in developing these areas of activity?

Having empathy for everyone involved is more skilful for the therapist:

For Mary's therapist, the invitation to side with Mary and blame Tony for his behaviour and for her unhappiness is a tempting possibility. Mary's position, as presented, invites sympathy, and, in offering this, it also invites collusion.

It would be easy for Mary and her therapist to fall into the same sort of dialogue as is common amongst friends, whereby they cemented their relationship by agreeing that Tony was the problem and that his behaviour was out of order. Such an agreement would have reciprocal pay-offs in that Mary could gain support for her role and self-view, and her therapist, in return, could bask in Mary's appreciation.

The pact would, however, represent a less therapeutic

response than one which revealed the underlying dynamics of Mary's view of Tony, even though this latter course might be less comfortable for both Mary and her therapist. It would have the effect of maintaining and reinforcing the current self-structure (which might, of course, be sufficient to help Mary feel better about life, and so gain the confidence to improve her relationship anyway) rather than challenging it.

Most of us become protective if our loved ones are criticised:

If the therapist 'sides' with Mary, the act of giving this support may backfire. It is not uncommon for a person to tell a friend all the faults of her spouse, but then, if the friend agrees, or even adds, "Yes, I've always thought your husband was a selfish lay-about," or something of the kind, to become defensive and angry. People often have an attitude which says 'I'm allowed to criticise him, but you're not'. Such a person may say all sorts of negative things about his partner, but jump to her defence if he sees her under attack.

This is not as perverse as it sounds. Usually it comes out of ambivalence. The person has positive and negative feelings. To be able to explore their negative feelings, the person needs the listener to hold a balancing neutral or positive perspective. Mary may unconsciously want her therapist to hold a neutral view of Tony so that she can express her rage at him without completely losing sight of the positive aspects of their relationship.

Taking Tony's perspective into account is a more ethically positive position:

Whilst some therapeutic gain may come from helping Mary to feel supported in a situation where she feels unhappy and unloved, if this gain comes at the cost of making Tony into the villain, there may be losses simply because this response involves taking a less ethically sound position.

Behaving ethically provides a sound basis for mental health and when we feel that we have been drawn into behaving in unsound ways, we may feel disturbed. The benefits which have come from such actions are tainted by the knowledge that we have not been quite fair. When we have spoken badly of another, especially if we feel we have been unjustly critical or fabricated a case against them, this can leave a bad feeling, which clouds any temporary relief we have felt.

For the client this may result in a feeling of having been disloyal. Whilst the therapist may be reassuring, the feeling of having been unjust or disloyal may have a basis in reality, and may undermine the work which has been done. Having regard for the real existence of the other people involved in a situation, and holding at least a general sense that they too have a perspective, creates a container for the therapeutic process which is more ethically sound.

Getting Beyond the Frame of Reference

In order to understand and explore the real objects in the client's world, the therapist needs to become adept at moving between perspectives, and in doing so, needs to encourage the client to do likewise. This requires a somewhat different understanding of empathy. We need to expand our sense of what is possible.

In some ways the wider form of empathy which we are describing arises from our deeper faith in the client. We trust that they will not be overwhelmed by the truth of their situation. They will be able to look at their relationships and situation from new angles, and even be able to face ways in which they might have been mistaken or prejudiced. As we become more empathically aligned with a person, we start to perceive their strength as well as their weakness, or, in some cases, conversely, their weakness as well as their strength. We see them as complex people with complex motivations.

This more complex view of the person's potential leads us to appreciate their capacity to think in new ways. It also enables us to see the person in the context of their object world and to see beyond them to appreciate what that world might be like viewed from other perspectives. We notice their reactions and appreciate their struggles, but then we also take a wider vantage point which incorporates empathy for others who might be involved in the situation. This other-focused empathy invites the client to also explore the other viewpoints.

Having an ability to hold more than one position is important. For example, it can prevent the therapist from getting drawn into the same negative spirals as a despairing client. If the focus of empathy is too narrow it is easy to fall into a client's overwhelming negative feelings or a sense of hopelessness. As therapist, if one loses the ability to create distance, one may feel sucked into the dark pit of a situation, from which there seems no escape. If one can move between a closely empathic position and a more objective one, one can retain a supportive space without 'catching' the client's hopelessness.

Entering the pit with the client, and experiencing the feelings of despair with which they are struggling, can be immensely supportive. As Rogers described in examples quoted in session two and three, the feeling of having been understood by another person is deeply affecting, and can be the catalyst for immense changes in a person's life. In Rogers' view, this deep empathic connection, coupled with the other core conditions of positive regard and congruence, is a necessary and sufficient condition for change. If we offer a deeply empathic presence, we can have faith in the human potential to heal; the self-actualising tendency[141].

There are certainly arguments for seeking to remain in this sort of profound empathic intimacy with the client, and for Rogers it was an act of faith to keep following the process even when the landmarks of understanding had disappeared and the process felt very heavy and painful. At such times, the therapist and client may together face the most profound human experiences, and, through the fire of this uncertainty, find an alchemy of transformation. Sometimes, intuitively, we know that this is what is needed.

Other times, however, our empathy for the client's process points us towards a broader perspective. On the one hand, we hear the immediate distress of the situation, but, from our longer term relationship with the person, we also know that this is part of a track which will cycle indefinitely, re-creating the conditions for the narrow identity formations which are the root of their distress to be replicated and strengthened.

Sometimes too, even in new therapeutic encounters, we sense that all is not quite as it is being presented. We feel an impulse to question assertions and test the resolve with which they are offered. Then, taking a wider view, we may broaden our empathy to include not only empathy for the client, but also empathy for the others who they interact with.

At such points it can be useful to step back. Without losing a basically empathic position towards the client, who remains our first concern, one may temporarily take up a second perspective and explore other avenues, and in doing so, one might invite the client too to step out of their habitual view, and take a fresh look at the situation. This depends upon a well established therapeutic alliance and a sense of shared purpose. For the other-centred therapist, such a position comes about through the establishment of fellow-feeling.

The Commonplace Attitude

We have already seen how taking the position of a third party in the scenario which the client is presenting can bring insight and help to move the client out of a fixed view. Another perspective which can be introduced into the therapeutic process is that of 'the person in the street'. What might the ordinary person, faced with this circumstance, make of it? How might someone without the personal investment in the scenario respond? Offering the 'person in the street' perspective is often useful. It can be used to float alternative ideas or to test out unseen factors in a situation.

When someone comes to therapy, it is usually because they have exhausted their own resources in trying to sort out or resolve a situation. If they are presenting their problem as a practical dilemma, they have almost certainly thought through the obvious solutions to it and discounted them for one reason or another. There is probably more to the situation that meets the eye, or else they would not be bringing it to therapy.

It may be that the client knows some aspect of the situation which he is not voicing to the therapist, either because it embarrasses him, perhaps raising feelings of guilt, or because he has suppressed the knowledge, or simply not thought it relevant. There may be an extra dimension to the problem which is not apparent, and which may not even be easy to put into words. If there seems to be an obvious solution, then the client may have some psychological reason why he is not adopting it. He may have resistance to a particular course of action, perhaps because it conflicts with his self-image or habitual patterns of thinking or acting. Or it may be that he does not really want to change, and may be unconsciously be looking to therapy to prove that his situation is insoluble.

Jonathan tells his therapist about his difficulties with his finances. He has been trying to start a business designing web pages, but has not really got any orders. He did a small amount of work for a friend a few months ago for which he was not paid. This was largely because he offered to do the work without agreeing any payment, so that he could use the site which he created as a demonstration for other would-be customers. Now his expenses and debts are mounting and his position is clearly becoming increasingly untenable.

"I don't see a way out," says Jonathan

"Sounds difficult. I guess you've tried advertising," responds his therapist.

"Not yet," Jonathan hesitates, "I wanted to wait till I'd got this web page finished..."

"You've no money coming in at all..."

"No, and the interest on the loan is eating away at what I have in hand..."

Jonathan's therapist is aware that Jonathan seems to be presenting his situation as impossible. Her responses so far appear to be intended to address the situation on the practical, solution orientated level. She is questioning the story presented and asking for more factual detail. In this she perhaps sounds more like a guidance counsellor at this moment, but in fact her intention is therapeutic. She is gently testing out the reality of the situation which Jonathan is describing. How serious is he about making this business work? What is motivating the stagnation which seems to have set in? How much is the therapeutic need concerned with accepting the hardships involved in starting a new enterprise, in facing reality if the business is not viable, in identifying mental barriers to this and other enterprises, or in some other as yet undisclosed factor?

After some enquiry in this manner, she reflects on what she has heard. Clearly, either Jonathan is completely lacking business skills or there is an unspoken factor at work.

"I don't know," she says, "but I guess the person in the street, if they heard you talking, would wonder why on earth you keep going with this. I'm sure they'd say 'Why on earth doesn't he just get a job. It's easy enough to get computer jobs at the moment, and he could do this website business in his spare time. After all, he doesn't seem to be doing much of it.' I guess there must be other factors that they wouldn't know about. I wonder what you'd say to them...?"

In offering this response, his therapist expresses a perspective which may be difficult for Jonathan to hear. Doing this, she is partly discharging her own curiosity and bafflement. What is going on? She hopes that Jonathan will explain the hidden aspects of his position.

In this way, her first aim is to rule out the obvious and bring into the open any undisclosed practical issues. This first function of the 'person in the street' approach helps her to keep sympathy for Jonathan's situation at a point where it is possible she might have lost it through not understanding the real nature of the pressures upon him.

Secondly, however, she is indirectly challenging him to look more deeply at what he is saying and to explore what the real inhibitions to the process are. Jonathan may respond with some sort of emotional reaction to the intervention. He might say, "yes, that's just what my mother says," for example, in which case is therapist might surmise that this issue may have some roots in his relationship to his mother, or his concept of his mother, and that this may be preventing him from really engaging with it.

Invoking the view of the 'person in the street' allows his therapist to introduce a third- party perspective from which to challenge Jonathan's story. The manoeuvre is helpful in that it distances her personally from the challenge and allows it to be experienced with some neutrality. It is as if she places the person in the street on the empty chair and invites them to speak. This frees her to remain empathically supportive to Jonathan. She can even take a slightly collusive attitude and imply that 'they would say that sort of thing, wouldn't they'. This is in fact implied in the therapist's last comment, that there are probably other factors which the person in the street wouldn't know about. The comment opens the possibility for Jonathan to respond, linking the issue to his mother, a comment which seems to draw the therapist, at least for the moment into a slightly collusive shared understanding that that is 'the sort of things mothers say'.

We can see that the 'person in the street' response creates new possibilities for the therapist's role. For example, the therapist can ask the naïve question from a position which is separated from herself. This means that the question can take the form of an awkward question or a sharp challenge to the client's position. The technique gives the therapist two voices simultaneously. She can challenge the client from the 'person in the street' voice, whilst at the same time offering support and understanding from her 'therapist in the chair' position. From the latter position she can even relate to the client as the supportive buddy, knowing that any collusion this involves can be countered by the voice which has been externalised as the 'person in the street'.

In addition to these two voices, the therapist can take a third position. She can step back into a role more akin to the psychodramatic director which we encountered earlier. From here she can invite Jonathan to explore his response to the 'person in the street' and look on the one hand at the validity or otherwise of that point of view, and, on the other hand, at what prior conditioning might be colouring his response to it.

Of course, we should not overlook the possibility that the 'person in the street' voice is actually a counter-part role or counter-transference response which the therapist experienced in response to Jonathan's ways of voicing his problems. This is, in fact, quite likely, since his manner will have thrown up reactions in his therapist which will have led her to feel frustration and ask questions. If this is the case, externalising this response to the 'person in the street' position can be helpful in allowing it, and its impact, to be explored whilst freeing the therapist to hold a more neutral role.

This use of the commonplace attitude to investigate unspoken material can be used in two ways in particular:

Elephant in the room: Voicing taboo material, which everyone knows is there, but no one dares to name.

Emperor's new clothes: Making apparent what should be obvious, but no one has noticed because a compelling story has made the obvious impossible.

EXERCISE SIX: INVOLVING THE COMMONPLACE ATTITUDE

Reflect on the work Jonathan was involved in.

What do you think of Jonathan's therapist's approach?

What other directions might she have taken?

What results might they have had?

Think of your own work with clients. Have you encountered clients who present their problem in terms of practical difficulties? If so, how have you responded?

Empathy for the Other and Role Reversal

Earlier in this session, we saw how the therapist may invite the client to become more empathic towards a third party in their story. By empathising with Tony, Mary was invited to explore why Tony might have reacted as he did when he came home from work. Mary was encouraged to see his point of view, and, in so doing, to become less attached to her own sense of hurt and rejection.

It is not a large step from looking at Tony's perspective and talking about what his reasons for acting in a particular way might be, to questioning how he sees the situation and what thoughts he has about his life, and even about Mary. This position is called *role reversal*. The term role reversal comes from psychodrama. It describes a common method of inviting the person who is exploring an issue to swap roles with another character in his drama.

Role reversal is an important step in other-centred work as it allows the client to imaginatively become 'the other' and, in doing so, to step completely out of the self-perspective. Of course, the process is an imaginative one, and as such, is clearly going to be imperfect. Nevertheless, it is surprising how powerful the technique can be. People often realise things with great clarity as soon as they step into the 'other' position, which had not occurred to them in their own position.

In psychodramatic work the process of reversing roles involves a physical exchange of positions. This movement cements the exchange. It can sometimes be useful in one to one work to use an empty chair for this purpose. When you intend to invite a client to explore what a third party is seeing and feeling, you might first suggest that the client visualise the person sitting on a particular chair, then ask him to move and sit on that chair as he 'becomes' that person. This can help the client to really enter into the role of the other.

On the other hand, some clients will not be ready for such enactment, and may be better able to work if simply invited to think about how the other person is thinking and feeling whilst remaining in their own chair.

Returning to our example, Mary's therapist might say, "So, if you were to imagine you were Tony, lying down on the sofa... like you have just come in from work... Mary is in the kitchen cooking... you switch on the telly... what are you thinking about?"

You will notice here that the therapist's first invitation is made in a naturalistic, conversational way. There is a suggestion that Mary imagine being Tony, but it is presented as something that Mary might do of her own accord, 'if you were to...'. Immediately, though, having created the possibility for the scene with this invitation, the therapist leads Mary imaginatively into role as Tony, shifting into present tense speech and addressing her as Tony. This shift into present tense, other-directed dialogue cements the client into the role reversed position. The therapist then reinforces the position by speaking to 'Tony' about Mary, emphasising to the client that, at this moment, she is not Mary.

This shows how the client in role reversal can not only explore the feelings and thoughts of the third party, but can also look at the world through the third party's eyes. This world view includes the third party's view of the client. Therapist might well take the exploration a stage further by asking Mary (as Tony), "and what do you think of Mary, Tony? How do you think she feels about you..."

Role reversal demonstrates the capacity that people have to access parts of their awareness which may be out of range of conscious thought. They can step out of the mind-set of their normal identity and discover knowledge which they had not realised they possessed. Mary's response when she is 'in role' as Tony will give a quite different response from that she might make if she were simply asked what she thinks Tony thinks of her. If she has really entered into role as Tony, she will probably know with some clarity what Tony feels about her. This phenomenon demonstrates how conditioned our knowledge and intuitions are by the roles and circumstances we find ourselves in.

You have already had an experience of working with role reversal if you tried the second variation on the empathy-lab exercise in session three. There you worked from role reversed position when, having been counsellor, you took the role of client and talked about the issue which the client had previously been sharing. Recall the effect of this shift of position in allowing other dimensions of the story to surface, which perhaps you had not even been aware of as counsellor, and probably had not voiced.

Guidelines for Role Reversal Work

We will return to the mode of working known as role reversal in the next session and look in some detail at a piece of work involving this technique. For now, let us establish some general guidelines:

- Role reversal comes out of an empathic relationship between the client and a third party who is normally not present in the therapy session.
- It is not usually helpful to try to do role reversal work with someone whom the client does not respect, or is very angry with. It is also unlikely a client can do this kind of work when reflecting on someone who abused them seriously.
- In establishing the reversed role position, the therapist needs to offer clear, decisive instructions. Confused instructions result in incomplete immersion in the experience.
- Respect the spatial positions of the roles. Move the person physically into the space 'occupied' by the character, whether this is an empty chair or a position in the room. Move them out of role afterwards. (Role reversal can be done imaginatively without movement, but this is often less clearly differentiated from the rest of the therapeutic dialogue and takes more skill on the part of the therapist).
- Notice what the client is naturally doing. If the client repeatedly talks about the person with whom they are supposed to be role reversed in the third person, they are consistently not 'in role' and should be taken back into a neutral position. (ie if, when you ask the client, who is supposed to be in a role reversed position, a question, they think about the answer and respond "Well, he'd think...", they are not in role, but are perceiving the person they are supposed to be enacting as a third party.)
- Pay attention to getting body posture of the person who is

being played right.

- Speak to the person 'in role'. Address them in the present tense by the name that the person whose role is being explored is or was known by; that is as 'Mrs...' or 'Fred'.
- Avoid pantomime. If the client is not taking the role reversal seriously, it is not working, so stop. As we will see in the next session, there may be times when humour breaks in, and indeed, this is quite healthy, but the general tenor of the work should be serious and respectful.
- Pay attention to whether the client needs help to leave a role. Usually in one to one work this is not a problem, since subsequent discussion tends to bring the client naturally back into their own experience.

Different Viewpoints in Other-Centred Work

In other-centred therapy, the client may be guided to look at their world from a number of perspectives. Switching between different perspectives is a useful technique in that it disrupts pre-conceived patterns of thinking and takes the client beyond the limits and conditions of his habitual viewpoint. There are endless possibilities for variation.

The identity is not one fixed entity. A person has a number of identities, each conditioned by a particular set of circumstances, and each with its own mental formations, expectations and preoccupations; each with its conditioned view of the world. These different identities may be explored directly by changing the object of attention. Different scenes, or different objects within the same scene, create new insights.

Other exploration focuses on the object world itself. Here too, there are a number of possibilities for exploring different view points. Objects may be explored, both as they appear to the client as rupa, coloured by his experience, and as they exist in their independent state, as real things.

Whilst these many possibilities may seem confusing, they can be represented by the five categories into which they fall. These categories describe the five key lines of enquiry which a client might be invited to take. The diagram below summarises these. Each element in it represents a way of working which has many possibilities, but each is distinct in the angle of view which it offers:

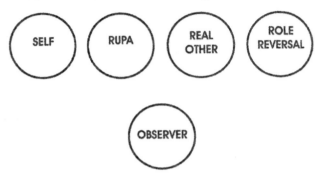

We have already discussed all these possibilities in some detail, so we can now briefly summarise them as follows:

- **Self Exploration:** This enquiry involves the client's exploration of his own personal experience. It is a mode of working commonly used in counselling, and involves the client's experience of 'me'. It might be evoked by questions such as "how is it for you?"
- **Rupa Exploration:** This enquiry focuses attention upon perceived objects. It explores the object as it is seen, with whatever personal distortions naturally arise. These distortions may be made more powerful through the process of amplification. Resulting emotion may require containment. Rupa exploration is facilitated by questions such as "what do you see"
- **Exploring the Real Other:** This enquiry centres on an attempt to see and understand the object in its own right. It is based on an attempt to reach a position of clarity and honesty about the others in the client's world. Rupa explo-

ration is facilitated by questions such as "what is he/she/it really like?"

- **Using Role Reversal techniques:** This form of working involves taking the client right out of his own perspective and putting him in the position of the other, so that he can attempt to see the world through the eyes of the other. Role reversal is facilitated by the action of physically moving the client into the other's place and by questions such as "if you were him/her what would you be thinking and feeling?"

To these four perspectives, which might all be described as being within the scene, we can add a fifth position, which is that of **the observer**. The observer is outside the situation and so takes an overview of it. The observer brings clarity or insight. It has something in common with the director role. The client might be invited to step into the 'observer' role by way of a question such as, "If you step back and look at this situation in which you and he are in conflict, what do you see?"

Moving between these roles, the client experiences the situation from multiple viewpoints. This facilitates an exploration which is in itself freeing for the client, moving him out of the fixed position of the self perspective, as he learns to play creatively with experience.

References and Background Reading for This Session

Brazier D *The Necessary Condition is Love* in Brazier D 1993 *Beyond Carl Rogers* Constable UK

Dayton, T 1990 *Drama Games: Techniques for Self-Development*
HCI Publications US (although the general approach of this book is more self-orientated, it contains a lot of practical exercises which can be adapted to explore the *other* perspective.)

SESSION TWELVE

Meeting Others from the Past

In this session we will explore:

- Options in other-centred process
- Exploring the real other when working with past relationships
- Act hunger and role reversal in the therapy session
- Naikan method
- Biographical and other research based therapeutic work

Other-related approaches in therapy explore the client's world. This world is the current configuration of the client's experience. It includes the factors that condition identity and support the ever-repeating cycles of its continual renewal. Among these are the current focuses of the client's attention, the real objects which are present in daily activity, but also the shadowy imprints of past people and events, and hopeful projections of future dreams and plans.

This personal world presents itself to the senses, the doors through which our experience is mediated. Besides our sight and hearing, touch, taste and smell, these unruly faculties[142] include our mental function itself. The mind's eye, in this model, is a sense which perceives objects which are known as mind-objects: thoughts, dreams, ideas, fantasies and other apparitions.

The client's world, as it is perceived by him, has rupa quality. Experience is constantly subverted, taken as an indicator which points towards the self[143]. At very least this process is one of filtration, but often it involves distortion and even fabrication of data. We see what it suits us to see.

So far in this book we have explored how the other-centred therapist might focus on this area of experience which might be described as conditioned perception. We have seen how, by amplifying its power, the client and therapist can explore how it shapes and influences the process of self-creation. We have also seen how behind the perceived world, with its inevitable distortions of the personal frame of reference[144] lies a real world of 'others', and how the attempt to see those others may also provide a therapeutic direction.

The real world of others is, at once, inaccessible to direct perception, and a reality which disrupts our expectations and offers a means of adjustment and change within the self-world. The fact that other people around us do not meet our expectations is a blessing in that their failure to fulfil the roles to which we assign them challenges us to revise our perceptions[145]. Without such checks we might sink further and further into delusion, and indeed, many who live isolated lives, unless they are particularly spiritually mature, do become a little idiosyncratic.

So it is that the challenge of living with others is a gift. It modifies our oddities and smoothes our rough edges. It forces us back into dialogue with reality. The self becomes a negotiated phenomenon, establishing itself between feedback from others and preconceived views of our own making. Maturation involves learning to live with increasing degrees of complexity and uncertainty.

Object-related work may sometimes focus on the distorted view, the rupa, but often it makes its focus in the real world which lies behind the client's perceptions. In this way, it involves the client in exploration the reality of the objects, people or things which exist but are subject to the distortions imposed by his conditioned view.

As we have seen, this process is often based on a sober evaluation of the others who are important to the client's personal story. Sometimes this is done through reflection and observation, but other times the object-related style of working moves a stage further and uses the technique of role reversal which we looked at in the last session.

When something is presented in therapy, the other-centred therapist working in this way will follow a process which involves:

- Identification of the significant objects
- Bringing attention to those objects and holding the client's focus with them
- Either a) amplifying the rupa aspect of the object or b) exploring its real aspect.

We can represent this diagrammatically:

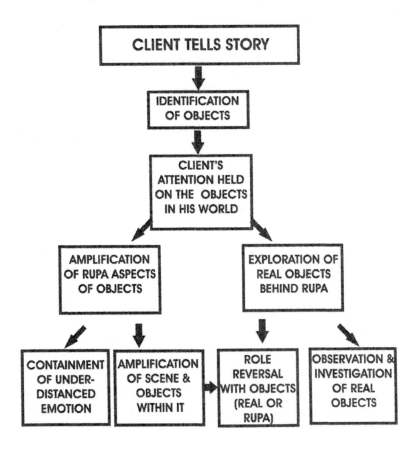

In the previous session we looked at examples of how the real nature of the other's experience might be explored, and how the therapist might encourage the client to question his perception, and, in stepping out of rigid attachment to his own perspective, to attempt to see the world through the eyes of another person. This work was illustrated with examples of people with current life difficulties who used the methods to explore the perspectives which they saw as belonging to people whom they knew personally.

Such methods, of course, are still open to distortion, and although the counsellor may push the client to question his assumptions and really try to understand what the other person might be thinking, the facts and feelings which emerge in the session are still bound to have some colouration arising from the client's perceptual bias. At the same time, in theory at least, when working with material relating to current relationships, the client could check reality with the person concerned, and may well leave the session and start to observe the other person more closely, developing greater empathy for their position and taking an interest in their views.

The methods can, however, also be used to explore the other perspective of those who are no longer present in person in the client's life. Of course, such work is without the same checks and balances as come when a person is going to be facing the real other after the session. Nevertheless, the effects of investigating the experience of others who have been important in our lives in the past, as if through their eyes, can be powerful. In this sort of work, although in one sense we are investigating reality, in another sense we are not confined to the realistic. Despite this, the insights that arise from other-related work of this kind can be profound and life changing.

In this session we will explore the possibilities for other-centred work centred on people from the past.

EXERCISE ONE: THE THERAPEUTIC PROCESS

Looking at the diagram above, think about work which you have done with clients recently and look at whether you have used any of the possible directions which it suggests.

Notice the choice points during the process and think about what basis you might make such choices on, and what would affect your choice of option.

Meeting Others from the Past

Let us return at this point to the example we used earlier. Let us go back to Susan's story. Susan, as you will recall, arrived in therapy following an incident in which her supervisor at work had upset her. In talking about her response to the incident, Susan realised that she had made the connection between the supervisor and a person she had known years before; a teacher she had had when she was at school called Miss Richards. She had found this teacher frightening and threatening.

In the therapeutic work that followed, we saw how it was possible to re-visit the past as it presented in Susan's memories, and how these could be made more vivid through a process which we call *amplification*. Having identified a particular occasion on which she recalled Miss Richards being angry with the class, Susan was encouraged by her therapist to imaginatively re-create the scene in which an incident had happened in the classroom. It was on a day when Miss Richards had put the whole class in detention.

In the piece of work that followed, we saw how, having first re-constructed the scene, paying particular attention to the fact that it was set in a specific location, Miss Richards was re-introduced to the scenario as a rupa-charged figure.

This imaginative re-creation of a childhood situation was powerful and real enough to evoke a strong emotional response in Susan. It represented not only something which had been significant in her past, but also something which was live in her current psychic configuration, in that the incident had probably impacted upon her relationship with her supervisor at work.

When the scene was established, Susan responded with the surprising observation that now, as a result of the work done in the therapy session, she thought Miss Richards had been frightened. This observation emerged because Susan was trying to understand Miss Richards' facial expression. She was puzzled by the way Miss Richards' eyes looked tense and narrow and she had tried to work out what the expression really meant. In trying this expression out herself, she naturally experimented with a kind of role reversal.

This example of spontaneous experimentation illustrates that, although these techniques might seem artificial when they are described, in fact they are not so different from the ways that people generally think about situations, and if handled with sensitivity and skill, they can become part of a therapist's repertoire without importing a contrived or overly directive style.

The use of role reversal is a powerful tool in exploring the other perspective, and it can be introduced into investigation of historical or imaginative scenes as well as those from the present day, as happened for Susan in a small way. To look at how this might work, let us imagine that at this point, Susan's therapist decides to encourage her to take the spontaneous role reversal a stage further.

As Susan screws up her eyes, her therapist sees that she is closely identifying with her teacher. She has already made a move towards stepping into her shoes of her own volition, and her therapist feels that Susan may be willing to take the work a step further.

Recognising when a client is already mentally entering a scene is a skill that psychodramatists develop. They call this readiness which a person has *act-hunger*. When a person has act-hunger, they are already mentally entering the scene and so will make the transition to action smoothly. It will simply be a confirmation of their existing mind-state. If act-hunger has not developed, the person will find it more difficult to engage with the material in an experiential way and will tend to talk about the situation more cognitively. Act-hunger is often evident in the person's body posture and facial expression. These give evidence that they are experiencing sufficient level of *entrancement* to step into the scene.

EXERCISE TWO: ACT HUNGER

Reflect on pieces of work which you have done recently. Can you identify points at which clients with whom you were working, or other students in your group, might have been expressing 'act hunger'.

What sort of signs did you observe?

"OK, suppose you try being Miss Richards," Susan's therapist offers.

"You mean, be her?" Susan is a little taken aback. Although she has been experimenting with trying out the expression which Miss Richards had around her eyes, she has not anticipated taking this experimentation further. The suggestion temporarily takes her out of the school-room trance.

"Yes, if you want to." Her therapist is encouraging, but also open to a different direction if Susan does not feel this course of action is right.

"OK, I'll give it a try."

You can see here that the process of exploration has been temporarily paused whilst Susan and her therapist negotiate the next stage in the work. This kind of interruption is not necessarily problematic, as the work has reached a natural pause with Susan's insight. Susan was well enough established in the scene to be able to 'put it on hold'. As we have already seen, it is quite possible, when a client is in the flow of a piece of work, to engage their observer aspect in discussion, whilst another part of them remains immersed in the storyline.

Since Susan's therapist wishes to suggest some work in role reversed positions, she will need to give some explanation of the method, but this needs to be kept to a minimum, since, as with any work of this kind, too much discussion will keep the client in a more cognitive mode for too long and so break the trance state in which they are working.

"So Miss Richards is standing over there at the front of the class," the therapist points to the location across the room, re-establishing as she does both the scene and the present tense. "Suppose you go over there and try being Miss Richards?"

This latter instruction is still directed to Susan's adult, observer self.

Susan gets up and goes over to the place. She stands with her face towards the classroom.

"OK, now take some time to feel your way into being Miss Richards," her therapist suggests. "How would she stand when she was in front of the class?"

Notice that the therapist does not rush into addressing Susan in role. She is still negotiating with Susan's observer self at this point.

Susan stands rigidly, her shoulders forced back, facing stalwartly ahead of her.

"Does that feel right?"

Susan thinks. "Perhaps even more…" she says.

She tightens the muscles in her legs, forcing her abdominal muscles to clench up and her breathing to constrict. Her face tightens, and her eyes become narrow and tense.

"That's it, that feels right," Susan says.

"OK, so now what's going through your mind? You look at all these girls. They are expecting something from you. Do you think they like you? Are you a popular teacher?"

Now Susan is in role, so her therapist switches to addressing her directly as Miss Richards.

Susan gives a little laugh at this, "No! They all hate me." She pauses and looks across the imagined classroom. "Goodness, all those eyes, just looking at me, full of resentment. It's scary."

"Tell me a bit about yourself, Miss Richards."

EXERCISE THREE: GETTING INTO THE BODY

When we try to understand another person through role reversal, getting a body sense of their experience can be an important first step.

If you are in a group:

Work in groups of three. In invite one member of the group to stand in their usual posture. Now, let one of the other members become a 'sculptor'. That person will mould the third member of the group into the body posture of the first member. Treat them like a 'bendy toy' and adjust limbs, head and torso to create as good a replica as possible.

Do not use speech. Just move the body gently into position. Pay attention to detail. Make sure that the angle of the shoulders and of the jaw mirror those of the first person.

This is an exercise in observation for the sculptor and in experiencing a felt-sense of a different body posture for the person being moulded.

For the subject it can be a revealing experience too, as they see and hear feedback about their habitual stance.

Afterwards, the person who was moulded should share their experience of being in the first person's body posture before a more general feedback session in which all three group members participate. Take turns so that everyone has a chance to try out the method in all three roles.

If you are working on your own:
Think of someone whom you have difficulty understanding. Take some time to try to move your body into a position which mimics theirs.

You will have to work from memory, though you could use a photo to remind you of them. You can do this by feel, or you could use a mirror to help.

When you have found the closest posture you can to theirs, close your eyes and spend some time getting a felt-sense of it.

Allow any images or thoughts which associate themselves with the posture to surface. Write down your impressions.

You will notice that, having made the move into the role-reversed position, Susan experiences the scene in a completely different way. When she was looking at Miss Richards, she was able to discern something of what the teacher might have felt, and, through her detailed testing out of the tension which she observed in her eyes, gained some insight, but this still had a quality of speculation about it. Now that she is 'in role', her responses have a confidence about them which comes from an experiential recognition of their validity. Susan now knows how it feels to stand in front of a class full of hostile teenage girls.

Of course we cannot re-visit Miss Richards to discover how accurate Susan's experience in role is to historical reality. This does not really matter. Susan has stepped out of her habitual view and is starting to see other possibilities. She starts to understand in a felt way what may have been the case for another person.

Susan responds to the therapist's invitation, "Well, I'm a teacher at Bridebridge High School. I've been here for twelve years. I teach French. I am head of department."

"How old are you?"

Susan laughs, "Oh very old!" she says. The question has pulled her out of role a little. Her response probably comes from the role of 'Susan as a schoolgirl'. It is perhaps conditioned by the amusement which schoolgirls take in speculating about the ages and other personal details of their teachers. She then regains her seriousness, and adds, "I'm about forty. But I feel much older."

"And you're not married."

Again, Susan laughs, but then quickly regains the role, "No... some chance!"

"You'd like to be?"

"I don't know... maybe. But I like being a teacher. Maybe getting married would stop that."

"Do you like being a teacher?"

There is a long pause. Susan is thinking. "I used to..." she looks at the class in front of her, "but maybe I'm wondering..."

The therapist waits. Will Susan say more? When she does not, she tries a new angle.

"What do you do when you get home from school? Where do you live?"

Susan thinks, "I've got a little flat overlooking the park. Its very neat... and I've got a cat."

Susan is now having to use her imagination to create a world for Miss Richards to inhabit. She doesn't know anything about her teacher's life outside school, but she builds up a picture, probably on the basis of other single women she has known. It is speculative, but congruent with her experience of those aspects of Miss Richards which she does know.

"What do you do when you get in from school?"

"I make myself a cup of tea. I've got a china tea pot and a matching cup and saucer... and a tray... with an embroidered tray cloth..." Susan is enjoying creating the peripheral details of this woman's life, the little things which bring it to life.

"Did you embroider it?"

Susan pauses, then laughs gently, "no, I'm not an embroidery sort of person. It came from my mother."

"Is your mother alive?"

Again, Susan thinks, testing the thoughts against her felt-sense of Miss Richards. "No," she says, "she's died."

"Do you have any relatives?"

"No... not close ones... I might have distant cousins ..." she tries out the possibility, then more decisively, "No. I feel all alone."

"And what do you do with your evening?"

"I guess I just do my marking... perhaps I read..."

"Do you eat?"

"Oh yes... not much... beans on toast maybe."

At this point, Susan looks suddenly emotional, struck by the pathos of the situation. "God, what a life! Poor woman! No wonder she was so sour."

Susan's remark indicates that she has come out of role. She is no longer 'Miss Richards'. She is back in her own perspective, looking at Miss Richards with new insight.

"It sounds like you have stopped being Miss Richards," her therapist comments, recognising the reality. "Let's bring you out of the scene."

The piece of work has been effective in changing Susan's view of Miss Richards. Now her therapist will be interested to know whether this insight has had any impact on Susan's feelings about her supervisor.

"How does this relate to your experience at work today?" she might ask, once they have regained their seats.

EXERCISE FOUR: IMAGINING AN UNKNOWN PLACE

Recall one of your teachers from school. Choose anyone who comes to mind, regardless of whether you liked them or not, or how well you knew them.

Now imagine your teacher at home in the evening after class. Think about what their home would have been like (probably this is complete speculation).

Include details of their house, the things which they have around them, the details of furnishings and objects which they use, and the people or animals with whom they share the space. Think about how they spend their evening. What do they do? What interactions do they have? What do they eat?

Write a creative piece about your teacher's home life. Use your imagination to create a world for him or her.

After you have finished, reflect on how the exercise has coloured your feelings about the teacher.

Reflecting on this piece of work we can see that Susan's therapist uses a number of methods to help Susan to step into the other position and gain an appreciation of how her teacher might actually have felt.

We can also see that the use of role reversal enhances this process. Paying attention to detail is significant in creating the conditions for a spontaneous insight. Although some aspect of the scene, such as the food which is eaten, or the description of the woman's flat, are completely speculative and incidental, they create the ambient conditions which bring Miss Richards alive for Susan.

EXERCISE FIVE: FACILITATING ROLE REVERSAL

If you are in a group, work in triads, facilitating imaginative role reversal with a figure from the past. When you are in client role should choose someone with whom you sufficient empathy to enter into their life and world. Do not choose someone who was abusive or towards whom you still feel a great deal of anger.

Use the guidance given in the last session and in the description of Susan's work to help you.

> If you are not working in a group, think about trying this sort of work in your therapy practice. Begin by gaining experience in simply inviting the person to think about how the third party might have felt. As you gain experience, you can gradually intensify your work by amplifying the process using present tense, drawing attention to the body element, then moving into a degree of dramatisation with an empty chair.
>
> Reflect on the progress of this work in supervision

Blame the Parents

It is popular in some Western therapies to blame the parents. As our earliest influences, our parents have provided much of our early experience, our education, our emotional climate in childhood, so if we are not to blame ourselves, where else can we lay the responsibility for our troubles? In addition, given that parents generally inevitably fail to live up to the high ideals which we, and society, wish of them, it is no small surprise that many clients and their therapists either subtly, or not so subtly, place parents in a bad light.

At the individual level, our self-referenced world view, in its extreme, sees other people simply as players in our personal stories, rather than as people who have stories of their own. Whilst egalitarian principles and social awareness mean that we often over-ride this tendency when it comes to our peers and friends, not least because they frequently assert themselves in similar vein, parents may not be given such opportunities to counter our critical views of them. So, typically, we either think badly of them, or conversely we hold onto fantasies of their perfection and cling to an idealised perception of them. With so many layers of associations and stories attributed to them, they become powerful rupas for us, second only to the self.

It is hard for us, even as adults, to see the person behind the reality when it comes to our parents. Whether blamed or idealised, these projected images vie for attention and carry with them the conditioning of our old selves, which we can easily regress to.

Exploring the reality of parental relationships through other-centred methods of therapy is valuable and liberating. Discovering the human being behind the layers of expectations and assumptions, we can find our lives are enriched, as are those of our parents themselves. An other-centred model tends towards this sort of exploration, and pushes us to look beyond the easy interpretations which our habits of view throw up. A therapist with this perspective may ask pertinent questions which upset the assumptions which the client holds, and may use any of the methods we have seen to date to take the exploration further.

In the remainder of this session, we will look at two further methods which fall within an other-centred approach. These can be used to explore early relationships, and particularly the relationship with parents, encouraging us to see them in a new light. Firstly, we will look at the method of Naikan. This generally focuses upon this parental relationship, though it can be used for examining any relationships. Secondly we will look at biographical work and how it can be used to help a client to explore the reality of the lives of others who were important to him.

Naikan

In *Listening to the Other* we introduced the form of therapy called *Naikan* or *Nei Quan*[146]. Nei Quan or Naikan originated in Japan. It is a therapeutic method which focuses on the relationships which a person had with significant people in his or her early life. With its focus on primary relationships[147] from the past, Naikan is helpful in enabling exploration of the other perspective in those past relationships.

Historically, Naikan's origins go back to the middle of the twentieth century. It was developed by a Pureland Buddhist priest called Yoshimoto Ishin, who lived 1916-1988. Ishin practised a form of meditation called mishirabe, which was noted for its toughness. Having found a lot of benefit in this form of training, he developed a modified version of the practice which could be offered to people who did not wish to take on the level of spiritual discipline that the original practice had involved. He called this new practice *Naikan*, which meant 'looking inside'. The term carries the implication of placing oneself and one's life at the focus of the mind-sense. It implies engaging in objective contemplation of one's being.

Naikan is traditionally offered as a retreat. In Japan there are a number of Naikan centres, some of which present the method in this original form, whilst others have adapted to a more secular style of presentation. In the West, Naikan is offered in a number of centres in Europe and North America, though as a method it is not well known. Among those who have specialised in this area of work, David Reynolds was a pioneer who offered training and retreats and has written a number of books on the topic[148]. Another pioneer in this field is Gregg Krech[149] who currently directs the Todo Institute[150] in Vermont, where he and his wife Linda offer Naikan both residentially and in online programmes.

Naikan as a method is intended to shift our perception from the self-referential view that we commonly cling to, towards a perspective which takes into account the others who have supported us in practical and emotional ways, and who have thereby provided the conditions for our existence. It is other-centred in its outlook, putting its focus on concrete, practical enquiry into the facts of one's life. Krech writes of Naikan:

Naikan broadens our view of reality. It's as if, standing on top of a mountain, we shift from a zoom lens to a wide-angle lens. Now we can appreciate the broader panorama - our former perspective still included, but accompanied by much that had been hidden. And that which was hidden makes the view extraordinary[151].

During a traditional Naikan retreat, it is common for a person to start by reviewing the earliest period of their life, normally looking at the time from birth to three years old. The investigation usually begins by focusing on the relationship with the person's mother or the person who was in the mothering role. This is done with the aid of a set of questions.

The Naikan questions are:

- What did this person do for me?
- What did I do for this person in return?
- What trouble did I, or my presence, cause?

Those undertaking the retreat are asked to work from memory, to be as concrete and detailed as possible and to recall what actually happened. In particular they are instructed not to speculate about psychological factors, but to try to find concrete memories of events. Where there are no memories, as in the early years there generally are not, the person may fill in the gaps in their information with knowledge of what must have been true. The mother must have done practical things for the baby, so the person can say 'she fed me, she changed my nappies' and maybe even, 'she sang to me', with reasonable confidence. The small child also probably behaved as all small children do, and gave in small child-like ways – a picture from nursery, or a handful of flowers from the park. The young child no doubt also had their share of sickness, frustration and temper tantrums, as well as requiring round-the-clock care. All this created joys and trials for the mother. Mostly these things were ordinary occurrences and no-one was blameworthy. This is the point of Naikan.

Some deduction comes from general knowledge of the lives of young families. Other things can be worked out from knowledge of the circumstances. A baby born in war-time would bring particular pressures for the family. A child born out of wedlock might have caused great shame in the past. Some families struggled financially, suffered unemployment, hardship or poor living standards, sickness or pressure from relatives. Some mothers juggled career with household duties, others were widowed or divorced. Some mothers were frustrated by domestic life, whilst others relished it and hated mess. Such factors will colour the understanding which a person can reach through the exercise.

During the Naikan retreat, the person leading the event will go to each participant in turn and invite them to report on what they have been reflecting on. The retreat leader will not usually comment on this report, but, rather, will receive what is shared with reverent attention. Afterwards she will thank the retreatant and ask him to continue with his enquiry. In this way, the retreatant is held in the silent bubble of his memories, allowing the scenes of the past to run before him, and seeking the truth of his early years. There is no distraction or direction, save that in his own mind.

After a period of time, often about half a day, the person will be moved on to look at the next block of three years; to the period of time from the age of three till he was six years old. Once more the focus is on the primary relationship with his mother. Thus the process moves on in stages, usually taking periods of three years at a time and working through childhood, exploring the relationship with the same maternal figure. Later the person may move on to look at another relationship; frequently the father, then teachers or other significant people.

The important thing about Naikan work is that it is about exploring the reality of the relationships, and seeing the other not just as an adjunct to one's psychological comfort, but as a person who exists in their own way for their own reasons. Through it, the retreat participant often comes to a deep appreciation of the way that his life has been conditioned by the provision that others have made for him. He discovers his dependence upon conditions and on other people.

In particular, Naikan helps people to develop a deeper appreciation of the experience of the other person; to feel empathy for their situation. When this happens, they start to see parents or carers as separate people with their own life experiences. They had their own stories and their own times of joy and sadness.

The purpose of Naikan is not to attribute blame, but to reach a point of fresh understanding. Indeed it is the fact that it comes from a tradition in which the concept of judgement is not part of the equation that makes it possible for it to be undertaken with such bare honesty. In participating, retreatants often experience powerfully cathartic insights and may feel regret and even remorse, but, most frequently, the residual feeling at the end of the retreat is deep gratitude and a sense of having been blessed with many wonderful things.

EXERCISE SIX: NAIKAN

Set yourself a period of time, perhaps an hour initially, to work with the Naikan questions.

Find yourself a quiet place, away from interruptions or distractions. Reflect on your relationship with our mother or caregiver during the first five years of your life.

Make notes of your observations. Remember to keep your observations practical. Do not include any psychological speculations or reflections. Think in terms of numbers and quantities. How many nappies did your mother change? How many hours of sleep did she get? How did she transport you to school? How much did your clothes cost?

After completing your Naikan, think about whether you could use any of your learning from it to inform your work with clients.

Naikan and Therapy Settings

Whilst Naikan is traditionally offered in the formal context of a retreat, it has been adapted in a number of ways. Reynolds has combined the method with Morita therapy, referred to in session ten, and a number of Western methodologies, to create what he called Constructive Living[152]. This approach is presented as a personal growth or educational process rather than as a therapy, but is basically therapeutic in its intent.

Personally I have found the Naikan has been a positive and powerful influence in my therapeutic work, even though I rarely use the method in its pure form. I have on occasion run Nei Quan (Naikan) retreats, and find the format offers participants something which is both healing and cathartic. However, when I have run these retreats, it has been as a distinct experience, not integrated with my other therapy work. They are intense and life changing and as such, they suit people who have an interest and ability to work at this level.

Anecdotally I would say that, out of a group attending a five day Nei Quan retreat, roughly a third of retreatants have a very substantive, life-changing insight. Another third have powerful experiences which affect them deeply and no one goes away unmoved or without some new understanding.

In its pure form, Naikan method provides a particular sort of container which is different from that offered in the regular therapy setting. Where it is offered in a one to one weekly format, or in similar small steps, Naikan is closer to regular counselling, and more suited to clients who have no prior experience of retreats or intensive groups.

I do not personally work in this latter form, but practising Naikan has given to me a change of view in my regular therapy work. When I first encountered it, it showed me the conditioned Western assumptions which I had previously bought into, and opened my eyes to the way that most Western therapists fail to notice the immense imbalance between what most of us have received, both from our parents, and from the universe at large, and what we are able to return.

Bringing this viewpoint into my work, sometimes through a questioning approach, has shown me how even those who have spent years in conventional therapy berating their parents for numerous understandable omissions or abuses, can discover another side to the story, and can feel moved by seeing their parents' stories in a new way. It has taught me to step out of the popular Western assumptions and encourage exploration, and to find the freedom of knowing that sometimes their parents got it right, even if other times they didn't.

Biographical and Research based Work

A second method which might be used to explore family history and parents' lives is that of biography and other-related research approaches. Creating a record of another person's life can be a pleasant and revealing experience. It can be a way of celebrating their contribution to the world and to one's own life.

From on other-centred perspective, an important factor in this work is the attitude which informs it. Any of these methods might be used in ways which put the client at the centre of the project and reinforce his prejudices about others and about his own privileged place in the scheme of things. The therapeutic value in this sort of work, fro an other-centred perspective, is generally in placing the other at the focal point and enabling a new perspective to emerge.

Biographical work is something which might be undertaken for a variety of reasons:

Understanding why

One of the most powerful reasons for doing biographical work with clients is because it helps them to understand why their parents' lives were as they were, and their relationships with those parents are as they are. Since children rarely get the full story of their parents' lives, it is often only when one starts to investigate as an adult that one discovers factors that were previously hidden. The child that died, the previous disappointment in love, the impact of war or poverty, dynamics with in-laws and other relatives, thwarted ambitions and hidden losses may all have created waves within the family which impacted on the children but were never acknowledged.

Family research can throw up surprises and insights, and can explain. If facilitated in a way that assists the client to feel empathy for the people involved, who are, after all, their relatives, but who struggled secretly in their own ways, the results can be healing and can put the past to rest.

Honouring History

For people who are displaced or have lost connection with home and family, whether as refugees or for other reasons, creating a record, story, or personal biography may be a valuable adjunct to the therapeutic process, and form part of the journey towards integrating their roots with their present situations. Creating a tangible record of places and loved ones left behind, provides the sort of memorial which can be treasured and looked back on as time passes. Whether a scrap book or a narrative, a memory box or a picture, the product itself becomes a container for the memories of people and places and for feelings which are associated with them. Such an object can take on the sort of power we spoke of in earlier sessions associated with artwork[153].

A Memorial or Gift

Much biographical work is done for personal therapeutic purposes, and is not intended for others to view. Nevertheless, this kind of work can also be used to create something that will become a more public record.

Such a memorial or gift is usually something which places another person's life at the centre of the account. This kind of work might take the form of a *'This is your Life'* book to mark an important occasion, such as a significant birthday, a retirement or a marriage. It might be a memorial for someone who has died. It might take the form of a collage or wall hanging, a scrap book or a collection of writings. For example, I was at a wedding where a relative of the couple organised other members of the family and friends to each create an embroidered patch that was then sewed into a quilt for the bride and groom. This became a precious reminder of those who had been present on the occasion.

Making a memorial or gift of this kind can involve creating objects which will be treasured by the person to whom they are given. In some cases, it may involve a process of researching the person's life and collecting contributions from others who have known the person, as well as assembling anecdotes, photos or other images. Such a process is healing at many levels. It can bring insight into the other's life. It can change the view which the person involved in creating the object has of the person for whom it is intended. It can bring family members together is a common activity.

A Gift from a Dying Person

A somewhat different gift-making project is the creation of a memory box, letters or other record by a person who is terminally ill for his or her children or for other loved ones. This is an other-centred activity in the sense that its purpose is to communicate to an important other, namely the child, in years to come. An act of love, it requires the dying person to develop empathy for the future needs of that child.

We have seen how object-related work can be used to explore relationships from the past. Creating a gift for the child to receive in years to come involves exploring the future experience of the adult which their child will one day become. Such work is clearly extremely emotional. The dying person is likely both to experience the painfulness of loss which comes from knowing that they will not see their child grow up over the years, and also comfort or sadness in imagining that loved one's experience in receiving the message. Will the gift be precious or a painful reminder of past grief? Will it be embarrassing for the young adult or a focus of tender feelings? What will be most poignant and what will be remembered? To see the adult in the six-year-old is not easy, but to try to do so may help the gift become meaningful and in the process support the client on their journey.

EXERCISE SEVEN: CREATING A BIOGRAPHICAL
RECORD

Choose someone whose life you would like to celebrate. For the purpose of this exercise you can keep the project small and simply make a picture, but you may choose to create a larger item such as an album or book instead if you prefer.

Take a large sheet of quality paper or card and assemble as many images as you can which relate to the life of the person whom you have chosen. These may include photographs and other mementos, but may also include pictures from magazines, or scraps of coloured paper or cloth.

You may want to add short quotes from favourite poems, notes of significant dates, memories, or events, or written tributes, but keep these brief. Use a suitable glue which will not spoil the pictures and create a collage which celebrates the person. You may choose to frame it and either keep it yourself or give it to them on a suitable occasion.

Reflect on how this method might be used with a client.

Laying Ghosts to Rest

When we explore the lives of figures from the past, other-centred work can be very powerful in healing hurts and bringing new perspectives. The method brings to life characters who have been held in the memory, making their presence more vivid. In recalling some of the people who have been significant for us, and reflecting on the lives they led, we encounter some figures who are benign and some who are troublesome, some who are ordinary and some who are a source of distress.

Among these figures, for some people there may be terrifying memories of those who have abused or hurt them. For people in this position, memories may be too vivid and flashbacks and nightmares may keep the perpetrator all too present. How does one work with such situations in an other-centred way?

In fact, I have found that an other-centred approach is

extremely helpful in such situations. Firstly, as we saw in session six, the therapist may need to help the client to understand the processes of under-distancing. Whilst flashbacks are happening, the client will find grounding methods helpful and needs reassurance that the terrifying rupa is the creation of his own mental processes. Working together, the client and therapist learn to navigate the turbulent sea of emotions and create safe places from which, gradually, the story can be voiced.

Secondly, the story probably needs telling. During this process, the therapist becomes the fellow traveller, establishing a deep empathic link, and hearing the client's experiences scene by scene, gradually approaching the material with the client. This sort of investigation allows the characters in the story to emerge as real people, rather than remaining the caricatures which fear has created. The therapist maintains an attitude of concern and interest which is warm, yet neutral. By avoiding judgement or the easy solution of condemning those not present, she holds to a non-judgemental attitude as her precept.

This radically non-judgemental stance is fundamental to an other-centred approach. Whilst not judging the client is essential, not rushing to judge the perpetrator is also wise. The situation may have been desperately sad, hurtful, even bad, and this may need saying in a forceful way sometimes, but the truth of the human dynamics involved is no doubt far more complicated than simple condemnation allows. Such complexity can only be appreciated if we resist the emotive pull towards judgmentalism.

Thirdly, as the exploration unfolds, a window of understanding opens up. Gradually as the clouds of fear start to diminish, it becomes possible to remember. The client is ready to look more closely at the reality of the past. At this point, the therapist of this tradition may gently start to invite a more challenging exploration of the material. This might involve investigation of the real person who was the abuser.

"I'm wondering what your father experienced when he was six?" the therapist asks as the client finishes describing the way her father used to beat her at that age.

"His father used to beat *him*. He ended up in hospital with a broken arm..."

There is a moment of recognition. Although it does not diminish the brutality of the harsh abuse her father meted out to her, the realisation that he too suffered abuse brings the client to a point of tenderness; of common feeling towards her father.

"He had a tough time," she says wryly.

Even in the most horrific situations, the people involved in perpetrating abuse are human. Appreciating this humanity does not require us to condone their actions. It does not even require us to like them, or to understand, or to think that we might have done the same in their circumstances, though we might wonder. The conditions of another's life are so different that we cannot know. Would I, in some other circumstances have been a saint? Would I in others have been a murderer? Probably in the right or the wrong circumstances we could all have taken either route. We are not as much the masters of our own behaviour as we like to imagine.

Other-centred work is powerful because it reveals the person behind the rupa. The rupa tangles with our psyche, conditioning our mind to terror or revenge. It ensnares us. It becomes the sign to which we look to find our nature. It holds us in its spell. The perpetrator holds the victim even from beyond the grave through the power which the victim continues to give him. This is the power of rupa.

Other-centred work diminishes the rupa quality. By seeing the reality of the human within the perpetrator, even if we only partly glimpse this reality, we cut the ties of rupa energy and attachment. We see, instead of a threatening presence which haunts us in our dreams and waking times, a man or woman, pathetic perhaps, maybe selfish or sad, but someone living in the mess of their own conditions. Seeing this person, we are liberated.

References and Background Reading for This Session

Harris J, 1999 *The Nurture Assumption: Why Children Turn Out the Way They Do* Free Press US

Krech G, 2001 *Naikan: gratitude, grace, and the Japanese art of self-reflection* Stonebridge Press US

McLeod, J 1998 *Narrative and Psychotherapy* Sage UK

Reynolds, D 1980 *The Quiet Therapies*, Univ. Hawaii Press, US

SESSION THIRTEEN

The Truth is Friendly

In this session we will explore:
- Re-visiting past places and people
- The positive effects of hearing the truth
- Reality checking
- Challenging the client to explore truth
- Truth in relationships
- Inhibitions to truth: judgement and fear

In my twenties I had a series of nightmares. These were vivid and disturbing. The content varied somewhat, but the location remained constant. I was always back in my old school. Although at the time when the nightmares occurred, I was an adult, in my dreams I would find myself wandering the corridors which were familiar from my school days, going from classroom to classroom, or sometimes through the dark basement where we stored our coats, or out into the bare yard behind the tall buildings. I don't recall any events that happened in these dreams; maybe I just wandered; but I do remember a feeling of dread and gloom which hovered over me in them. I guess in some way they reflected a residue, left over feelings from my adolescent struggles in a place where expectations were high, feelings intense, and I was often in trouble.

When I was about thirty, I was persuaded by a friend to revisit the school. There was a reunion of old girls and she wanted to attend and was keen that I join her. With a mix of fascination and resistance I agreed to go. Despite my misgivings, the idea excited me. We met outside the school gates at the end of the street so that we could go into the building together. I had my three small children with me, perhaps for support, perhaps out of pride, for most of my friends had yet to have families, or perhaps just out of practicality as there would be a crèche organised by sixth-formers.

Walking into the old school hall was a strange experience. The room was so familiar. It had dark wood panels and a balustraded gallery, a huge arched window at one end, and beneath it a small stage made of large wooden blocks. There was a grand piano on the stage and reproductions of paintings on the walls. I knew the details well: the deeply incised grain of the wooden rail upstairs, the smell of warm dust settled on the cast iron radiators, the clock with the school motto below it. All these seemed carved into my being, as much a part of me as my fingernails or hair.

Yet now, as I stood in the room, I saw the place in a different way. Light flooded in through the high window, catching the green cloth below the clock. The wooden floor was newly varnished, and at one end a buffet had been spread out for us on a long table with a white cloth. A clamour of people, some of whom I recognised as former classmates or as staff, milled together, chatting happily whilst balancing wine glasses and plates in their hands.

Joining the crowd, I soon found myself caught up in conversations, discovering who had done what in the twelve years since we had left. Which girls were married with children, and which were making their way in careers? Which members of staff were still teaching at the school, and who had retired or moved on?

The distinction between girls and teachers no longer created a great divide, and it now became apparent that the younger teachers had actually not been many years older than we were. They too were still young women, having babies and juggling work with family commitments.

Even now, though, I felt a little strange re-entering the school which had held so many mixed emotions for me. The atmosphere was warm, the faces familiar, and yet I still felt haunted by memories and the dreams.

Then I met my old art teacher.

"Oh, you were the naughty one!" She greeted me with a jaunty humour, then thinking better of it, apologised, "I'm sorry, I've had too much of this." She waved her wine glass awkwardly and looked sheepish.

I felt a rush of affection for her. Her tipsy comment seemed to cut through all the polite conversation and spoke of something real. I was grateful. Later, as I left the gathering, her comment stayed with me, a breath of fresh air, which swept away the dusty memories.

I did not dream about my school again.

After that meeting, I gradually began to remember other things about my school days: the kindness and support of some of the teachers, the excitement I had felt when encountering new ideas, the imaginative freedom of lessons in art, drama and dance, the play times spent in the wonderful open space which the school grounds provided with their trees and grassy banks. Gradually I began to appreciate what this place had given me.

So, memory changes with insight. A different perspective leads us to recall different details. A new present creates a different past. The selectivity of the self-story ensures that only part of our history is held up to scrutiny and much is buried. So too, the truth, when spoken directly, even if it is uncomfortable, can often liberate. It cuts across the shadows of expectation.

The experience was complex and perplexing. Sometimes the clouds of memory can be so dense that it is hard to see through them to the ordinariness of people: a group of women, whose lives had converged for a while, reminiscing. The two images superimpose. Dark and light jostled for supremacy, memories of childhood struggles with authority, juxtaposed with this polite gathering of educated adults. There was not just one truth.

My art teacher's comment brought clarity. Its down to earth honesty and humour was both honest and charming; light-hearted, and yet honouring that, indeed, I had had a bit of a reputation. My impression of being different, of having had a less smooth transit through the system than my peers, was confirmed. Thank goodness! The comment changed more for me than years of therapy might. It confirmed a truth I had believed, but had only circumstantial evidence for, giving it external substance. It allowed it to be real.

And so the facts are friendly. Half remembered incidents can haunt us for years, whilst discovering the truth, even when it is painful, can be easier to deal with than living with uncertainty. My own story is just a small example, a minor incident compared with many of the stories which I hear from other people, but it illustrates the way that external confirmation can quell the emotion which a sea of uncertain memories can generate, just as turning on the light dispels night time horrors. It illustrates how straightforward honesty is often the most healing thing that we can offer. Bluntness may be more caring than polite evasiveness.

EXERCISE ONE: TRUTH AS LIBERATION

Think of an example from your own life of hearing the truth from someone about something which troubled you brought liberation.

What do you think made the difference?

The Voice of Reality

Returning to places, objects and people of the past can touch us profoundly. It is interesting that, in the case of my school reunion, the experience of going back to a place I had known so well not only affected my feeling, but also changed something beneath the surface in my psyche. The dreams stopped. Beyond my conscious awareness, something in the construction of my personal world was changed. A seed was discharged and a pattern of perception and reaction disrupted. Reality broke in and swept the images which had haunted me away.

In part, I think the change was attributable to the meeting with my old art teacher. Her remark was one factor. She spoke the truth and this changed my perception of the whole experience. Voicing the part of the story which other people in the room for one reason or another were not expressing, she cut through some of the surface gloss of social niceties. Without this blunder, the ordinary politeness of the meeting might have prevented me from really engaging with the others there. Such 'niceness' leaves a feeling of dissatisfaction like that which comes from dining on chocolate cake and candyfloss; a slightly nauseous feeling of having indulged in something that was pleasant enough, but which lacked the substance to sustain. Instead, the down to earth honesty grounded the experience.

I think primarily it was the human connection which changed things. I might have been the naughty schoolgirl once, but there was an implication of conspiracy and naughtiness in the tipsiness and the warm, good humoured greeting which my former teacher gave me. My heart went out to her, person to person. I appreciated her sense of fun and the way that she was, somewhat subversively, getting through a Saturday gathering at the school on wine provided by the old girls.

Besides these human factors, the place also impacted on me. Revisiting places from the past, we are challenged to revisit our memories. The old haunts become barometers of our changing perceptions. The *me* who walked into the school hall on the day of the reunion was not the same person as the *me* who had left it twelve years earlier. She saw the furnishings and structures through different eyes. Memories were superseded by fresh encounters. The real sun shone through the window. Outside a different life was unfolding, and that provided a safer vantage point from which to view the scene.

Just as it is hard for the affronted child to hang onto anger when the parent lovingly embraces him, laughing and stroking his heated head, so too our minds can only cling for so long to out of date impressions when the force of evidence tells us otherwise.

In the therapy room, which is, after all, a cut off bubble of experience, it is easy to construct a nightmare, but such a construction may be fabrication based on scant evidence. The client can build a castle of memories on foundations which are at very least uncertain. The therapist listens sympathetically and attentively, providing a context in which the truth can remain unquestioned. During the hour, the client's story becomes more concretised. He builds his case so that it becomes water-tight. Whether a prosecution or defence, he summons evidence and weaves together ideas which, as they grow, take on a life of their own. The therapist has no reason to doubt, and in any case, is well schooled in giving full credence to the client's case. Receiving the story empathically she seems to offer approval. So, through reiteration, a story is created. But is it true?

I am sure most of us have had the experience of talking with someone intensely about a personal issue. Perhaps it has been in a counselling session, or perhaps we have been talking with a sympathetic friend. As we have continued to explain the situation, clarity has seemed to dawn. We reach a point of certainty and see what we need to do to resolve the situation, to make decisions. We frame words to say to others who are not present. Such times can feel uplifting in their simplicity. 'Now I've got it! I know what to do.' But then, strangely, walking out of the room into the fresh air and the daylight, a new sort of clarity arises. Nothing has changed. The insights were simply moonshine and creative imaginings. Faced with reality, they no longer seem to ring true.

We can create stories, and our clients, without the checks offered by the day to day reality of their lives and relationships present, can experience imaginative processes running riot. Life hovers in suspended animation, and nothing is real.

Possibilities seem to open up, but they are often fatuous and ungrounded.

In this way, the self-story grows. The time spent in the therapy room is a blank screen onto which our mind-structures can become projected. Memories are used as illustrations for personal theories and scripts, and in the process are adapted. The power of projection is the grist of a more analytic therapeutic approach. Indeed, if one's interest is in wandering the fascinating avenues of mental formations, this is rich territory. But do the stories hold up to examination? Are they true? There is a danger that in exploring what are effectively speculations and inventions in therapy, we simply create more layers of delusion upon those which are already there. The self is created by the endless turning of a wheel of expectation and response. Conditioned mind creates conditioned worlds, which in turn condition more ruts within the psyche; more mental formations.

Thankfully, reality has a way of surfacing. The world of others breaks in and disturbs our complacent perambulations. We do not even need to seek reality out, though perhaps we have a drive to do so[154]. By being alive, we inevitably have experiences which challenge and disturb us. Although we tend to distort them with our self-invested interests, our perceptions nevertheless are based, not just on some internal process, but also on the real objects which we encounter. Reality is real, and sometimes it doesn't let us get away with claptrap.

EXERCISE TWO: FABRICATIONS AND REALITY

Have you ever had the experience of discussing something in therapy, supervision, or with a friend and feeling convinced of a truth, only to find that once you left that discussion, you saw things differently?

Counselling exercise: If you have an opportunity, practice counselling in triads. Afterwards in your discussion of the piece of work look at whether, and to what degree, you moved into consensus with your client. If so, was this consensus useful, or might it have been based on false foundations?

What purpose do you think it served in terms of:

- The client's agenda
- The counselling relationship
- The counsellor's agenda
- The interests of third parties

But Is It True?

Mary talks to her therapist about Tony. Tony comes home from work and flops in front of the television, flipping channels and ignoring her. This has happened repeatedly, and Mary is fed up with his attitude. She cooks his meals and he just eats them without speaking to her, slouched on the settee, watching football. Afterwards he leaves his plates on the floor beside him for her to clear up.

Mary has complained about Tony on a number of occasions. The story is much the same each time. She feels frustrated and angry, but every time she tries to talk to him, he doesn't seem interested.

"But is this true?" her therapist asks.

Mary is taken aback. It is not her therapist's role to question the truth of what she is saying. Surely, she is paying her therapist to be on her side. She feels affronted. The woman is out of order, or is she?

"Is it true?" her therapist repeats.

EXERCISE THREE: IS IT TRUE?

What do you think of Mary's therapist's intervention?

Is it the therapist's role to be 'on the client's side'? If you think the answer is yes, what do you understand by this?

Might you make an intervention like this therapist did? If so, when might you do so?

Mary pauses. She thinks. Is Tony interested in her? Is she always the one who is hard done by? Is it true?

"I suppose it depends what you mean by it," she says reluctantly.

Her therapist is interested. There is an opening in Mary's story about Tony. Perhaps there will be room to explore new dimensions of the relationship.

"So how are things between you and Tony?"

Mary hesitates, clearly thinking about this. "Well he's pretty boring to be with."

"But you are staying with him despite all these problems. Some people might think that was a sign that things can't be that bad," she presses.

Here Mary's therapist is using the 'person in the street' response. She is aware that she has already challenged Mary, and that this has probably been effective, so she does not want to destroy the therapeutic alliance by putting too much pressure onto Mary or to leave her feeling unsupported.

"It would be difficult to leave him. I've nowhere else to go."

There is a pause.

"Really?"

Mary's therapist has a twinkle in her eye as she says this.

Although this remark could be perceived as very challenging, the therapist's humour softens it. It adds a slightly conspiratorial edge to the interaction. The tone in which the remark is made implies that the therapist knows that Mary has more personal resources than she is letting on, that she is quite capable of finding herself a new place to live. By pulling her leg a little, the therapist offers Mary a friendly nudge, preventing her from falling into a 'pathetic little woman' script which she, and Mary, both know that Mary is capable of falling into.

"OK," Mary acknowledges the truth. She was not being quite straight in her earlier comment. It is not the lack of alternatives which keeps her with Tony.

"I do love him. Things used to be good between us. I just don't know what has got into him at present."

"Things have changed." The therapist accepts the truth of this remark. She does not yet accept that this is Tony's fault.

"I wish he'd just talk about it."

"And if he did, what do you think he would say?"

Mary's therapist now invites her to look at Tony's perspective. Her question is an invitation to role reverse with Tony, though she does not go so far as to invite an actual switch of positions.

"He'd say it's all my fault." Mary laughs.

This response reveals that Mary knows that the situation is actually more complex than she has been suggesting so far.

"Uhuh?" her therapist smiles.

Now they have reached a point of greater honesty, they can start to explore what might actually be going on in the relationship.

EXERCISE FOUR: EXPLORING THE TRUTH

Now that Mary is beginning to talk about her relationship with Tony in a more objective way, how might you facilitate the process?

What concerns would be uppermost in your mind?

Are there methods which you might use to help the exploration if Mary were open to them?

Exploring Realities in Relationships

Having established a more robust basis for looking at the relationship, Mary and her therapist can now look in a more sober way at what might be going on between Mary and Tony. In this matter, the therapist is open-minded. She does not know the truth, but she does see the contradictory evidence. On the one hand, Mary complains about Tony's behaviour and paints a picture of life together as completely unfulfilling. Taken at face value, it is hard to see why she would remain in the relationship. On the other hand, Mary does stay in the relationship and continues to look after Tony, despite having few practical ties to him.

There might be many different explanations for such an anomaly. Mary might actually be getting more from the relationship with Tony than she is saying. She may have practical reasons which have not yet become apparent for staying. There may be some unspoken bargain between them. Perhaps he is better salaried and pays the bulk of the bills. It may be that the reasons for staying are in Mary's psychological constellation. Perhaps her identity is somehow supported by seeing herself as the victim or the martyr. It might also be that she is not disclosing, and probably not even aware of, the ways in which she treats him badly, and the ways that these behaviours contribute to the dynamic between them.

Such possibilities could be the subject of speculation and discussion. It may be that in exploring the relationship more honestly, Mary will start to be aware of other factors which she has not yet spoken of. In all probability, before the next session Mary will observe things which happen between Tony and her more closely, or may even talk to Tony about his feelings about their interactions.

Such observation will give Mary and her therapist evidence about the relationship. Working with a brief element of role reversal has already proved useful and brought some clarification. A more focused role-reversal exercise might yield more. On the other hand, there is always a danger that the exploration in the therapy sessions will focus the problem on Tony. This could be erroneous. Having established that there are two points of view, other strategies may be more helpful. We have already looked at many practical methods in this book which could be applied to couples work, but let us look at a few examples of how some of these techniques can be adapted so as to preserve balance in the exploration:

Creating a balance sheet

When a relationship is not working well, it is frequently because one or both partners feels that the balance of what is being put in and what is being taken out is skewed in the other's favour. This may be due to differential valuing of various aspects of each person's behaviour. One partner may put a high premium on the material input which they make to the partnership, for example, while the other values spending time together more than such practicalities and would prefer their partner work fewer hours. In such a case the 'hard working' partner may feel that he or she is contributing to the relationship by working overtime whilst the other partner may see the same behaviour as being selfishly motivated.

Taking a systematic look at the checks and balances in a relationship, as well as at how these are assessed by each partner, can help to bring some facts into the discussion, and it can also reveal what biases each partner has in prioritising their own contribution and that of their partner. It provides a way of looking more objectively at data, although of course, data is itself highly influenced by subjective forces.

A balance sheet could be drawn up by one person in a therapy session, or the exercise could be done by both partners, assuming both are interested in doing so, in between sessions. Such methods are useful at two levels. Firstly they give hard data which can then be discussed, but secondly they becomes a focus for a process which itself reveals the client's patterns of thinking. In facilitating them, the therapist needs regard for both processes. Of course, if the exercise is done at home, it also creates a focus for the couple to work together on their relationship.

EXERCISE FIVE: CREATING A BALANCE SHEET

Create a balance sheet for your own relationship. If you do not have a partner, try doing it with a friend or work colleague.

Use a large sheet of paper and divide it into two columns, one for each person in the relationship. Now try to fill in the columns as honestly as you can with information in the following categories:
• Practical things you do or contribute
• Emotional support you give

- Practical things you ask for or take
- Emotional things you ask for or take
- Other pressures

The last category can include any factors which influence your ability to give to the relationship, so might include work pressures, children, or other family duties.

When you have finished filling in the balance sheet, look at what it seems to say about the way you see your relationship. Do you think it is fair? What would your partner write in the columns? What would he/she say if you showed him/her the sheet you have drawn up? (You could each do this exercise and compare notes)

Might this exercise be useful to any of your clients?

Naikan reflection

The Naikan questions which were explained in the previous session can be used by one or both members of a couple to explore their relationship[155]. They might be applied to the whole duration of the relationship or to a specific period of time. Often the latter is more helpful, since it requires the people involved to be very specific and concrete in their reflections. Thus the client might ask: What has my partner done for me in the last week? What have I done in return? What trouble has my presence caused for him or her during that time?

On the other hand, it can also be good to be reminded of how things were in the relationship in its early, 'honeymoon' phase when each partner was being more caring towards the other. Sometimes exploring these early times can reveal ways in which the couple have begun to do less for each other and to take each other for granted.

To use such questions requires a pre-existing level of respect for the partner. If done with good intent, they can help a person to develop more appreciation for the contribution which the other person makes to the relationship.

Looking at a specific incident in detail

A sober investigation of facts can be helpful, and revealing, when something seems to have gone wrong in an interaction. Where there has been a conflict or misunderstanding, looking at what factors led up to the incident from different perspectives, and at the preconceptions which each party might have brought to it, can sometimes help to make sense of what has gone amiss.

One approach to such an exploration might involve drawing the incident and the events leading up to it as a flow chart or other diagrammatic representation. Where there are different perspectives on what happened, this might be shown by including each person's path on the same diagram, or by creating two versions, one to show each point of view. Investigating such detail helps because it brings clarity where there may have been assumptions. It also helps to move a situation on because it gives extra weight to the will which the person has to sort the problem out. Trying to make sense of the factors in a conflict, where the enquiry is undertaken in good spirit, demonstrates a willingness to take responsibility on one's own part, rather than just to look for someone who will commiserate about it. It shows that the relationship is being taken seriously.

Sculpting histories

Sometimes the difficulties in a relationship come out of differences of expectation, and often these have grown from previous experiences of relationship. Exploring both people's histories in as dispassionate way as possible can be revealing. One method which could be employed for doing this is sculpting. We saw in session six how sculpting techniques provide methods which are both containing and illuminating. They can be used to look at patterns in groups and relationships between people. Thus, for example, in exploring an intimate relationship, a person might create three sculpts, one representing his own family of origin, one his partner's family, and one showing their current relationship. This method might reveal striking similarities between the relationships involved, or may show up reasons for differences of expectation between the partners.

Sculpting methods can be used in other ways to explore relationships. They might be used to look at the ideal families to which each partner aspires. They could be used to represent the wider circle of friends and relatives and show each partner's support system. A series of sculpts could show the development of the relationship over time, including the arrival of children, or changes in living situations.

Honesty in the Client-Therapist Relationship

The role of honesty in the therapist-client relationship is something which Carl Rogers wrote about. He stressed the need for *congruence* as a core condition for therapeutic growth. Congruence means being authentic and not just playing a role or trying to be the 'good therapist'. It may also mean being explicitly open about one's reactions and sharing feeling responses as they relate to the substance of the therapy session. Congruence does not mean sharing personal material which has to do with the therapist's personal life outside the therapy relationship, except in as much as, in extreme examples, it might cause the therapist to act in ways that could be puzzling to the client.

For example if the therapist is suddenly touched by emotion connected with a recent bereavement, there might be reason to tell the client briefly that this is the case, since not to do so could cause the client to wonder if he has upset her. The usual guidelines offered by professional bodies would be that the therapist should a) tell the client in a factual way and not dwell on the matter, but return attention to the client's situation as quickly as possible, b) deal with the feelings that have arisen in such a situation outside the client-therapist setting, in her own therapy or supervision and c) if the feelings are likely to get sparked off frequently, consider taking time out of working as a counsellor, managing this process of withdrawing from work in consultation with her supervisor.

Such guidelines seem common sense, and are probably appropriate to most situations, though very occasionally there may be value in the therapist sharing personal material in a little more depth, since this may offer an opportunity for the client to relate in a more 'real' way. In such rare instances, however, it is still essential that the therapist holds the client's interests paramount and does not get drawn into being the client herself.

Mostly, congruence is expressed in a therapy session through the 'here and now' relationship between therapist and client. The degree of 'realness' in this relationship can be a significant part of the therapeutic process, not just because it allows the client to experience the therapist's response to him as genuinely caring, as opposed to the therapist 'just doing her job', but more importantly because it gives the client an experience of being in a real relationship. The therapist is less likely to remain a screen for projections, but rather is experienced as a human being; as a real other. In a limited way the client will learn to feel empathy for the therapist, though of course, as has already been emphasised, the therapist needs to be wary of allowing this to encourage inappropriate personal disclosure.

If the therapist is congruently present, and is actively so, she offers a relationship which is a challenge to the client's self-world. As we have seen, according to Kohut's thinking, it is the small failures of empathy which, against the background of a perceived good will, bring about therapeutic change. These demonstrations of the therapist's presence as a real, fallible person provide the client with evidence of the real effects of his words and behaviour. They also reveal the fact that, as a person who exists and has her own responses and agendas, the therapist is not under his control. His isolation, and also his grandiosity, are both challenged by this knowledge.

Realness in the therapy relationship can be demonstrated not just in positive responses, but also through challenging and even negative ones. Whilst it is hardly ever helpful for a therapist to be volubly angry with a client, occasional expressions of frustration or shock, where they are genuine and offered against a back-drop of a good empathic relationship, may break through the client's assumptions about the therapist and demonstrate her separateness.

When feelings of this kind arise, however, there is a strong likelihood that they come from a counter-transference type reaction. It is likely that the therapist is being drawn into a counter-part role which has been invited by the client's habitual script. In this case, the pros and cons of expressing the feeling, as opposed to commenting upon it, or simply guarding the information, is a therapeutic decision. It is worth taking such interpersonal process to supervision if it occurs repeatedly, but in single instances, the therapist may need to decide then and there whether to react or to suppress the response which wells up in her. Should she express a feeling reaction, that response should itself be open to discussion both with the client within the session and later with her supervisor.

Whilst some dynamics expressed in the therapy session echo relationships from outside the therapy setting, conversely, some things which the client says about his life outside the therapy may contain within them indirect messages to the therapist. If the therapist can spot such occasions, a gentle challenge to such remarks may bring about a more direct and honest encounter. This requires both vigilance and a willingness to accept criticism on the part of the therapist. A particular example of this is given by Irvin Yalom in his excellent book, *The Gift of Therapy*[156]. Yalom suggests that if a client admits to having told lies on one area of his life, this provides a particular opportunity for challenge.

I find such an admission an excellent opportunity to inquire about what lies they have told me during the course of therapy. There is always some concealment, some information withheld because of shame, because of some particular way they want me to regard them. A discussion of such concealments almost invariably provokes a fruitful discussion in therapy...[157]

Registers of Truth

Whilst many of us today would hold an ideal of achieving honesty and openness in relationships, in practice, living a completely honest and open life is neither possible, nor, probably, desirable. There are times when being too 'up front' simply becomes insensitive. Some things are better left unsaid altogether. Sometimes the decision about what to say comes down to choice. One thing is focused upon and another left unspoken. Sometimes privacy needs to be respected, and sometimes people do not want to know uncomfortable facts.

For example, whilst the trend toward openness in the previously closed medical profession is generally a good thing, for some elderly people, a diagnosis of cancer or some other terminal illness may be something which they would prefer glossed over with comforting niceties. It can be quite distressing to see a young doctor sitting beside a frightened and confused elderly person, insisting on telling them about the multiple risks of the treatment which they are about to undergo and trying to negotiate with them which option they would prefer. Sometimes it can even hasten the person's death. Some people prefer their doctor to take control. They do not want to be told everything.

In part, the difficulty arises from attempts to impose a single value of honesty and openness without taking into account cultural differences between diverse groups of people. Different cultures have different attitudes to self-revelation, but also different ways of saying the same thing. They may have their own language for conveying bad news or displeasure, which will be understood by others brought up in the same system. In a culture that is very reserved, for example, much can be said in few words, or even simply with a raised eyebrow. Open discussion of sensitive topics is either viewed as uncouth or distressing. I knew just what my grandmother meant when, as a teenager, I showed her a new dress which I had just bought, and she responded, "Oh, do you like it?" Louder cultures often miss such subtle cues, however. They are used to more expansive expressions of feeling and may have fewer taboos.

In Britain, we have moved from the rather reserved culture of the mid-twentieth century, to a more open, 'let it all hang out' culture in the late twentieth and early twenty first centuries. Virginia Nicholson's book *Singled Out*[158] describes the lives of women who had been left single or widowed as a result of the huge number of deaths of young men of their generation in the First World War. In this book she describes an exchange between a woman, Gertrude, and the mother of the man whom she had loved many years earlier, and who had been killed in action. The exchange is poignant for the depth of feelings which must have been hidden behind it. These feelings are not openly spoken of, but, rather, are alluded to in an understated way. In the exchange we see both a suppression of overt feelings and an acknowledgment of the unspoken bond of grief.

Mrs McFarland was next to speak, 'You loved him.'

It was a statement, not a question. But this time it needed a reply... *'He was loved by everyone who knew him,' she said.*

The generalisation, with its tacit confession would suffice. There was nothing to be gained by self-indulgent histrionics. He was dead, and she had her life to get on with.[159]

For many therapists in the West, such a person might be viewed as repressed and needing to learn to be more expressive, and yet Gertrude was a successful academic. She had put her grief behind her and indeed made something of herself. Nor was she as emotionally illiterate as she might seem. She left behind a personal memoir for her friends, which expressed in a private way the grief which she had felt all her life, and which had perhaps inspired her work and fulfilment. Her avoidance of a public declaration of her grief came more from propriety than emotional illiteracy.

We should be careful in expecting our clients to speak our language. This means being sensitive to the ways in which, for some people, difficult emotions can be expressed with the lightest of phraseology. Such expressions may involve a depth of feeling which can be masked by more brazen expression.

EXERCISE SIX: LANGUAGE AND TRUTH

Think about different people whom you know, and particularly older people.

How might such a person talk about a bereavement? If they went to speak with a professional, and that person were pushing them to talk about their feelings, how might they react?

If you were counselling someone who was reserved in the way that they expressed themselves, how might you help them?

Inhibitions to Truth

Many factors may inhibit a client's expression of the truth. In the remainder of this session, we will look specifically at two of them. These are the expectation that the person will be judged and the presence of high levels of fear or distress

Expectation of judgement

We live in a society in which there is a great deal of judgement. When we read the newspapers or watch television, talk to people at the bus stop or in shops, or enjoy conversation in our families, we are likely to hear criticism voiced. People criticise others in order to assert a viewpoint or to coerce them into changing. They criticise in order to establish their own position and create a sense of their individuality. They form alliances and friendships on the basis of being different from others and judging them. At the same time many people suffer legacies of anxiety, and lack confidence as a result of feeling criticised and judged by others. They may limit their activities or hide their real feelings through fear of such responses.

Judgement is part of a way of thought which predominates in the West. To an extent, it probably grows out of the Western religious paradigm. This paradigm is one in which a single divine authority is central. Although modern Christianity is complex and diverse, and often at pains to move beyond its earlier emphasis on divine judgement, the legacy of a Judeo-Christian belief system which centred on God's laws and an after-death division of the good and the bad, the saints and the sinners, the believers and the infidel, has been to establish ideas of judgement as a central organising principle in the Western psyche. Even for those with no religious leanings, judgement-based thinking is still a central force in creating a predominating mentality. Indeed, it is often among those who count themselves as non-religious, who have not been exposed to modern theological debate that such a paradigm is strongest. Ideas of justice and human rights are, for example, strongly represented in the Western socio-political arena.

The judgement-focused mentality is founded on principles which include presumption that:

- It is possible to distinguish right and wrong
- Those doing wrong are to be condemned
- Punishment should follow
- Getting found out is inviting condemnation

Such ideas also lead to an assumption that justice and forgiveness are fundamental human values, that humans are given responsibility for the care of all forms of life on the planet, and that a divine hierarchy overlies human decision making. Whilst this paradigm has positive aspects, people influenced by its more negative manifestations tend, on the one hand, to be wary of being caught out in the wrong, and on the other hand, to be critical of others. The Western preoccupation with judgement and guilt conditions many psychological manoeuvres, and many of the 'games'[160] which people get into. It can lead to evasiveness and a sort of endemic dishonesty which is constantly trying to adjust reality so that we do not appear in a bad light.

The therapy profession espouses non-judgementalism, but, operating in a cultural paradigm which is so strongly weighted with expectations of criticism and negative assumption, it struggles to find real neutrality. The desire to avoid judgement is at odds with the, often unconscious, underlying paradigm of judgementalism. Together they create an anomaly which the therapist has to solve. Despite wishing to be honest and non-judgemental, the ambient culture of judgement and criticism has been internalised to a greater or lesser degree by both therapist and client.

One the solution to this anomaly which is prevalent in the profession is to assert positive values over negative ones by attempting to counter the prevailing tendency to judgement with positive affirmations and reframing. Popular therapy culture has placed a great deal of emphasis on self-actualisation, personal improvement, affirmation, and other concepts which pay tribute to the myth of human perfectability.

As I have already described in my books, *The Other Buddhism*[161] and *Guilt*[162] this inflated striving for perfection found in the modern Western world is problematic in a number of ways. Firstly it sets up an ideal of personal sufficiency, and denies our dependent nature. Secondly, it leads us to 'play up' ways in which we are successful and hide ways in which we fail. Thirdly, it leaves us feeling failures for not having achieved the level of self-improvement which society idealises and, fourthly, it leads us to feel fraudulent, since we know, despite the reassurances of others, that in general we are not perfect and, in specifics, we have distorted the truth to show the world our 'best face'.

Acceptance of our ordinary fallibility[163] is both a challenge and a relief. In therapeutic terms it can be immensely healing. If we can recognise that it is in the nature of things that we make mistakes, and that we are even sometimes intentionally nasty, we will be able to look far more honestly at our situation. For the therapist, adopting a position which accepts the ordinariness of people and their bad as well as good intentions is essential if one is going to undertake the sort of work which is being described in this book.

Fear or distress

The creation of the identity and the self-world is, as we have seen, a process which is basically defensive. It is a response to our fear of life's uncertainty and the pain which comes from engaging with, and loving, others. As soon as we commit emotional energy to relationships, we place ourselves in a vulnerable position, for every relationship will inevitably eventually involve loss. This is true whether the relationship is a friendship, a marriage or a therapy relationship.

The loss that we will experience is, in turn, proportional. The greater the commitment we make, the deeper the pain of the potential loss of that relationship will be. For this reason we hide behind walls of partial commitment. We hold others at a distance, and we try to mediate their love through filters of conditioned thinking. We are afraid to risk wholehearted loving.

Therapy offers lessons in limited, but open, communication. In it the client and therapist may try to relate with fewer restrictions, knowing that the circumstances are bounded by the time allocation and especially by professional behavioural codes. For these reasons, the level of honesty which a therapist and client achieve are not just valuable in achieving insight, they are also valuable in helping to restore the client's faith that it is worth taking the risk or relating.

The ending of therapy is an experience of loss. In some cases it has only limited significance in itself, but for some clients, reaching an ending with honesty and facing the feelings that surface at that time can be an immensely important experience, providing evidence that it is possible to really encounter another person and then to part without one's world collapsing. In such situations, discussion of the impending separation, and of the felt reactions to it, can be helpful and healing, giving language to previously taboo areas of experience and maintaining the process of honest encounter right up to the end itself.

References and Background Reading for This Session

Brazier C 2009 *Guilt* O-Books UK

Brazier D 2007 *Who Loves Dies Well* O-Books UK

Worden, W 1983 *Grief Counselling and Grief Therapy: A Handbook for the Mental Health Professional* Tavistock Press, UK

Yalom, I 2001 *The Gift of Therapy* Piatkus UK

SESSION FOURTEEN

Living in the Real World

In this session we will:
- Reflect on the presence of others as therapeutic conditions
- See the effects of places as other phenomena
- Explore wilderness experience as an encounter with other
- Look at the impact of body changes on the person
- Explore ways of seeing life as a therapeutic experience
- Recognise the way that the other arrives in people's lives of its own volition

Tonight as I finished writing, my head was full of tangled words and ideas. So much so, I wondered how I would find it within myself to go to sleep. It was late. I had, as so often is the case, been writing into the night. Everything around the house was quiet. Everyone else was in bed. Only my thoughts churned on; so much still to include, so many questions. Had I covered enough? Had my explanations been clear – or simply pedantic? Was it too longwinded? Or were essential links missing? Would I have the manuscript edited in time for my imagined deadline? How could I hope to hold so many thoughts?

Inside the kitchen, the woodstove still burned, its last embers glowing, throwing out its comforting sleepy warmth. The smell of Susthama's baking filled the air, and there was a slight steaminess from the airing washing overhead, and the occasional hum of the refrigerator as its motor switched on and off.

As I stepped out of the kitchen door to go to my room, I was suddenly in another world.

Outside the air was sharp. A quarter moon hung in the sky over the barn, throwing a pale light between the clouds. Shrubs in the garden lurked; heavy, brooding shapes, merging into the indistinguishable darkness of the soil. Across the yard, the great bulk of the temple stood out against the night sky, hunched on its low stone walls, its gabled roof catching the glint of reflected light on its wet tiles. The night called me.

Instead of going to bed, I walked across the grass, which was already soaked with heavy dew, towards the meditation hall. It was dark and deserted.

I fumbled in the darkness on the edge of the shrine to find the box of matches. I opened it. Then, striking a match, which spluttered damply, managed to light the three nightlights placed before the Buddha. Then I sat.

It was actually not cold. The clearness of the air cut through my thoughts, and, despite having no coat on, I remained there for perhaps ten minutes, enjoying the quiet of the space, the old stones, barely visible in faltering light of the three candle flames, and the rafters and tiles above my head.

I breathed, enjoying the peace that seeped into my being from the place.

The Therapeutic Other

I reflect on the process which I have just gone through. So far in this book, we have looked at the ways in which the mind is conditioned and the way in which this conditioning affects our experience of the world. We have looked at our relationship with the world, and how we are changed by our encounters with the people and objects which we are in contact with. We have considered the practice of therapy itself, and what might make it more or less successful. All this is useful, and as a counsellor or therapist one needs to be able to think intelligently and reflect on one's experience and absorb the learning from it.

But becoming a therapist is not really such a rational process. To learn to be with another person in a way that will change their life is not a matter which any book or training course can define. It is about our hearts and not our heads; about how we grow and who we are, not what we have learned from books. The training of therapists can only be a rough approximation. Time and experience are the real teachers. We are but fellow travellers[164], other poor examples of human nature, doing our best to be honest in the face of confusion.

The process of therapy is itself unpredictable. We can measure outcomes, formulate treatment programmes, and monitor results. We can investigate the methods which seem to work and we can share experience with the masters. All these give us some indicators and provide rough and ready guidance. They are probably the best we have, if we want to know what may work.

But at the end of the day, for all my years of therapy and spiritual practice, my mind is still too busy to go to sleep. And still it is a chance occurrence, the sight of the moon and the stillness of an autumn night, which draws me out into the darkness, long after I should be in my bed. And then, without intention, the place where I have so often found that special calm welcomes me in.

I can take no credit. The other has found me, and, from the infinite possibilities which the world could offer, has spoken to my heart.

So here perhaps we find the true nature of other-centred therapy: the power of the other to reach us. We cannot control the conditions life offers, but we can maybe become braver in letting them in. Rogers' potatoes grew towards the light despite their poor situation[165]. Even in the darkest corner of the cellar, they found enough support to grow. Perhaps what we give our clients, more than anything else, is the confidence to walk with us where the light is shining.

EXERCISE ONE: OTHER THINGS, OTHER TEACHERS

Think back over the last week and identify times when you have had a surprising encounter or chance experience which has changed your mood entirely.

Notice what happened, what triggered the change and whether the change was lasting. Was the experience accompanied by insight at the time or since?

Places as Conditions

Conditions change our mental states. In this book we have explored the impact of relationships with objects, both other people, and environmental, on our feelings and behaviour. Places offer powerful conditions. They can be redolent with memories, associations and personal significances. When we think about the different places which we have visited over a period of time, or the chance encounters with the natural world, or the created environment which we have had, we start to see how powerful an influence these outside forces have upon our mentality. Looking at such experiences, we see how our moods and our patterns of thinking can be affected by what seem to be the irrelevant details of everyday situations.

In the last session, for example, I described my experience of returning to my old school. For most people re-visiting a place with this kind of past association kindles many memories and these lead to reactions. It can be a highly emotive experience. A town where we have lived, a house, a workplace; each has its indefinable qualities, each has its associations.

In part, of course, such associations are our own, constructed from all those mental processes which we have been exploring, but this is only half the story. The place itself exists in its own nature. It exerts its particular influence which has its own character. An open moor, a town park, a library, a doctor's waiting room; what do these spaces bring of their own and what do we superimpose through expectation? It is impossible to define where one begins and the other ends.

What we can observe is that the places in which people live are highly influential on their mental states. Whether city or rural landscapes, flatlands or hills, hot Mediterranean sunshine or dark Northern winters, in common place conversation, we are well aware of the way that humans are shaped by their environments. Each individual adds his own stamp to the situation, and this is understandable. Each of us has peculiarities in the conditions which we experience, but broad generalisations still hold. We are all the products of our circumstances.

This being so, how much should we, as therapists, enquire into the landscape of a person's life? Should we, instead of spending hours behind closed doors discussing the minutiae of people's thoughts, try to improve the conditions of their lives, and not distract ourselves from the real task by trying to improve their minds? Should we be investing our energies in housing improvement schemes and community arts? How much are we rooted in those ideas of individual autonomy which are simply part of the grandiosity of human thinking? Should we not be looking to the wider group, the city and the nation? Or should our concern be with planetary problems and the threats to life which make our future as a profession, and as part of the human race, perilous?

Clearly there is space for balance. Our task as therapists addresses that part of the story located in the person, and, as we have seen, there is plenty to be done. But let us not lose sight of the bigger picture, of people within their landscape, small players in a bigger game.

EXERCISE TWO: PLACES AND CONDITIONS

Take two large sheets of paper and some coloured chalks or paints. Put the first sheet of paper in front of you. If you are in a group, someone may like to lead this exercise as a guided fantasy, but if you are on your own, you may simply like to read the instructions and then carry them out.

Think of a place out of doors that you know well, where you feel comfortable. Sit quietly and close your eyes. Imagine yourself sitting in that place. Spend time bringing the details of scene to mind.

Recall the natural features of your location. Be aware of the plants or animal life that might be around. Notice any human-made buildings or other features. Notice the quality of light and the sky, if you can see it. Notice the predominant colours. Notice the time of day and the weather. Sit with the image.

Now take the first sheet of paper and draw your impressions of the place. Make your drawing more about your sense of the atmosphere and qualities of the environment than about its physical appearance.

Now choose a second place, this time choose somewhere indoors. Repeat the exercise, once again paying attention to detail, this time of furnishings and colours, light levels and objects which are on view.

When you have finished both halves of the exercise, reflect

> upon the two drawings.
>
> How do these two places condition your mental state? What have they given to you? What can you learn from them?

Wilderness and Outdoor Approaches

Some therapeutic approaches, more than others, point towards a view of the person embedded in their environment. The use of wilderness experience[166] as a therapeutic tool fits well with an other-centred approach in this respect. Allowing the natural world to provide the challenges and the inspiration, the therapist may step back from proactive facilitation, and act instead as guide, facilitator, and companion whilst the natural world becomes the arena for reflective change. Not trying to be too interpretive or too active in directing the process, the therapist offers space, containment and accompaniment to the client.

About fifteen years ago I was co-leading a psychodrama group in the French Alps. Among the participants, one man, a wiry outdoor type, told us about his usual occupation which involved taking management trainees out into the mountains. He had noticed, he said, that on the mountainside nearby there was a fixed rope track-way running along the cliff face which was intended as a route for beginning mountaineers. He offered to hire equipment for us all and take us out. It was an easy route. It had taken him around half an hour to cover it. Would we like to go?

The group were keen to give it a try. I was rather less enthusiastic, being terrified of heights, but even so, a part of me was tempted by the challenge. Whatever my inclinations, as the group facilitator, I felt some duty to join in, and maybe also feared the loss of face in refusing. The expedition was agreed.

So it was that, on the last day of the course, harnessed up with hooks on loops of webbing to attach us to the rope course and prevent us falling too far should we miss our footing, we started out.

After walking to the base of the cliff, we stood together, looking up at the prospect of what was to come. Bare rock extended upwards, marked only by small ledges and crevices, and the occasional stunted tree. The task looked impossible. At the same time, there on the stone face was the start of the rope track; a metal ring, cemented into the rock, with a plastic covered cable attached to it. Here we were to hook our harnesses onto the line and begin. Despite the impulse to give up and go back to our centre, there felt no real option but to go on.

The route began with an initial climb of perhaps ten feet, then gradually, edging along narrow ledges, over crevices, up scree slope scrambles, as ground dropped away beneath us, our ascent created a height of several hundred feet between us and the trees below. We progressed slowly along the rock face, one by one, sometimes finding our own footholds, but other times helped by our guide. Occasionally one of us would feel panic rising in us and freeze, and there were times when each of us felt we could not go on, yet knew that, having now embarked on the route, we had little choice but to continue to the end.

The gap between us and the ground widened, and sometimes the ledges on which we placed our feet narrowed and even disappeared, so that we came to rely upon small handholds or rocky projections to support us. Other times we found ourselves on wider rock shelves, able to pause and take in the surrounding area. The view became spectacular. Great vistas of further mountains opened up. Birds of prey wheeled below us. The air was clear and fresh.

The strange thing was that I found I liked it. Once the initial climb was done, established on ledges too narrow to take my feet completely, or even braced against the rock, hauling myself along the rope, hand over hand, I found my fear had vanished.

There on the great bare rock face, I learned to trust that, even when I anticipate that something is impossibly frightening, I may not in practice be afraid.

Eventually we reached the end of the course and descended to the valley floor. What had taken our guide half an hour, had taken us the best part of the day. We were tired but exhilarated; not just at finishing, but at the whole experience.

We discovered things about ourselves and about the group that we had not discovered during the previous week in the group room, and probably could not have experienced through sitting together talking in that comfortable space. We learned that we could rely upon one another and that everyone had different reactions to the experience; that each had times of fear and times of elation, times of calm and times of doubt. We learned that everyone was subject to the same range of human reactions, but, more, we all shared the experience of being, for that time, simply small creatures clinging to the huge rocky face of the mountain. We felt the privilege and awe of our situation.

EXERCISE THREE: WILDERNESS WORK

Take an opportunity to go for a walk in a wild space. The place you choose will depend upon your locality. If you live in a city you may have to make do with a park, but if you can find somewhere that is in as natural a state as possible.

A piece of waste ground may be better than a formal garden. Of course, in doing this, be aware of your own safety. Do not take risks either in places where humans may be a threat, or, if you have access to wild country, where there is a danger of getting lost or from exposure to

---

weather, animals or accidents. You do not need to go far off the beaten track on this occasion. Make sure you stay within your own safety limits and go prepared, or, ideally, take a companion.

When you start your work, begin by centring yourself. Stand quietly and do a grounding exercise, or sit and breathe quietly. After five minutes of stillness, walk in silence to the place where you intend to work, or through your chosen area of country, for half an hour or so, keeping awareness of your surroundings.

Follow your intuition, exploring your felt sense of the different spaces you pass through. (At a level of practicality, do not get lost. In open country, half an hour of walking could take you out of sight of your original starting point, so take care to not be so wrapped up in the exercise that you lose your direction back[167].)

Look for a space which seems to speak to you in some way.

When you reach your chosen spot, sit quietly in that space. Allow the environment to speak to you. Remain in your space as long as you are able. This might be ten minutes or several hours. You may sit or walk about.

Allow yourself to take in the impact of the natural features of the space. See if they bring images or associations for you. See whether there is a message for you in the space. See if there is anything you would like to leave there.

When you have finished, walk back to your start point

quietly.

Later take time to reflect upon the experience which you had doing this exercise, and write about it.

Life Processes

Life gives us experiences. Some are pleasant, others painful. Many involve changes which may well be uninvited or unexpected. Our bodies themselves change and develop with time. Adjusting to such changes can provide us with fresh life-challenges.

Sometimes our bodies seem to let us down, other times they surprise us. Much of the time people ignore their bodies and try to get on with their lives as if their activities take no physical toll on them. Other times people cannot ignore the consequences of their actions on their health. Accidents and sickness sometimes arise from carelessness or abuse, but often have no foreseeable or known origin. Many body changes have no obvious causes, and arise unexpectedly, sometimes disrupting our lives substantially.

We cannot control most of the changes our bodies go through. We may try to live healthily and keep the effects of age at bay for a while with cosmetics and lifestyle, or even surgery, but sooner or later, inevitably, changes will come about. Everyone grows old unless they die first.

The changes which our bodies go through have their effect on our mental states. Some changes are physiological. The influxes of hormones and other chemical messengers which accompany different life phases can have powerful effects upon the mind, as can day to day fluctuations of blood sugar levels or sleep hormones. Adolescence and menopause are often times of mood swings and emotional outbursts. Starvation leads to polarised, black and white thinking. Jet lag befuddles the mind. Excesses of caffeine create anxiety symptoms.

Other mental effects are more psychological in their origins and arise in response to our changing abilities and changing appearance. Our self-image struggles to adjust to the effects of time. We look at the face reflected in the mirror each morning, and often the mind lags behind reality. We do not see what we expect to see. The grey hair shocks. The wrinkled face staring back at us becomes a stranger. Perhaps we believe ourselves to still be the youngsters that we were years ago. Oh yes! Other times, we welcome change. The young lad looks for stubble on his chin; the girl inspects her changing outline with pleasure or anxiety.

With such changes come both fears and opportunities. Sometimes we dread the coming years, and resent the effects of passing time. Other times, awareness of these changes brings maturity and new insight. Perhaps we come to trust life, even as it pushes us again and again to adjust to new conditions and to face new challenges. In the strange unfolding of our body processes, we discover riches we had never expected.

In the following extract, which is from an article called *Buddhism and the Feminine* which I wrote for the online Butterfly Journal[168] in 2002, I described how the experience of giving birth to my first child was something which I found touched me deeply. This was not just for the obvious reasons of becoming a mother for the first time, but also for the sense it gave me of the spiritual nature of life. The direct contact with this process in which new life was created within my own body affected my experience of the continuity and eternal nature of the forces involved.

Giving birth to my first child was perhaps the most profound spiritual experiences of my life so far. Reaching down and grasping in my hands that slippery, taut little form as it emerged between my legs, I made contact with life in a way I had never before. No one needed to tell me of immortality. Here was the miracle of life sucking at my breast; the link to past generations and to the future, another small vessel in the process of unfolding evolution. No airy concept, this was the reality of life passing through my body, of my body and yet beyond my body, linking me into the greater; the process that has unfolded from time begun, and will unfold till time done.

This experience was completely unexpected. As a young woman, I had been frightened at the idea of giving birth. Before becoming pregnant, I had imagined that the whole nine months would be filled with anxiety at the prospect of childbirth, but once the process became inevitable, I was surprised to discover how enjoyable the whole experience was, and how transforming. Rather like the experience on the rock face, the reality of the situation was quite different from the experience I had imagined it would be. As with many experiences which lead us into spiritual and psychological maturation, that which we expected to be painful becomes the arena within which the change evolves.

Giving birth is generally viewed as a positive situation, even when the process is painful. Terminal illness, on the other hand is often anticipated with dread. But even in facing serious illness, the gift of the unexpected often arrives. It is striking how many people experience some sort of opening of the heart or life confirming insight at such a time of extremity. I have seen many people facing serious illness on the one hand suffering terribly from pain and terror which one would not wish on anyone, and yet also, within those awful experiences, finding a crucible in which profound meaning could emerge. Right into the last moments of life, the processes which carry our animal nature, powerful as a surge tide, offer benign blessings if we are fortunate. And so it is, our bodies teach us.

EXERCISE FOUR YOUR BODY HISTORY

Use a lifeline diagram to explore how your body has changed over the years. Start at birth on the left hand side of the page and draw a line across the page to the present on the right. This line can have ups and downs like a graph, marking your experience of your body.

On the line, mark specific things which have happened to your body. These might include changes which came about through the normal human change processes like puberty or ageing, pregnancies and child-birth, or they might have resulted from accidents or illnesses, changes in weight or fitness, or changes in appearance. Some will be things which happened at specific points in time, others will have happened gradually over a period of time.

Reflect on the ways that these changes have impacted upon you. What have they given you? How have they affected your psychological state?

Others as Teachers

Jim has taken his driving test four times. He keeps failing. He just gets too nervous each time and makes mistakes. He feels really stupid.

When he was at school he used to get really nervous about taking tests and would often get sick the night before he was going to have to take one. Sometimes he even ended up staying off school on the day of the exam because he had a bad stomach as a result of his nerves.

His fear of being tested has made him timid, and, over the years, has stood in his way. Although he is intelligent, he did not take the exams which he needed to in order to have a 'proper career'. Instead he has existed on odd jobs and casual work, which he has often found mundane and frustrating.

The fifth time his turn to take the driving test comes round, as he leaves his home in the morning, his wife says to him, "Please try to pass this test. I really think you can this time. If you do, then we can get a car and go out as a family at the weekends. It would make so much difference to the children."

Jim passes his test this time

****

Edith was widowed three years ago. When her husband Albert died she was distraught. They had been married for forty eight years, and had never had a night apart in all that time. His death was sudden, from a heart attack. She was not prepared.

For months, life seemed empty. Edith hardly knew how she kept going. Each meal, each domestic task, became a mechanical repetition of what felt like a meaningless process. At nights, alone in the bed which had been theirs for years, she lay, watching the shadows cast by passing cars sweep across the ceiling of the room, feeling nothing.

Two years after Albert's death, Edith decides to sort out the garden shed. The shed was Albert's place. It is only now that she just feels able to face the reminders of him which line its shelves: neatly labelled jam jars full of nails and screws, tools on hooks along the side wall, gardening implements in a bin in the corner, and boxes of labelled envelopes full of seeds, saved from previous years, their names written in his familiar, tidy handwriting.

Taking these down, Edith looks out of the window of the shed towards the garden. Their son has cut the grass, and pruned the apple tree last autumn, but the vegetable patch is covered with a new growth of weeds.

"Albert wouldn't have liked that!" she thinks.

Edith looks down at the envelope in her hands. Broad beans, it reads.

Edith puts the box down and takes the small fork from the bin beside the door. She goes out into the garden. By the end of the morning she has cleared enough ground to begin planting.

The spring sun is warm, and Edith notices a blackbird on the fence post. She rakes the soil smooth and even and creates a furrow. One by one she puts the beans into the drill, eight inches apart, just as Albert used to.

Three weeks later, the first small shoots of green are poking through the soil. Edith smiles as she looks at them.

****

Thomas comes into the kitchen. He has been staying in the retreat centre for a week now. He is a big man, perhaps in his late fifties; broad shouldered, but stooped over by the weight of his unhappiness. He has suffered from depression for many years.

Thomas has been asked to help with the cooking, but he is not enthusiastic. Glancing up at the others in the room, he reluctantly takes a knife and a carrot from the bowl on the table. Others are preparing vegetables for the communal meal.

Holding the carrot awkwardly in his hand, Thomas starts to peel, slowly and deliberately. The parings fall onto the table in front of him; big strips, with too much carrot still on them, but carefully, and with great concentration, he carries on. One strip after the other falls. He finishes the first carrot and reaches for a second. When the bowl is empty, he silently slips away, back to his room.

The next day he returns. Again he peels carrots in silence.

The third day, he comes again: again the fierce look of concentration, again the slow, careful paring, again the thick, uneven shavings scattered all across the table where he works. But this time he finishes the task and grins.

"We'll all be joining the RAF if we do carrots tomorrow," he says, "We'll have the best night vision ever!"

****

Angela is worried about her health. She has had all sorts of minor symptoms recently. Today her head feels strange and she has tingling in her left arm. Perhaps it is something serious. She goes back to bed.

Her flat-mate, Judith, finds her lying in bed and asks what the matter is.

"I'm not well. I think I'm really sick this time."

Angela has already been for tests at the doctors twice this month, but they didn't find anything wrong.

"Oh, for goodness sake!" Judith snaps, "You're always sick."

Angela gets cross, "That's not very nice, I'm really worried."

"You're always worried!"

Judith shuts the door and goes downstairs.

When she gets downstairs, she feels sorry for Angela. Perhaps she really is sick this time. Perhaps she should get herself checked out anyway. After all, she had a cancer scare a couple of years ago. It was successfully treated at the time, but one never knew if these things might recur.

Judith is just about to go back upstairs to apologise and ask if Angela wants her to ring the doctor, when Angela comes into the room.

"I feel a bit better," she says, "You're right, I'm not really ill, but I was frightened I might be."

****

People are changed by circumstances. The chance remarks of a stranger, the buildings they inhabit, the love which they feel for family and friends, the physical objects which they use, the processes of birth and growth and death, the places they travel to, even the confrontations and misunderstandings which they have with other people; all these create the conditions which break through the isolation of the self-world.

The real world is unpredictable. It surprises us. Some changes are welcome, others not. Experience is sometimes raw, and other times it is tender. Life events can turn our expectations upside down. From time to time they delight us and leave us standing in awe at the blessings which we receive.

People's lives shape themselves around such events. Whilst, as therapists, we may like to believe we make a difference, the effects of our work are often small compared with the effects of real life. We are the midwives of change in the psyche, but not the parent of the child. The real source of inspiration and change is the measureless world of otherness, the real world to which our clients relate and through which they have their existence.

What we offer is our faith, our confidence in meeting the challenges in life, and our capacity to observe the details and find the possibilities in what it offers. Life provides the conditions which can help the client to grow and develop instead of stagnating and retreating. In our ordinariness, we are fellow travellers in this adventure, making our own misjudgements and mistakes, and sometimes, by providence, getting things right. We walk alongside, not ahead.

We share the process of living and growing with our clients and yet, often, we simply marvel at the strange and wonderful possibilities which appear, seemingly out of nowhere. We too are surprised by the gift of the unexpected. Together with our clients, we discover the richness of life's beautiful territory.

Final Reflections

As we reach the end of this programme, take time to look back.

Reflect on the journey which you have come, and the companions who have travelled with you. Perhaps you have studied with others, in which case, recall the moments of sharing and meeting one another. Even if you have followed the book alone, many others will have helped you. Reflect on the contributions which they have made.

Think of the teachers who brought you this far. Who taught you to read? Who inspired you to care about people? Who taught you the value of experience? Who gave you guidance in your spiritual journey?

Think of the people whose examples have given you inspiration. Think of those who taught you courage and wisdom, compassion and humour. Think of those who fostered your creativity and those who helped you cry.

Remembering these people and this process, look into your heart. From the great store house of experience which life has given you, offer your gratitude and your love.

Walk on in the light.

Notes

1   Brazier, C 2003, Buddhist Psychology Constable-Robinson London

2   Conditional and Object relation theory is set out in Brazier, D 1995, Zen Therapy Constable, London

3   Furedi, F, 2004 Therapy Culture Routledge, London p18

4   Furedi, F, 2004 *Therapy Culture* Routledge, London p12

5   Spinelli, E, 1989 *The Interpreted World: An Introduction to Phenomenological Psychology*. Sage Publications. London.

6   These two categories of meditation are found in most schools of Buddhism, but may be called by different names.

7   Fourteenth Century English woman mystic

8   Paper presented at 8th International Person-Centered Approach Forum in Japan, 2001

9   Buber, M 1970 *I and Thou* Charler Scribners Sons, US

10   Rogers C R 1980 *A Way of Being* Hougton Mifflin Boston

11   ibid p20

12   ibid p20

13   ibid p8

14   This theory of *conditioning* is central to a Buddhist understanding of the human mind. You can read more detailed explanation of the theory in David Brazier's book, *Zen Therapy* (pub. Constable Robinson, 1995)

15   An other-centred approach makes considerable reference to our relationship with the object world. Mental states are described as being object-related. Objected-related theory has its roots in a particular understanding of conditioning presented in the Abhidharma, the key Buddhist psychological text. The term in particular can cause confusion as it is similar to the term object-relations theory used by Fairburn, Winnicott and Guntrip in Western psychodynamic psychology. The two can be distinguished by the observation that Buddhist object-relation theory is framed in the

singular.

16 Brazier C 2003 *Buddhist Psychology* Constable Robinson UK

17 In Buddhist teaching such afflictions would be called Dukkha (Skt) meaning affliction. Dukkha is explained in the teaching of the Four Noble Truths.

18 The six senses, Shadyatanas (Skt), are the eye, ear, nose, tongue, body and mind's eye.

19 These three levels of escapism are mentioned in the teaching on samudaya (Skt) the second Noble Truth, and are Kama, Bhava and Abhava; sense pleasures, becoming and non-becoming.

20 Rowan J 1990 *Subpersonalities: The People Inside Us* Routledge UK

21 Beech, C and Brazier, D 1996 Empathy for a Real World in Hutterer, R, Pawlowsky, G, Schmid, P and Stipsits, R (eds) 1996 Client Centred and Experiential Psychotherapy: a paradigm in motion Peter Lang, Frankfurt am Main, Germany

22 Skt Lakshana

23 Rogers, C. R. 1951 *Client-Centred Therapy*, Constable London p29

24 see lesson one

25 Rogers, C. R. 1961 *On Becoming a Person*, Constable, London p53

26 Rogers, C. R. 1961 *On Becoming a Person*, Constable, London p284

27 Rogers C R 1980 A Way of Being Houghton Mifflin Boston

28 ibid p.10

29 As reported by David Brazier who was attending that event.

30 Brazier, D *The Necessary Condition is Love* in Brazier D 1993 *Beyond Carl Rogers* Constable UK

31 Brazier, D 2009 *Love and its Disappointment* O-Books UK

32 ibid

33 ibid

34   We will be looking at aspects of this process in the remainder of this book. If you are looking for a more comprehensive coverage of the underlying theory, it is described in detail in Buddhist Psychology by C Brazier, Constable-Robinson London, 2003.

35   In phenomenology, this world would be called the *Eigenwelt* and refers to things we think of as "me".

36   In phenomenology, this would be called the *Mit-welt*, or with "with-world" and refer to things we feel close to or identify as part of "my world".

37   Lakshana (skt) is a pointer to the self. All things are lakshana.

38   Beech, C and Brazier, D 1996 *Empathy for a Real World* in Hutterer, R, Pawlowsky, G, Schmid, P and Stipsits, R (eds) 1996 *Client Centred and Experiential Psychotherapy: a paradigm in motion* Peter Lang publishing, Germany p. 333

39   Brazier C 1997, *Reflected Selves: an exploration of the concept of self as manifested I a group of women who identify themselves as compulsive eaters.* MPhil thesis presented at Keele University

40   This view is expressed in some Buddhist traditions as the idea that the world is all projection of mind.

41   Brazier C 2009 *Listening to the Other* O-Books UK

42   Rogers C.R. 1961 On Becoming a Person. Constable, London p153

43   Lakshana (Sanskrit)

44   rupa is a Sanskrit word meaning phenomenon, or colouration. It is used technically in Buddhist theory. Capeller online Sanskrit English dictionary, defines rupa as: *any outward appearance or phenomenon or colour (often pl.) , form , shape , figure*

45   Aditta-pariyaya-sutta found in the Samyutta Nikaya 35.28

46   For each sense, the text describes a process: '*The eye is burning, rupas are burning, eye-consciousness is burning, eye-contact is burning, also whatever is felt as pleasant or painful or*

neither-painful-nor-pleasant that arises with eye-contact for its indispensable condition, that too is burning.

[47] In the Buddha's teaching these are represented by the three types of entanglement, greed, hate and delusion

[48] The Buddha concludes the description above. *'I say it is burning with birth, aging and death, with sorrow, with lamentation, with pain, with grief, with despair.'*

[49] These do in fact correlate with elements in a process known as the skandha process. We will explore this later in the book.

[50] As we have seen, the Buddha used the metaphor of fire to describe the forces which draw us towards the world of attachments

[51] These basic requirements could be seen as corresponding to Rogers' core conditions: empathy, congruence and unconditional positive regard.

[52] In Buddhist theory, this trance state would be called *avidya*, or ignorance. Literally it means not seeing. We are all continuously going round habitual tracks without perceiving things as they are.

[53] There are interesting parallels to the ideas about the multifaceted self in the work of Paul Federn. Federn wrote about the segmented or stratified self, and the way that it was created in association with different fields of experience. He also saw the self as retaining layers of earlier experience and modes of response in a kind of archaeological stratification. Federn, P 1953, *Ego Psychology and the Psychoses*, Imago London

[54] We can allude here to the theory of karma and the idea that karmic seeds are the traces of past action, which are stored in the *alaya*, the repository of the mind, to be reactivated when conditions repeat themselves. See Brazier, C, 2003 *Buddhist Psychology* Constable Robinson London p 112

[55] Erik Berne's approach, Transanctional Analysis provides a simple and useful model for describing and working with

some aspects of the different selves which are conditioned by different self-worlds

56 Whilst in the ideal case a Buddhist view is that such self-building is not useful, the ordinary person in such extreme circumstance does not usually have the spiritual resources to stay present with the experience. Rarely, however, experiences of extreme trauma have been a trigger for spiritual breakthrough.

57 Beech, C 1993 *Looking In, Looking Out* in Brazier, D 1993 *Beyond Carl Rogers*, Constable, London

58 The concept of occupying the middle ground has some parallels in the Buddhist notion of the middle way

59 Sculpting is a method which uses objects to represent psychological phenomena. Commonly, small objects such as pebbles, buttons or coins are used to represent elements such as family members, people in a scenario or sub-personalities. There is a fuller description of this method in *Listening to the Other*

60 Sand-tray work is a Jungian method which the client uses small toys in a tray of sand to create a "world" for further information see: Mitchell, R and Friedman, H 1994 *Sandplay, past present and future* Routledge UK.

61 There is useful analysis of the way that art work becomes a transference object in Schaverien, J 1992, The Revealing Image, Routledge UK

62 ibid 114-6

63 The theory of transitional objects was developed by Donald Winnicott, and particularly relates to the mother-child bond, however the process described here as relating to the therapist can be seen to be similar in its function.

64 Gendlin, E 1981, *Focusing*, Bantam, New York

65 Leijssen, M 1993 *Creating a Workable Distance to Overwhelming Images* in Brazier, D 1993 *Beyond Carl Rogers*, Constable, London

66 Gendlin, E 1981, *Focusing*, Bantam, New York

67 Leijssen, M 1993 *Creating a Workable Distance to Overwhelming Images* in Brazier, D 1993 *Beyond Carl Rogers*, Constable, London p130

68 ibid p131

69 ibid p132

70 ibid p136

71 ibid p130

72 ibid p132

73 Skandha is often translated as aggregate, but literally means heap or bundle. The teaching is often taken simply to mean the elements which make up a person, but, taken as a whole, these elements can be interpreted as a cyclical pattern. This interpretation is confirmed by parallels with other Buddhist teachings and offers a useful clarification of the processes of self-formation. For more discussion of this see: Brazier, C 2003, *Buddhist Psychology* Constable-Robinson London

74 ibid

75 The teachings of the Common and Rare Factors and that of the Twelve Links of Dependent Origination both map onto the teaching of the Skandhas, elaborating the detail in the original cycle.

76 The Ant Hill Sutra MN23

77 You will find that the translation of some terms are open to discussion, so I have here used those translations which are most helpful in understanding the psychology implicit in the teaching. Whilst I personally think these translations are correct, you will find other interpretations in other sources.

78 This derives from the five skandhas, however, the fifth skandha, *vijnana*, (ordinary view) can be split into two elements, *chetana* (intentionality) and *manaskara* (attention) which are elements in another teaching: *the common factors*. The rational for this, again, is explained in *Buddhist Psychology*.

79   Rupa is sometimes translated as form or body, but the real meaning is colouring or phenomenon

80   vedana is sometimes translated as feeling, but its meaning is basically reactive as described.

81   Sanskrit: samjna. I have used two terms to describe this stage. Both terms are useful as they refer to different aspects of the process and neither completely describes the meaning of the term. Often translated as perception, it means the conditioned engagement we have with events in which everything is fitted into old scripts or assumptions.

82   The arising of energy in the stages of reaction and entrancement, vedana and samjna, can be seen as parallel to that arising which occurs in the stage of samudaya, the second stage in the teaching of The Four Noble Truths. In other words if we link these two teachings we can see that as we encounter the world, which is potentially afflictive, we feel energy arising in us, and in most cases we use that energy in the process of self-building.

83   Samskara

84   The idea that the mind is conditioned by action is elaborated in the theory of karma

85   This is a reference to karmic seeds. Thich Nhat Hanh writes about karmic seeds in a number of his books, but you will find a good explanation in *Understanding Our Mind* Parallax Press 2006

86   an example of this would be Thich Nhat Hanh's practice of '*watering good seeds*'

87   Vijnana, sometimes translated as consciousness or mentality, this term carries an implication of a split or two-fold mind-set

88   The teaching of the *common factors*

89   Chetana

90   Manaskara

91   Brazier, C 2003, *Buddhist Psychology* Constable-Robinson

London

92   alaya

93   In The Fire Sermon, Aditta-pariyaya-sutta found in the Samyutta Nikaya 35.28, the Buddha spoke of the whole world being on fire, because we are constantly getting caught, craving for objects which support our identity.

94   Trishna, thirst, is used to describe the part of the cycle in which we are hooked into reaction and entrancement.

95   Jacob Moreno 1889-1974, inventor of psychodrama, a contemporary of Freud in Vienna, he later moved to New York where most of his work was developed.

96   Through a process called role reversal

97   Through a process called mirroring

98   Taking something 'out of role' means returning it to its ordinary status. We will look at de-roling objects later in this session.

99   Role reversal means the exchange of roles with another character. This technique will be explained further in a later session.

100   In psychodrama the double is a person who stays with the protagonist (the person working on their material), standing by their side often with a hand on the shoulder, maintaining empathic connection. When the double speaks, they do so in the first person, as if they were the inner voice of the protagonist, rather like the "thinks bubble" one sees in cartoons.

101   Protagonist would be the correct term here if we were describing full psychodramatic method

102   David Loy writes about the role of lack in the formation of human process and society in his books Loy D, 1996 *Lack and Transcendence: The problem of death and life in psychotherapy, existentialism and Buddhism*, Humanities press, New Jersey USA and Loy D.R. 2002. A Buddhist History of the West : studies in lack. New York, Suny.

103   Mano-vijnana, one of the six senses in the Buddhist model

[104] There is also a section on creating anchors in *Listening to the Other*

[105] Sculpting was introduced in session six. Further explanation of the method can be found in *Listening to the Other*.

[106] Genograms are diagrams like family trees which represent the family structure over generations. They can be done as sculpts or as drawings. For more ideas on this way of working, see Schutzenberger, A 1998, *The Ancestor Syndrome: Transgenerational Psychotherapy and the hidden links in the family tree*. London: Routledge

[107] A method of exploring spatial relationships between objects, representing people, things or concepts by using small buttons, stones or other things.

[108] See *Listening to the Other* session five

[109] Schaverien, J 1992, *The Revealing Image: Analytical Art Therapy in Theory and Practice*, Routledge UK

[110] ibid p138

[111] See session four

[112] *Watering Good Seeds* is a practice taught by Thich Nhat Hanh

[113] Skt: sparsha

[114] In another Buddhist teaching, that of Dependent Origination, the cycle of self-building is rather more elaborated. Here *rupa* leads to the *senses*, which in turn lead to *contact* and *contact* leads to *reaction*. We can therefore see that rupa and contact are closely related. In a different teaching, that of the rare and common factors, contact (*sparsha*) transforms into mindfulness (*smriti*). These teachings and their implications in understanding mental process, are set out in my earlier book *Buddhist Psychology* so I will not attempt to repeat the discussion here.

[115] Skt: Smriti

[116] Kabat-Zinn, J, 1991 *Full Catastrophe Living: Using the Wisdom of Your Body and Mind to Face Stress, Pain, and Illness* Delta USA

117 ibid p21
118 Skt Samadhi. This might otherwise be translated as vision. Samadhi describes the focused mind state which arises in high states of meditation in which vision spontaneously appears.
119 Skt Prajna. Wisdom, or, more literally, seeing deeply into
120 Hanh N 1988 *The Sun My Heart*, Parallax US
121 ibid p29
122 ibid p17
123 Shakyamuni Buddha, the historic founder of the Buddhist tradition who lived in India in the fifth century BCE
124 This practice is called Nembutsu which means 'Buddha in mind' or mindfulness of Buddha.
125 Brazier C 2007 *The Other Buddhism* O-Books UK & US
126 Such observations lie behind the focusing work of Eugene Gendlin: Gendlin, E 1981, Focusing, Bantam, New York
127 Morita Therapy developed by Shoma Morita uses a variety of methods, many of which are designed to disrupt our assumptions. For a full description see Reynolds, D 1980 *The Quiet Therapies* University of Hawaii Press, Honolulu
128 see session nine
129 In Pureland Buddhism, we keep in mind the Buddha, Amida. Amida means without measure.
130 Skt avidya; literally meaning not seeing
131 Brazier, D 2009 *Love and Its Disappointment* O-Books UK
132 Brazier C 2007 *The Other Buddhism* O-Books UK
133 ibid p55
134 song by Paul Anka popularised by Frank Sinatra
135 this would happen through the step called entrancement; Skt samjna
136 Brazier, D *The Necessary Condition is Love* in Brazier D 1993 *Beyond Carl Rogers* Constable UK
137 ibid p73
138 ibid

[139] This can particularly be a problem where one partner is involved in personal change, and explains why people may experience problems in their relationships as a result of going into therapy or joining a counsellor training programme which involves a lot of personal growth.

[140] These five elements were included in the initial summary of the Foresight report on Mental Capital and Wellbeing, published October 2008.

[141] Rogers C.R. 1951 *Client-Centred Therapy*. Constable, London pp 487-491

[142] The senses are literally called the six uncontrollables, Skt *shadyatanas*

[143] Skt: *lakshana*

[144] Frame of Reference is a term deriving from Carl Rogers and commonly used in Person Centred Approach

[145] Based on his work with narcissistic clients, Heinz Kohut proposed that it was the small failures of empathy on the part of the therapist which led to positive psychological change.

[146] Nei Quan is the Chinese form of the name, which we tend to use at Amida. Naikan is the more commonly used Japanese form of the name.

[147] ie those with parents and other significant caregivers

[148] For example, Reynolds, D 1980 *The Quiet Therapies*, Univ. Hawaii Press, US

[149] Krech G, 2001 *Naikan: gratitude, grace, and the Japanese art of self-reflection* Stonebridge Press US

[150] http://www.todoinstitute.org

[151] Todo Institute web site:
http://www.todoinstitute.org/naikan.html

[152] Reynolds D, 1995 *A Handbook for Constructive Living*, W Morrow US

[153] see session nine

[154] Brazier, D 2009 *Love and its Disappointment* O-Books UK

155 Todo Institute currently run online Naikan courses for couples

156 Yalom, I 2001 *The Gift of Therapy* Piatkus UK

157 ibid p74

158 Nicholson, V, 2007 *Singled Out: How Two Million Women Survived Without Men after the First World War* Penguin UK

159 ibid p272

160 Berne E 1964 *Games People Play* Random House US

161 Brazier C 2007 *The Other Buddhism* O-Books UK

162 Brazier C 2009 *Guilt* O-Books UK

163 Jp: *bombu* nature

164 Yalom, I 2001 *The Gift of Therapy* Piatkus UK pp6-10

165 Rogers, C 1961 *On Becoming a Person* Constable UK

166 One needs a little wariness here as the term 'wilderness therapy' can be used in various ways, and does not necessarily imply a sympathetic, receptive relationship with the environment.

167 It is not necessary to venture off the beaten track to do this exercise, but if you are going into wild country and are not used to walking in such terrain, take guidance. At very least, be prepared for sudden changes of weather and carry a whistle or other means of attracting attention for emergencies.

168 This on-line journal no longer exists as far as I can discover

BOOKS

O is a symbol of the world, of oneness and unity. In different cultures it also means the "eye," symbolizing knowledge and insight. We aim to publish books that are accessible, constructive and that challenge accepted opinion, both that of academia and the "moral majority."

Our books are available in all good English language bookstores worldwide. If you don't see the book on the shelves ask the bookstore to order it for you, quoting the ISBN number and title. Alternatively you can order online (all major online retail sites carry our titles) or contact the distributor in the relevant country, listed on the copyright page.

See our website **www.o-books.net** for a full list of over 500 titles, growing by 100 a year.

And tune in to myspiritradio.com for our book review radio show, hosted by June-Elleni Laine, where you can listen to the authors discussing their books.

mySpiritRadio